HOUSES FROM THE FACTORY

HOUSES FROM THE FACTORY

System Building and the Welfare State 1942–74

Brian Finnimore

Rivers Oram Press
London

First published in 1989 by
Rivers Oram Press
144 Hemingford Road, London N1 1DE

Published in the USA by
Unwin Hyman Inc
8 Winchester Place, Winchester, Mass. 01890

Set in Times 10/12pt
by Columns Typesetters, Reading
and Printed in Great Britain
by T.J. Press, Padstow

ISBN 1 85489 002 6

CONTENTS

LIST OF ILLUSTRATIONS

PREFACE

Like most people in this country, much of my life has been spent either in the type of building discussed on the following pages, or just down the road from one of them. One of the most exciting events at primary school was watching the erection of a prefabricated classroom which seemed to happen almost overnight.

As one would expect, I was completely unaware at the time that these buildings were in any way different from others. However, having started this research I became aware of how much of our built environment has been shaped by building methods which were considered revolutionary at the time. While it is unlikely that construction methods could have had an effect on the development of my childhood generation, it is very possible that the social circumstances which gave rise to them did. If ideas and events determine how buildings are made, then surely they also affect people. For the author, therefore, the research described in this book has a meaning beyond simple academicism: not only did it provide a clearer sense of the historical events which in some measure shaped us but it occasionally recalled earlier years. In addition to its academic utility I would like to think it could have the same effect on future readers.

It writing this book I am particulary indebted to Mark Swenarton and Adrian Forty not only for their encouragement but much of historical rigour which I hope is evident.

For help and support I would also like to thank Tim Baylay, Ed. Cooney, Elizabeth Fidlon, Murray Fraser, Sara Faulkner, Ann Finnimore, Jim Gear, Ray Moxley, Ruth Owens, Mark and Anna Povell, Andrew Saint, Audry Stafford, and Hetty Startup.

London, February 1989

INTRODUCTION

> I have been looking eagerly, ever since I took office, for some system of prefabrication which would enable us to build houses in the same way as cars and aeroplanes. So far my search has been in vain, but I do not despair.[1] (Aneurin Bevan, Minister of State for Health, 1945)

To the historian, system building is a remarkable subject for study because of the way in which it amalgamated social theories and building practice – for the way in which it was a response by construction firms to the requirement for state housing and, for the ideologue, a global remedy for social ills. The use of system building in post-war Britain, therefore, can only be understood as the outcome of a combination of social and economic policies.

While system building has been used in other countries, under other circumstances, its use in Britain was associated with the Welfare State which, for a period of thirty years or so, generated unprecedented demands for public housing.

Aneurin Bevan was only one of many politicians who saw mass production as the solution to Britain's housing needs. The search for methods to build houses in the same way as cars and aeroplanes were made also helped bring about the widespread use of system building, and it was the most dramatic way by which Modern Movement theories of architectural design and production affected everyday experience. Indeed, the failures of system building in housing explain much of the virulence of the subsequent reaction against Modernism. Yet few innovations have carried higher hopes.

To Bevan and many like him, system building was the path not only to a revolution in building methods, but to better quality housing and to improved conditions for those in the industry. To the historian, it is evident that system building was not the revolutionary solution that was hoped for, but simply a phase in the evolution of building processes. But system building was more than just a different way of putting buildings together; it changed the role of each of the major participants in a construction process that had developed over the previous two centuries: involving the client, the architect, the building materials and components producer, the building contractor and building labour. The importance of system building in social policy was bound to decline as needs changed: the much reduced programme of public sector housing, and the stress on urban renewal rather than wholesale redevelopment, called for a different approach. What was not inevitable was that it should not only decline, but should be largely discredited in the very field in which the greatest opportunity was seen – housing.

To the general public, system building usually conjures up images of the worst forms of modern architecture – above all, tall buildings that leak – and is, therefore, considered the most vulgar expression of the state's involvement in housing. To architects and administrators, the term brings to mind a tragically misguided attempt to introduce higher levels of order and method to buiding design and construction. Technical mistakes might have been forgiven; but a design process dominated by technology, and supported by the ideology of the Modern Movement, ignored the needs of the user, and that has not been forgiven. The verdict of the market has been crushing: many "model" developments, proudly carrying the names of local aldermen, are, today, almost impossible to let.

Concepts of new technology

Yet denuded of its emotive connotations, system building was not a heartless juggernaut but an organisational approach to construction which is quite difficult even to define precisely. In particular, it has frequently been confused with a number of developments in twentieth-century building technology and, before further discussion, it is necessary to define its nature.

Standardisation was an early theory in building

2

technology. Borrowed from manufacturing industry's attempts to maximise repetition – and therefore economy and precision – in methods of manufacture, it was proposed that variations in the design of buildings should be reduced to a minimum. This led to the more radical concept of prefabrication, or the manufacture of standardised building components away from the building site. Bricks, of course, had been supplied in this way since pre-Roman times, and prefabricated components such as windows and doors had been used in building well before the twentieth century. After the Second World War staircases, trussed rafters and pre-cast concrete panels were normally standardised and manufactured off site. But system bulding as a doctrine, popularised as a theoretical concept by the European Modern Movement, looked to something higher than convenient economy.

Of particular significance to supporters of the Prefabrication Movement of the 1930s and 1940s were the links seen with contemporary manufacturing methods: "The possibilities of economy and improved design through prefabrication are great, but its main advantage . . . depends on the next stage: large-scale production".[2] It was hoped that houses could be almost entirely assembled from major, prefabricated components and that these components could be mass produced in factories like other commodities. Prefabrication was thus closely associated with new methods of construction and, in particular, system building. Indeed, other writers, such as R.B. White, have regarded the two as synonymous.[3]

Nevertheless, many systems were not based on the use of prefabricated components: No-Fines, a method (pioneered after the First World War) of pouring concrete into re-usable shutters, was by far the most successful, and was used to build some hundreds of thousands of dwellings. Within the shell, the No-Fines dwellings were fabricated on site in much the same way as the traditional house. While prefabrication was of crucial importance to the development of post-war housing, and a concept referred to many times in this study, it was not the same as system building.

During the 1960s the term Industrialised Building, or "IB", became the popular description for rapid technical advance in building. This term was adopted as it became apparent that mass producing buildings was a more complicated matter than "prefabrication" implied. IB was the application of a broad range of features associated with industrial production methods, and was described by the government in 1965 as:

> all measures needed to enable the industry to work more like a factory industry. For the industry this means not only new materials and construction techniques, the use of dry processes, increased mechanisation of site processes, and the manufacture of large components under factory conditions of production and quality control; but improved management techniques, the correlation of design and production, improved control of the selection and delivery of materials, and better organisation of operations on site. Not least, IB entails training teams to work in an organised fashion on long runs of repetitive work, whether the men are using new skills or old.[4]

A broader term than prefabrication, IB encompassed all forms of system building, and indeed the more efficient forms of that which it was intended to replace – traditional construction. However, so far as the government was concerned, IB and system building were the same: by encouraging the latter it promoted policies to industrialise the construction industry.

New approaches to building, such as standardisation and prefabrication, gave rise to the notion of traditional construction – the way buildings were produced before the introduction of alternatives. Indeed, "non-traditional" was the term used for system building during the 1940s. In the early 1950s the term new-traditional was invented by a government eager to encourage apprehensive local authorities in the wider acceptance of unconventional building methods. Nevertheless, rhetoric could not obscure the fact that traditional and system building were different. Inevitably, discussion of this difference concentrated on the composition of the building fabric.

The economics of innovation

In 1917 a government committee identified the, seemingly, eternal truths of house construction. By taking the cost of labour and materials together they found that of the eleven trades involved in housebuilding, bricklaying accounted for 31 per cent of the total cost, and carpentry and joinery for a further 26 per cent.[5] But, while carpentry and joinery lent themselves to prefabrication and the introduction of mechanisation, brickwork did not.

Traditional building was often characterised as a method in which bricklaying remained the major cost – the structure into which other materials and components were built. A feature certainly common to most building systems was the tendency to replace brickwork with other materials. However, even this was not always the case: "rationalised traditional" systems used brickwork for structural crosswalls, and timber frame systems as an external cladding.

It is clear then, that system building involved more than just replacing bricks. Nevertheless, using other wall materials had a number of advantages. Given the right circumstances, site time and the need for site labour were frequently reduced. So, though less often, were costs. Furthermore, at times when both bricks and bricklayers were scarce, the use of alternatives was essential. These potential benefits of new walling techniques were constantly used to promote system building, though they were often over-estimated.

The new methods required to replace bricklaying and other labour-intensive site operations had a fundamental effect on design and on commercial relationships. Traditional building had used methods of construction familiar to all parties in the building process. The architect designed the building to the last detail and tendering contractors attached prices to each item of work. This competitive discipline, was not usually available in system building.

New forms of contract integrated (it was claimed) the design and the construction of buildings in a way traditional contracts had not. They allowed the introduction of complex labour-saving techniques, ranging from a more systematic use of conventional approaches, such as the combination of timber panels with brick crosswalls, to entirely new techniques, such as forming the building shell with large pre-cast concrete panels connected by specially developed joints.

Often standard designs for complete buildings were offered: in these cases, purchasers and their architects were excluded from the design process altogether. Furthermore, to realise the full time, labour and cost

5

savings implied by new techniques, larger numbers of houses had to be offered in a single contract. The solution to detailed design problems differed from one proprietary system to another, so normal competitive tendering on the basis of a complete design was impossible. Where untried methods were on offer, the details were often worked out by the construction firm only well after appointment. However, what clients gained in innovation, they tended to lose in choice, entering into major commitments on a take-it-or-leave-it basis.

These difficulties gave rise to a number of new forms of contract, designed to introduce the producer to the architect at an early stage; so that a design could thus be prepared for the particular construction method in use. Serial contracting, one of these new approaches, was developed and first used in 1947 by Hertfordshire County Council for its school building system. This programme was an internationally admired success, and has been widely imitated. New contracting methods were also used for traditional construction to improve efficiency in large projects. System building was not solely a story of technical failures.

The organisation of system building

Although little in evidence to the casual observer of monolithic tower blocks, the developments described above, united many independent professions and suppliers, and could only be brought together on a significant scale by a new party to the building process: the sponsor. The sponsor was responsible for initiating and operating a building system and made the investment required to use labour-saving methods of construction. The presence of the sponsor was the crucial difference between system building and other methods of construction.

One sponsor might operate a number of systems, or the same system might be operated by a number of sponsors: but, every building system had a sponsor. The sponsors of building systems were various but could be categorised as three types; building firms, non-building firms, and clients.

Client organisations were usually groupings of the larger local authorities (consortia), or government building departments. Building firm sponsors tended to be larger regional or national contractors; while non-building firms ranged from primary materials producers (such as steel firms wishing to enter new markets) to small building component manufacturers. In most cases the non-building-firm sponsors subcontracted building firms to erect their systems on site.

As well as investing in the design, development and manufacture of prototypes, a sponsor had to finance the production plant and higher management costs associated with operating labour-saving building methods. While these costs might be offset by higher profits when the system was operating at full capacity, they represented a considerable burden when demand was low. Although investment varied considerably depending on the system, it was calculated in 1966 to be two-to-three times higher on average than traditional construction.

The willingness of sponsors to bear these expenditures on a large scale in post-war Britain was all the more exceptional in light of the building industry's historical aversion to capital investment. Indeed, throughout the twentieth century, the contracting industry has generally been considered exceptional for its lack of investment in methods of production and was frequently the subject of rebuke from progressive politicians and housing experts. In 1965 the building industry was reckoned to have less fixed capital relative to output than any other industry with the exception of mining and quarrying.[7]

According to Donald Bishop of the Building Research Station, this state of affairs resulted from the nature of the market. Except in the case of speculative housing, where the building process and property development were combined, building was traditionally a bespoke activity – the construction of individual buildings to the directions of individual clients. Furthermore, the demand for building work was highly unstable with regional fluctuations, uncertainties in timing and capricious clients. In response to this, contractors avoided specialising in specific building types taking whatever work was offered, increasingly using subcontracted labour and plant:

> In these circumstances there is little incentive for firms to invest heavily either in forward planning or in development because there is no certainty that the work in hand will be required again.[7]

The building industry's reluctance to invest resources in sophisticated techniques directed towards specific building types was, in fact, its adaptation to an uncertain market. Indeed, rather than being producers in the normal sense of the word, Bishop concluded that "Building firms viewed in this light are merely organisations capable of building".

Under the unique conditions created by the Welfare State, system building was the antithesis to this state of affairs: there was substantial investment in technology directed towards specific building types and to the marketing of a rationalised product by the sponsor rather than the sale of a building service by a general contractor.

A social framework

System building was the response by producers to changes in a major part of the market in which they operated. This book describes these changes, and explains why industry altered its methods of production. As important as the actual changes which took place were the aspirations of politicians and housing experts for more fundamental transformations in building technology.

At its peak system building accounted for approximately one-quarter of national housing output. The same social pressures that encouraged the use of new technology also engendered the hope that system building would be more than a partial solution to housing provision. According to the architectural theories of the European Modern Movement, all construction would eventually be carried out this way.

This belief itself was the product of a social theory which developed in the wake of industrialisation, and was honed in the politically traumatic years which followed the First World War. Modern Movement ideas influenced the house building policies later adopted by the British state. In the event, these theories were often tragically misapplied in housing, and the technical and planning failures which marked the system building era may well have played a significant part in discrediting the social and political ideas which partly inspired the experiment.

Chapter 1
COMMODITIES FOR MASS CONSUMPTION: 1872–1942

System building in local authority housing was directly related to the social and economic policies of the Welfare State. Like most significant historical phenomena it grew from processes developed over a long period. In the case of system building these processes extended back to the turn of the century and were twofold: the increasing intervention of the state in working-class living conditions and a developing concern with the relationship between technology, social, and economic progress. Indeed, rather than separate, these strands of history should be seen as interlinked: together, they had a fundamental effect on the character of post-war society.

A preoccupation with technology created the climate in which traditional methods of building were questioned by politicians and architects. Central to this interest in construction methods was the ambition to mass produce houses in the same way as so many other products of industry. Early state housing programmes following the First World War saw the first use of what came to be known as system building. A generation later, at the time social policy makers were framing their plans for the Welfare State which would follow the Second World War, mass production had become the goal of progressive housing policy.

Machines and houses

Until the early twentieth century, technology was little discussed in relation to house building. However, with the development of new methods of manufacture, which introduced the mass production of complex artifacts, and with state intervention in working-class housing, the stage was set for technical innovation to assume a growing role both in the theory and practice of building.

Early solutions to the "housing problem"

The inability of capitalism to ensure adequate housing conditions at all levels of society gave rise to what became known as the "housing problem". A result of the industrial revolution, this phenomenon was first identified by social commentators in the middle of the last century. Early charitable attempts to remedy the "housing problem" were followed by tentative state interventions.

Although Frederick Engels had argued, in 1872, that the industrialisation of society and its subsequent urbanisation had created the slum, he did not suggest that a similar revolution in building methods would remedy low standards of housing.[1] Indeed, nineteenth century solutions to the "housing problem" concentrated on cheap methods of finance rather than new technology. Over 100,000 rooms were built between 1841 and 1914 by the Five Percent Philanthropy Movement which provided housing at modest rents by borrowing low-interest capital from charitably-minded financiers.

1 American Building Techniques (USA mid-1940s)
From the start of this century, the methods by which houses were built assumed a growing significance in social theory. Mass production became the commonly accepted goal

Similarly, the Garden City Movement sought to generate cheap finance by taking advantage of the increase in land values which came through laying out new garden cities. By this means 11,000 houses were built prior to the First World War.[2]

The failure of charitable methods to substantially improve housing conditions precipitated direct state intervention. This may be seen as part of a wider concern, developed towards the end of the century, to improve working-class living conditions. Early welfare provision was encouraged by the recognition of low health standards in working-class recruits for the Boer War. This "national deterioration", as it was termed, prompted limited legislation, directed not least to improve military and industrial efficiency. The growth of the Labour Movement and fear of working-class radicalisation were further stimuli to reforms which had as their primary aim the continuation of social cohesion.[3] Among these reforms were tentative moves by the state to assist in the provision of cheap housing. Beginning in 1866, a series of Acts financed local authority housebuilding at low rates of interest. In this way 22,000 houses or one per cent of the nation's output was provided up to 1914.[4]

The mass production of complex artifacts

The fact that house building and mass production were not associated before this century arose from the general level of industrial development. It was only when development had reached a particular stage, in the late nineteenth century, that the concept of mass-producing articles as complex and large as a house could be conceived.

The application of machinery to manufacture had long been a feature of industrial development and the moving line and mass production were techniques used throughout the nineteenth century. As early as 1829 Thomas Carlisle described his times as "the Age of Machinery, in every outward and inward sense of that word".[5] Nevertheless, despite Carlisle's awareness of technological transformations in industry wrought by the industrial revolution,the application of large-scale production methods to complex artifacts for mass consumption came only in the latter years of the last century with a second phase of industrial development. According to Eric Hobsbawm, this was characterised by the growth of a new generation of science based industry, the systematic extension of the factory system, an increase in the scale of economic enterprise and the discovery that the "largest potential market was to be found in the rising incomes of the mass of the working citizens in economically developed countries".[6] Under these conditions the mechanisation of house construction became a possibility.

The technology of working-class housing received increased attention in the early years of the twentieth century as a result of further attempts to solve the "housing problem" in the light of recent advances in industrial manufacture. Between 1905 and 1908 three exhibitions were held in Britain to demonstrate the cost-reducing potential of new methods of construction. At these exhibitions concrete blocks, expanded metal and steel frames were shown. Of Cubitts' reinforced concrete cottage, J. Cornes noted that "Economical considerations require that as far as possible there should be a repetition of parts".[7] Cornes also noted technical changes that were taking place to cheapen cottage construction in order to "erect healthy, sanitary well-lighted and attractive homes which will pay interest and return the capital . . . at such rentals as the class of people for whom they are intended can pay". These changes included the use of thinner walls, smaller roof timbers and, where bye-laws allowed, the increase of fireproof timber construction. A further experiment which took place in 1905 was the erection of a block of apartments in Liverpool by the City Engineer, J.A. Brodie, in a steel framework clothed in pre-cast concrete panels. The first decade of the twentieth century also saw the continual urging by W. Thomson, author of *The Housing Handbook Up-to-Date*, "that the cost of production of the dwelling, like that of other manufactured articles, ought to be capable of reduction as a result of experiment and production on a large scale."[8]

Scientific Management, the assembly line and social theory

Discussion on the application of manufacturing techniques to housing was influenced by two early twentieth century developments in methods of business organisation: Scientific Management and the assembly line. These products of American industrial progress had a major impact on theories of social development and were particularly influential in discussions concerned with remedying the destabilisation of Europe which followed the First World War.

The study of rationalising operations within the workplace developed in America during the latter decades of the nineteenth century. In 1895 F.W. Taylor began lecturing and publishing his theory of Scientific Management. The basis of Taylor's theory was that management could maximise the productivity of each worker by prescribing, as a result of exact measurement and detailed study, the most efficient way of carrying out any working operation.[9] Taylor's ideas gained considerable prominence in the American efficiency craze of the decade following 1910, making a fundamental impact on industrial methods and popular consciousness.

The introduction of the assembly line first took place in the automobile industry, itself a product of the late nineteenth century phase of industrialisation. The success of the Ford Motor Co. was based on the identification of a market for cheap motor cars. Ford then exploited this market by designing a standard model which could be produced economically and in large volumes. By 1913 this strategy had proved successful enough for Ford to apply moving line techniques to the manufacture of components. The assembly line brought the task to the worker, thereby eliminating fetching and carrying. With the aid of "scientific study", the worker's task was reduced to the simplest and most repetitive operation: "He does as nearly as possible only one thing with only one movement".[10] Both conveying the task to a stationary point and rationalising operations to a single repeated movement allowed the introduction of machinery. Ford's motor operation combined the three requisites to mass producing complex artifacts: identification of a market large enough to support volume production, standardisation of components to the minimum number of variations and the accumulation of sufficient capital to invest in expensive but eventually cost reducing mechanised production plant.

The destabilisation of Europe resulting from the First World War encouraged the dissemination of American concepts of industrial efficiency and their application to housing. The 1917 Russian Revolution was followed in 1918 by revolution in Germany and widespread social unrest in many nations. In Britain, unrest following the Armistice culminating in major disputes in the power and transport industries. Advanced methods of industrial organisation and production, it was proposed, would be the antidote to this deterioration in social harmony. The belief was that new technology would create sufficient wealth to satisfy working-class demands for greater equality without fundamentally altering the social and economic system. As J. Merkel has pointed out, the ideas promoted by Taylor and Ford had considerable attraction to politicians:

> The Scientific Management doctrine of technocratic control, central planning, and high productivity, leading to a golden age of mass production in which high levels of material consumption would banish class enmity and create permanent social harmony, had a core of truth that made it a powerful doctrine in the political sphere.[11]

This view was to prevail for the remainder of the period covered by this book and in turn had a fundamental influence on methods of housing provision.

If standardisation and the assembly line had made the motor car a commodity for mass consumption then, in the view of a number of politicians and experts, it could do the same for housing. By 1916 the architect S.D. Adshead, a member of the Liverpool School, had concluded that "The cost of producing a simple article of commerce depends very largely upon the number of similar articles produced . . . this holds good with standard cottages."[12] In *The Standard Cottage* (1916), Adshead proposed a method of wall construction combining brick, concrete and a light steel frame which he felt would be very economical if combined with the large-scale repetition of standardised cottages. The social advantages of applying Ford's production methods to housing in this way were pointed out by Pemberton Billing MP during a speech to the House of Commons in 1919, at the height of post-war industrial unrest:

> As regards motorcars Mr Ford, the American, has taught what can be done by standardising them, and I submit it would be possible to standardise every door and every window frame, to make them by the hundreds and thousands in Government factories and thus get rid of a good many difficulties . . . if next

winter finds us where last winter found us, the social state of this country will be far more serious than it is today.[13]

New Forms of Construction in Early State Housing Programmes

A number of new forms of construction arose during the first major government housing programmes following the First World War. While, in the first place, an outcome of shortages in skilled building labour and traditional materials, the circumstances which gave rise to alternative methods of construction and the techniques themselves, had a considerable effect on the subsequent development of building technology. In particular, they encouraged the state's initiation of research into new methods and were seen by the building establishment as evidence of the degree to which housing production was susceptible to the immutable laws of industrial advance.

Immediately prior to the war there had been renewed discussion by politicians of housing provision, but it was the post-war fear of social unrest which prompted the Addison Housing Programme in 1919 as "an insurance against revolution".[14] At the outset, half a million dwellings were promised. State housing, subsidised by the Exchequer for the first time, was adopted as the major element of post-war stabilisation policy. With the onset of economic depression and the consequent waning of labour power, the Homes Fit for Heroes programme was reduced to 176,000 houses in 1921. Nevertheless, the principle of social housing had been established and the administrative machinery set up to implement this new building type. The state continued to build throughout the inter-war period, providing a total of 579,000 homes between 1924 and 1935.[15]

From the point at which it started producing housing, the state initiated the scientific study of building methods. Building technology was a significant element of the 1917 Tudor Walters Report, which examined the implications of mounting a large, publicly funded housing programme. The section on Economy in Construction stated of the nineteenth century that: "while science and skill were devoted in ever-increasing measure to the development of industrial processes, no such attention was paid to housebuilding". In the opinion of the Committee, house building should be the product of up-to-date methods of "business organisation, scientific costing, standardisation, etc., which have been found effective in other industries".[16] However, having given it consideration, the Committee rejected the degree of standardisation found in automobile manufacture feeling it to be inappropriate to good dwelling design. Nevertheless, it recommended the adoption of a range of standardised plans, window and door opening sizes, fixtures and fittings.

The post-war interest of government in housing technology also gave rise to the appointment of the Building Materials Research Board by the Department of Scientific and Industrial Research, itself a result of the state's wartime promotion of technical advance in industry. The government also set up the Standardisation and New Methods of Construction Committee to examine ways of solving acute shortages in skilled building labour and to consider the advantages of standardising building components. This Committee gave consideration to the various standards which could be adopted for sanitary fittings, washing coppers, windows and rainwater goods. The Committee also recommended the establishment of a Building Board to carry out "not only research into building materials, but also the building of works of an experimental nature" in order to examine the benefits which new technology could bring to house construction.[17] As a result, the state created the permanent Building Research Board to carry out research into building materials and experiment in new methods of construction. In 1921 a modest research station was set up at Acton which later became the Building Research Station. From small beginnings, the BRS grew in importance throughout the period covered by this book.[18] The state maintained its keen interest in housing technology for the remainder of the inter-war period. partly because of recurrent shortages in skilled building labour and partly because of continued involvement in low-cost housing provision.

The Addison housing programme saw the first extensive use of radical alternatives to traditional construction to overcome shortages in skilled building labour and materials. New methods included 10,000 Dorlonco steel houses and over 12,000 concrete dwellings erected by Henry Boot and Wm. Airey. By 1939 over twenty-three new methods of house construction had been developed, some of which formed the basis for post-Second World War systems. The methods used had as their aim the substitution of bricklayers with alternative, factory based, techniques carried out by unskilled labour, such as pre-cast concrete frames and walling blocks. A number of timber houses were also developed. Where engineering and shipbuilding firms attempted to diversify into housebuilding, the techniques and materials used were frequently those of the parent industry and involved steel frames or rivetted plates.[19]

While essentially a solution to short-term scarcities of skilled building labour, there was a strong relationship between alternative housing types and the search for more efficient methods of production through factory based techniques. Indeed, this was essential if sponsors were to compete with traditional builders. The adoption of advanced industrial technology was noted in 1924 by the government appointed Committee on Methods of House Construction which examined the steel-clad system promoted by Lord Weir. The Committee noted with interest the fact that it had been designed with "a view to adopting such methods of standardisation as will lead to cheapness in large scale production and to rapidity of building".[20] Further comment on new house-building methods and industrial development was made by a government court of enquiry into the industrial dispute which later arose from production of Weir's house. The court took the side of progress and found against the unions, stating what had by this time become orthodoxy in relation to housing production:

> In the ordinary course of the progressive evolution of industry changes are made, as a means of increasing the volume of production and lowering the cost, which have the effect of substituting standardisation and mechanical processes for the individual effort of the skilled craftsman. The whole history of modern industrial development in this country and elsewhere shows that this is true.(1925)[21]

By the mid 1920s, theories of social and industrial progress, reinforced by the practical example of new methods of construction and state initiated research, had increasingly connected mass production and housing in the beliefs of the political establishment.

The science of abundant housing

Although frequently overshadowed by the world wars which preceded and followed, the 1920s and 1930s were times of steady and significant change in social policy and architectural theory. The transformation of the Labour Movement into a parliamentary institution and the extension of welfare policy contributed further to the development of the Welfare State which followed the Second World War. Furthermore, the architectural theories of the European Modern Movement, involving revolution in methods of building design and production, captured the imagination of politicians and architects already interested in the role technology played in industrial development. By the early 1940s mass production of housing had become the conventional wisdom and expectation of social policy makers.

The strengthening of welfare policy

Although a period of social conflict, the inter-war years saw the transformation of once revolutionary political movements into parliamentary institutions through the belief that class inequality could be remedied from within the system by welfare measures such as free health care, national insurance and state housing.

Working-class interests were represented in Parliament by the first Labour government in January 1924 under Ramsay McDonald. The Labour Party leadership's resolve to improve working-class living conditions from *within* the parliamentary system was evidenced by McDonald's role in crushing the General Strike two years later. According to Ralph Miliband, the defeat of the Strike in 1926 represented the culmination of inter-war labour disputes and "immeasurably advanced the transformation of the worker's movement into a tame, disciplined trade union and electoral interest".[22] Under trade union leaders such as George Hicks, working-class power was diverted away from the pursuit of revolution to securing welfare reforms through Parliamentary action.

Notwithstanding regressive measures, such as the 1931 dole cut and family means test, legislation passed under Baldwin, MacDonald and Chamberlain (between 1925 and the Second World War) alleviated some of the harsher aspects of working-class life. Furthermore, the state continued producing housing on a large scale: between 1927 and 1939 local authorities built more than 50,000 homes in each year. State housing, supported by Labour and Conservative governments alike, had become integral to twentieth century social policy.[23]

Poverty and prosperity juxtaposed

The inter-war juxtaposition of poverty and prosperity, each the product of particular aspects of industrial development, added a further strand to the growing belief of politicians, architects and scientists, that science and technology were the means of achieving social and economic goals.

Economic depression had followed soon after the First World War. This was heightened and extended to an international scale after the Wall Street Crash in 1929. By 1931 world trade had fallen below that of 1913. During this global economic stagnation, Britain fared particularly badly experiencing the highest levels of unemployment in Europe.[24] Nonetheless, despite the severity of depression in staple industries, such as heavy engineering and textiles, more recently established areas of the economy, which included synthetic yarns, cars and electrical goods thrived. The combination of new forms of employment and a reduction in the cost of living which accompanied falling world commodity prices created affluence for many in the Midlands and South East, who were able to enjoy the mass products of new manufacturing industries. Typical of these was the output of automobiles which grew from 34,000 cars and trucks in 1913 to just over half a million in 1937.[25] While not able to provide for all, technical advancements in the industrial system helped to provide, in unprecedented and evident abundance, for many.

The exceptional performance of advanced sectors of industry confirmed the view of an increasing number of politicians, scientists and housing experts; that social deprivation could be alleviated by a wider distribution of the fruits of new technology. Typical of this relationship between technology and social progress was the Social Relations of Science Movement. Throughout the 1930s, with members such as the famous scientist J.D. Bernal, this movement advocated scientific rationality to create a truly utopian society of abundant provision and the erosion of social conflict.[26] In *The Social Function of Science*, Bernal expounded his belief in the progressive power of scientific thought and the degree to which it could improve the state of society:

> Science reacts on Society unconsciously and indirectly through the force of its ideas. The acceptance of the ideas of science carries with it an implicit criticism of the present state of man and opens the possibility of its definite improvement.[27]

The degree to which Bernal and those of his Movement believed science could provide solutions hitherto undreamed of is shown in his discussion of housing. As well as urging mass production, Bernal described a scientifically designed window "guarded either by the wind itself or by jets of air forming part of the general ventilation system. The ultimate development would be the weatherproof room without wall or roof".

The European Modern Movement

The belief that poverty could be eradicated by technology created a fertile culture for the growth of the European Modern Movement in Britain. This body influenced the tenor of inter-war housing theory and came to dominate all aspects of the building process in later years. At its core, the Modern Movement advocated that contemporary methods of industrial organisation and manufacture should be the model for building design and production. Around this proposition developed a comprehensive theory of architecture.

The Modern Movement has its origins in the time of rapid industrial expansion in Germany following Unification. The nation's tradition of planned state industrial development and scientifically based education system, provided strong encouragement to industrial innovation. Indeed, German industry took a world lead in many of the late nineteenth century science-based industries, such as electrical and chemical manufacture. The principles of standardisation and industrial efficiency promoted by Taylor and Ford were eagerly adopted by German and French engineers during the early years of the twentieth century and were used to promote attempts at rapid

20

industrial development. By 1910 Walter Gropius was advocating the mass production of housing through standardisation, already achieved by his country in automobile and machinery manufacture.[28]

The years which followed the end of the First World War intensified the relationship between architectural theory and models of industrial production. Architects such as Charles-Edouard Jeanneret (later Le Corbusier) advocated Taylorisation as the panacea to physical reconstruction in France.[29] In Germany, the imperative for the new Weimar Republic to rebuild the economy and prevent a recurrence of the social instability which had followed the war caused it to become the most technically innovative nation in Europe, building on the industrial achievements of previous years. In 1921, a grouping of German state officials, industrialists, engineers and academics formed the National Board for Efficiency, with the aim of aiding a major reform of German industry in accordance with the latest principles of American management theory.[30] This movement, known as German Rationalisation, contributed to the formation of architectural theory during the 1920s, out of which came the *Neues Bauen* (New Building), a movement which adopted models of industrial organisation for a series of state-funded, low-cost housing developments in the larger industrial cities of the Weimar Republic.[31] In these projects, new methods of construction such as pre-cast concrete were used extensively. With the political ascendancy of the National Socialist Party after 1933, under which *Neues Bauen* architectural theories were outlawed through their association with Bolshevism, many German architects and writers, including Walter Gropius and Nikolaus Pevsner, sought refuge in Britain and America. In their new homes this group of architects and theorists assiduously propagandised what soon became known as the Modern Movement.[32]

The Committee for the Industrial and Scientific Provision of Housing

Having accepted that houses could be mass produced, the late 1930s saw architects and politicians discussing in detail the means by which this belief could be implemented and the revolutionary effect it would have on the building market. Reorganising the building market to enable mass production was often thought to involve state intervention. However, such discussions were soon overshadowed by the very involvement of the state in preparations for post-war rebuilding programmes. A number of politicians and housing experts framing these policies were also enthusiastic contributors to discussions on the mass production of housing. In the latter years of the Second World War, theories of scientific housing production and the practice of state building policy became increasingly interlinked.

One of the first to indicate the role government might play in developing housebuilding methods was the Modern Movement architect, F.R.S. Yorke. In 1934 Yorke stated what was, by now, becoming the conventional wisdom that: "provision of the economical house of good quality can only be made possible through rigid standardisation and prefabrication".[33] Writing on the eve of the Second World War, Yorke acknowledged that his vision was impossible within the current pattern of demand for new buildings. The tendency for these to be commissioned singly from the architect "leaving to posterity a series of little monuments that are scarcely seen in the chaos" and the domination of building by individual commercial producers made the scale of output required for mass production unrealisable: "The job is too big for the individual, and a government cannot undertake the work while it is reluctant to compete with him".[34]

The circumstances under which mass produced housing could be realised and its effect on the building market were considered in great detail by the Committee for the Scientific and Industrial Provision of Housing (CISPH). This Committee was important for attempting to establish a framework for mass production and, furthermore, for involving figures active in social housing policy at local and government level. Like many during the Second World War, CISPH members believed that under advanced industrial conditions, housing should no longer be an expensive capital investment but an abundantly available consumed commodity. The Committee was founded by Raymond Perry, a self-styled industrial economist and administrator, well known for his interest in the "social importance of a rapid housebuilding programme"[35], after the War. Perry started research for a thesis on the application of machinery to "the enclosure of space for human consumption", and eventually formed CISPH in November 1941. Perry and an early architect collaborator, Dennis Clarke Hall, then approached Harry Weston, who, as well as being the owner of a machine tools business, was the chair of Coventry's Housing Committee. Thereby, Perry and Hall were provided with an influential connection in the field of local authority housing:

> So they came to tell me all about it and I was rather proud. And I can remember when they asked me if I'd take the chair at the first meeting, which I did . . . Well now that meeting was a real sensation. All those clever men with only the thought of the country at heart, comparing notes, giving their suggestions. It would have cost millions of pounds to have set up a committee like that. This was free.[36]

In October 1943 Perry submitted a memorandum to the Ministry of Health, then considering a temporary housing programme, giving advice on "The Limitation of Life of Houses: its Industrial and Economic Implications". As with most informed opinion, CISPH acknowledged that a secure and large market must be obtained prior to production in order to amortise the capital costs of development and manufacturing plant, "after which production becomes unbelievably cheap". Using the light bulb as an example (the cost of which had been lowered two hundred times through mass production), the memorandum stated that housing could itself follow the "common curve" of price reduction. With mass production, the cost of a 1,000 sq.ft. house "with a hitherto undreamed-of amenity standard" would be between only £300 and £350 at pre-war prices. The revolutionary implication of such a cheapening of the dwelling on the property market was noted by Perry:

> by a small capital payment and continued income payments a man becomes a consumer of motor cars. This position has been brought about entirely by the application of quantity production . . . . If the idea of permanence in a house be once abandoned and particularly its permanent association with the land upon which it is built, similar conditions begin to apply, and if the quantity production element can be brought in as well the analogy is complete.[38]

In its first report, published in January 1943, the

Committee gave considerable space to a discussion of ways in which the work of firms involved in the production of house parts could be "co-ordinated both technically and in terms of production schedules". The solution to this problem, the Committee felt, lay in the establishment of a Housing Production Council relying on donations by industries eager to participate in new methods of production and operated by a full time staff. In 1944, with the publication of its second report, an extensive analysis of existing systems of construction, the Committee dissolved itself, and found in its own place the Housing Production Society comprising fifteen members, many of whom were on the original Committee. However, this initiative seems to have petered out and Weston explains that soon after the war, architect members of the Society left to begin their work on practical rebuilding projects.

Rebuilding programmes anticipated for after the Second World War were undoubtedly seen by the Modern Movement as an opportunity to apply its ideas in practice. Maxwell Fry, writing at the end of the war considered the marketing problem described earlier by Yorke more optimistically. In *Fine Building* (1944), Fry emphasised the significance of the market to the success of mass production by referring to Henry Ford: "he assumed the need was widespread and varied only within narrow limits".[39] Such a market for housing, Fry suggested, had been forced onto the nation by the Second World War: four years without "serious" town building and four years of bomb destruction concentrated in major cities. The demand that the war had created was so great and the social imperative for rebuilding such that standardisation and mass production would have to be extended to all parts of the building. The basis of Fry's strategy for mass producing houses was the unification of municipal building programmes. Taking a standardised bathroom and kitchen, Fry insisted that there was not:

a first class industrialist in the country who would not agree that if we could standardise five such models – five and no more – and get them adopted by five big cities for use in their rebuilding over a term of ten years, that a kitchen better than the best in the Ideal Home could not be brought within the means of all who need them. It was by such means that Ford made his "T" model universal.

Maxwell Fry and F.R.S. Yorke were influential figures in the theoretical development of architects practicing after the war. Furthermore, a review of CISPH's pedigree suggests that the CCDD philosophy of scientific housing production was shared by a range of influential figures. For instance the membership of the Committee included: Harry Weston, Chair of a major Midlands housing committee; Ove Arup, and F.J. Samuely, both of whom worked as structural engineers during the war and later built up major practices; Max Lock, head of the Hull School of Architecture; Lewis Silkin, a member of Parliament and a member of the Central Housing Advisory Committee to the Ministry of Health; Donald Gibson, City Architect to Coventry and after a prominent career in the public architectural service eventually Director General of Research and Development to the Ministry of Public Works and Buildings; Edric Neel, another architect at Coventry who upon leaving CISPH initiated the Arcon Group and Elizabeth Denby, author of *Europe Rehoused*, a widely read survey of social housing programmes in inter-war Europe. Furthermore, Weston describes Lord Portal, the wartime Minister of Works responsible for advising the War Cabinet on building matters and carrying out government experiments in methods of construction, as a frequent and "valuable" attender of meetings. Weston also refers to a visit he made to London to explain CISPH's ideas to a special meeting of the House of Commons. If the membership of CISPH is any indication, the solution of housing shortages through mass production was upheld by a number of individuals able to exert a considerable influence on the formation of post-war state building policies.

Chapter 2
POST-WAR STABILISATION:
1942 – 48

The years that immediately followed the Second World War saw the use of new methods of construction on an unprecedented scale. In addition to large numbers of temporary bungalows, by 1948, thirty per cent of permanent local authority house completions were in system building (*see* Appendix 2). This reliance on new technology was the result of plans carefully prepared for post-war housing policy which, it was anticipated, would require more houses than the traditional building industry could produce. Furthermore, sponsors were aware of the considerable commercial benefits which would come from the successful production of new housing systems.

The extent to which factory methods of production were adopted and the ways in which they were regarded must also be seen in relation to ideals of mass production. The early post-war years saw the promotion of system building for ideological as well as material purposes. Central to this was the proposition that the Welfare State could meet social demands placed on it through its reliance on science and technology. System building was regarded by politicians as evidence that a major breakthrough was taking place in which the country's housing needs would be met.

The Welfare State

Like its predecessor, the Second World War had a fundamental effect on both the fabric and culture of British society. While it undoubtedly gave rise to many entirely new features of life, its main effect was to accelerate underlying economic and social trends. Most significant of these was the movement towards a comprehensive Welfare State.

The years between 1939 and 1945 saw renewed

Temporary pre-fabricated
bungalows, using new
methods of production
were considered essential
to ensure a stable transition
from war to peace during
the "emergency" period

demands for more even distribution of resources which could not be ignored in the catalytic atmosphere of social change created by "total war". The notion that the working class was enduring deprivation and sacrifice to secure a more equal society was crucial to the prosecution of the war effort which required cohesion at all levels. In contrast to the First World War, the state gave early consideration to far reaching measures to fundamentally

improve the lives of working people. The perpetuation of class unity through social legislation underlay the following Terms of Reference for the War Cabinet Reconstruction Committee established in 1941:

> To arrange for the preparation of practical schemes of reconstruction . . . .These plans should have as their general aim the perpetuation of the National Unity achieved in this country during the war, through a social and economic structure designed to secure equality of opportunity and service among all classes of the community.[1]

So far as housing was concerned, in relation to its inter-war housing programmes, the War Cabinet recognised that "It is certain that the country will expect an even more vigorous policy after this war".[2] It was acknowledged that continuing rent controls and inflated post-war building costs would eliminate the profit from rented housing and, as a result, private enterprise could not be relied on to provide cheap accommodation on a large scale. In anticipation of this, the state prepared to become the major producer of rented housing in the immediate post-war years, projecting unprecedented numbers of completions.

The large-scale provision of state housing was only one feature of post-war welfare policy. In 1944 the Butler Education Act extended secondary education to the entire population and in 1945 the Labour landslide ensured that other welfare proposals of the Reconstruction Committee were laid before parliament. In 1946 the National Insurance and National Health Service Acts were passed with the avowed intention of "covering the whole population and all risks from the cradle to the grave".[3]

In the immediate post-war years three features of what has become known as the Welfare State emerged: nationalisation of essential industries, a taxation structure to finance the state welfare apparatus and state intervention in the economy to prevent a recurrence of the severe economic crisis which had generated widespread unemployment during the inter-war years. By 1945 the State had accepted Keynesian economic theories based on government regulation of demand and the direction of investment to reduce unemployment and use the work-force most effectively.

The *Employment Policy* White Paper of 1944 clearly described the government's intention to manage the economy in post-war years:

> The government accept as one of their primary aims and responsibilities the maintenance of a high and stable level of employment after the war . . . the Government have in mind the more general aim of securing for the nation the most effective use of its manpower and its material resources.[4]

These concerns were to have a considerable impact on state policy towards the building industry throughout the post-war period. Indeed, for a decade after the war the state retained many of the economic powers it had assumed as part of its "total war" effort. In the immediate years, known as the "emergency" period, complete control was exercised to implement policies considered essential to achieve a stable transition of the economy and social structure from wartime disruptions to normal conditions. One of these policies involved new methods of house construction.

State policy: the "Emergency" Period

Methods of house construction were given early thought by the War Cabinet. As a result of plans laid at the height of conflict, new forms of construction became the backbone of housing policy during the post-war "emergency" period. These policies were by nature Keynesian, in that the cardinal concern in ensuring a stable transition of the economy from war to peace was the balance of demand and supply. The demand for houses could not be reduced if social cohesion was to be ensured; therefore, where it threatened to outstrip traditional methods of supply, alternatives were adopted.

Balancing demand and supply

Balancing demand and supply was considered by the War Cabinet along with the first forecasts of post-war housing needs in the middle years of the war.

In November 1942 the Ministry of Health presented a paper to the Official Committee on Post-war Economic

Problems describing how, after the First World War, the housing industry had slowly built itself up, achieving four million completions between 1919 and 1939. In order to meet the anticipated need for three to four million new houses in the first post-war decade alone, the Ministry argued that the inter-war rate of production would have to be doubled, placing an intolerable strain on the building industry. In the hope of easing this strain, the Ministry was considering "alternative" methods of construction: "If practical methods are evolved which result in houses being provided quickly and at a reasonable cost they will have to be adopted".[5] Earlier that year the Inter-departmental Committee on House Construction (Burt Committee) had been set up to review the potential of new methods of construction but as yet no conclusions had been reached.

In May 1943 the Internal Economic Problems Committee presented its deliberations on housing policy to the War Cabinet. The Committee was particularly vehement that mistakes made in the Addison housing programme of 1919, when a huge strain was put on the building industry without any system of planning or control, should not be repeated. To neglect the need for planning, the Committee argued, would threaten the government's plans to ensure economic stability in the immediate post-war years:

> The worst of all possible courses would be to attempt with high subsidies to force through a programme of new construction immediately after the armistice in excess of the capacity of the industry: this would lead to higher prices and wages in the Building Industry which would not only tend to defeat the end in view but in its wider reactions might well upset the whole stabilisation policy.[6]

It added that to ignore this problem might lead to the suspension of the housing programme as it had in 1921. The War Cabinet promptly acted on this advice, preparing administrative controls with which to restrain demand and direct resources towards state housing. This was achieved through two measures; first, a licensing system required practically all building to be sanctioned by the government up to 1949, and second, the Control of Engagement Order ensured that until 1948 all building labour was directed in accordance with government policies.[7] While writers have questioned the success with which these controls operated, it was clearly the government's intention that the housing programme would be carried out within the limitations of available building resources.

The fundamental resource problem was seen to be that of skilled building labour which had been depleted by conscription to the armed services. In 1943 the government Command Paper, *Training for the Building Industry*, set out measures to increase the workforce to 1,250,000 through extensive training schemes[8] but acknowledged that this would take between three to four years during which housing demand would be at its most intense. To overcome this pressure, the government prepared to bring alternative resources to bear.

The temporary housing programme

One very conspicuous solution to housing shortages during the "emergency" period was the provision of temporary accommodation using engineering methods of production. The aim in this instance was to use surplus munitions capacity without impinging on resources required for permanent houses.

The provision of temporary houses was much discussed in the latter years of the war and in May 1943 two Cabinet committees recommended its adoption. However, with the end of the war approaching, the real impetus for what eventually became the Temporary Housing Programme was provided by the Prime Minister. In the Cabinet meeting of 24 February 1944, Winston Churchill announced his intention to manufacture half a million temporary homes from steel, the whole process being treated "as a military operation handled by the Government, with private industry harnessed to its service".[9] The object of the programme was to provide a large number of houses which could be constructed without increasing demands on conventional resources and jeopardising the progress of permanent housing. According to conventioal wisdom, the mass production of houses under factory conditions would require the minimum of skilled building labour. This was explained to Parliament by an over-optimistic Minister of Health in August 1944:

We felt that it was of the first importance that this

project should not delay the building of permanent houses, and, consequently, that it should make the minimum demand on the building industry. That consideration pointed to a type of building, so far as possible, factory made . . . whereas it is usually reckoned that it takes 100,000 building operatives to build 100,000 houses in a year, the building labour force required for 100,000 of these bungalows is not much more than 8,000 to 10,000.[10]

Churchill's hopes of half a million temporary bungalows were dashed in September 1944, when the committee set up to implement the programme reported that little more than 150,000 houses could be provided without taking resources needed for permanent dwellings. It was with this reduced target in mind that the programme was implemented.[11]

Although subsidised by the state, during the inter-war period local authorities designed, built and owned their houses. Under the 1944 Housing (Temporary) Accommodation Act, which authorised the expenditure of £150m., provision was made for the manufacture of the homes on government account.[12] The production authority was the Ministry of Works who contracted directly with individual suppliers for materials and components and with construction firms to erect the houses. The role of sponsoring firms was reduced to that of managing agent on behalf of the Ministry and the involvement of local authorities was limited to obtaining sites and preparing off-site services and roads. The instruction manual, which advised local authorities on layouts, maintenance, selection of tenants, rents and management, clearly set out the terms on which they received their allocation. The houses were to be provided and owned by the government, while "the authority will choose the tenants, fix and receive the rents, manage the property and keep it in repair. The authority will make an annual payment to the Ministry of Health of an amount to be determined".[13] As Churchill had predicted, the Temporary Housing Programme was indeed carried out on the lines of a military operation.

Permanent prefabricated houses

While temporary bungalows were a short-term expedient, the fundamental aim had always been to provide permanent houses. To achieve sufficient numbers, the government promoted prefabrication and helped sponsors plan and implement production and offered local authorities outright subsidies to offset the higher costs resulting from new technology.

In August 1944 a new urgency was added to preparations for post-war housing when the Minister for Reconstruction, Lord Woolton, announced that the destruction of 25,000 houses and the serious damage to a further million by flying bomb attacks had falsified earlier assessments of housing demand. Under the circumstances, Woolton proposed to re-examine "the means of harnessing to the problem of providing living accommodation every form of construction, however unconventional".[14] Of these he made particular reference to the experiments being carried out into permanent prefabricated housing by Lord Portal at the Ministry of Works which had indicated considerable economies in skilled building labour. The immediate tasks, he suggested, were to approve alternative designs and ensure that manufacturing capacity for fittings and components would be "given priority second only to essential war production" in order to ensure their availability at the end of the war. Woolton concluded by stating that "Of all the problems facing us on the Home Front, housing is the most urgent and one of the most important from the point of view of future stability and public contentment". In March 1945 the Government announced its target of 300,000 houses "built or building" within the first two post-war years.[15]

Implementation of the prefabricated housing programme was discussed in earnest with the setting up of the War Cabinet Housing Committee in January 1945. Two months later, Duncan Sandys, the new Minister of Works, presented his case to the Committee for the maximum use of permanent prefabricated houses arguing that "there was no doubt that novel methods would enable substantial economies of building labour to be effected". Although both the Minister of Health and the Minister of Labour and National Service questioned the advisability of departing from traditional methods – the former through a scepticism that local authorities would accept the houses and the latter through a fear for the detrimental effect prefabrication would have on recruitment to the building industry – Sandys's persuasive arguments on labour savings carried the meeting. The resolve was that:

the aim should be to secure that in the "emergency" period as high a proportion as practicable of permanent houses were erected by new methods using the minimum of building labour.[16]

To implement the permanent prefabricated housing programme the government played a central role, ensuring sponsors of a market and subsidising their products. In January 1945 the Cabinet Housing Sub-Committee gave consideration to the means by which full advantage could be taken of the prefabricated housing systems now available, approving a recommendation by the Minister of Works that: "manufacturers should be assured of a sufficient demand for these [prefabricated houses] to warrant their embarking on large-scale production. To the extent necessary to secure this, government bulk orders or production agreements would be useful". Indeed, for fear of prejudice against new methods of construction on the part of local authorities and the building industry, the Ministry of Works prepared legislation "for the manufacture of permanent prefabricated houses on Government account". Later in the year the Ministry's proposals were made statute in the Building Materials and Housing Act of 1945 which made provision for the government to purchase building materials and equipment, including complete prefabricated houses, sell these to local authorities and, where necessary, erect them on their behalf.

Although total powers existed, the eventual implementation of the programme relied on less direct measures. In September 1945 the Ministry of Works prepared its final paper recommending that local authorities should be notified of the various types of prefabricated house on offer, with an indication of the dates when deliveries could be made, and invited to place an order. These enquiries allowed an assessment to be made of the extent to which:

bulk ordering of components or of complete houses should be undertaken, production agreements made in order to stimulate production in advance of firm demands . . . or central negotiations undertaken to fix the price of components . . . in some cases no action by the Government will be necessary, but wherever substantial factory production is involved, either of complete houses or of steel frames or other steel or

34

concrete units, action by the government in one or other of the directions indicated above will probably be found to be desirable in order to secure proper organisation of production and distribution and economy in costs".

With regard to his proposals, the Minister of Works pointed out that prefabrication required a substantial development period, during which designs were prepared and factories tooled up for production, and urged that "the experimental stage" should now be regarded as over and local authorities approached as soon as possible. This was done in October 1945 when Circular 182/45 asked local government to place orders for steel frame houses "on the assumption that the cost will be comparable with the present cost of houses of traditional construction".[17]

In certain cases the government intervened directly in the production of prefabricated houses. A guaranteed order was given to the British Iron and Steel Federation (BISF) for the "large-scale production" of its design. The government used its full powers to order 20,000 sets of pre-cast concrete components for the Airey system and purchased 5,000 Swedish Timber Homes outright for sale to local authorities. In the case of the Howard House an order was placed by the Ministry of Works for 3,000 (only 1,303 were eventually built) which also supervised delivery and erection.[18]

However, the greatest support given by the state to prefabricated housing was Section 17 of the Housing (Financial and Miscellaneous Provisions) Act of 1946 which, until December 1947, offset the increased costs of prefabricated houses through the payment of a capital grant to local authorities. The Ministry of Works' optimism that new techniques would compare in cost with traditional methods, stated to the Cabinet as late as September 1945, was ill-founded. Fifteen of the nineteen systems which entered production received subsidies. The largest of these, £708, was received by the permanent aluminium bungalow followed by BISF (£244) and the Airey house (£175). Eight other systems received subsidies of more than £90. Given the average cost of a three-bedroom local authority dwelling at this time was £1,242,[19] these subsidies were substantial and could only have been offered by a government convinced they were essential to its post-war "emergency" housing policy.

Sponsors: post-war diversification

The firms which most quickly produced housing systems in response to government policy came from the engineering industry using the techniques and materials they had used to contribute to the war effort. Firms engaged in munitions manufacture had strong incentives to involve themselves in housing as it provided a ready market for products no longer required for military purposes. In this they were assisted by a state eager to prevent the collapse of post-war industry.

Earlier initiatives and inter-war innovation

The prefabricated housing programme of the late 1940s was by no means the first time engineering and steel producers had attempted to enter the housing market through new building methods.

Diversification began as early as 1905 when the Cheap Cottages Exhibition featured designs from a number of companies hoping to find new outlets for metal products. There is no evidence to indicate that these initiatives led to large-scale production and it was not until the post-war government housing programme was introduced that engineering firms realised their ambition. The most successful producer of a system based on steel products was Dorman Long, a steel manufacturing firm which produced 10,000 houses during the 1920s. A number of other attempts to promote steel systems were made during the years of inter-war depression which affected steel and engineering firms in particular. Although, as well as Lord Weir's design, models were sponsored by six firms,[20] R.B. White estimates that fewer than 3,000 dwellings were built using steel systems due to the greater cost than traditional construction.[21]

The subsequent use of engineering techniques in housing was helped by inter-war innovations which economised on the use of steel by replacing the riveting and bolting of heavy hot-rolled members with welding, cold-rolling and pressing. The use of welding, which achieved stronger and more economical joints, spread during the 1930s and was stimulated by the Second World War which caused plant to be installed and labour trained.[22] Cold-rolling of thin steel sheet, stimulated by the inter-war growth of the automobile industry, enabled complex structural profiles to be formed.[23] Combined, these techniques produced more efficient lightweight frames with economical methods of cladding and formed a more practical basis from which sponsors could approach the design of steel houses during the Second World War.

Fears of post-war industrial collapse

The government's intention to utilise prefabricated construction brought an eager response from steel and engineering producers who had geared up to war production. Indeed, many firms that had considered diversification from an early stage of the war were assisted in their plans by government committees considering non-traditional methods of building.

In November 1941 the War Cabinet estimated the employment of workers in armaments to have risen by 2.5 million since 1939.[24] Nowhere was this increase more dramatic than in the aircraft industry where employment had stood at little more than 50,000 in the mid-1930s; by 1943 this had grown to 300,000 as a result of the nation's escalating air defence programme.[25] In 1941 the British Iron and Steel Federation (BISF) wrote to the Cabinet Reconstruction Committee expressing member's fears for the collapse of post-war markets: "Many industries have extended beyond any possibility of having a post-war demand equal to present capacity, and unless the surplus capacity is liquidated and the policy controlled, unrestricted competition might result in a slump with serious unemployment".[26] Rather than liquidate capacity, many engineering firms, including the authors of this plea, prepared to enter the state housing market. Of the twelve systems of construction under consideration by the newly constituted Burt Committee in 1943, seven featured techniques requiring substantial amounts of steel.[27] In the Committee's final listing of approved schemes, no less than 29 of the 78 post-war proposals involved steel frames.[28]

The potential for new methods of construction to provide an outlet for surplus industrial capacity was welcomed by the government. The widespread unemployment forecast by the BISF was inconsistent with the state's recent adoption of Keynesian economic management policies. In 1942 the Burt Committee considered both the interests of housing production and the interests of industry in general when considering which of the new methods should be used:

> It is apparent that, at the end of the war, many firms may suddenly collapse owing to the stopping of all demand. If the products, machines and labour of these firms can be used for housing, a useful change-over will have been accomplished. To this end it is well to bear in mind, in considering one or other method of construction, how far they are akin to present-day war production as opposed to normal building processes.[29]

The Arcon Group

A successful diversification into housing was made by the Arcon group, which amalgamated the resources of engineering firms, materials producers and two architects – Edric Neel (formerly of CISPH) and Jim Gear – to design and produce a range of temporary and permanent designs.

The group's first project was a two-storey house based on the products of Stewart and Lloyds, a steelwork firm in Corby. Although not eventually used, protoypes were built and the system was one of the first to be developed in preparation for post-war housing policy. The house featured a tubular steel frame, this being the main product of the firm and one for which they wished to find a new market.

Although the first design was unsuccessful, the Arcon Group eventually produced 41,000 steel frame temporary houses.[30] Production of the Arcon House was a collaborative effort involving a group of industries, each assigned a portion of the project according to their manufacturing interests. The lightweight welded steel trusses were manufactured by Stewart and Lloyds at Corby where "the complete cycle, from digging the ore to making the tube, is carried out practically under one roof".[31] This was the first large-scale structural use of steel tubes in building and was a significant diversification for the steel industry. Another steel firm, Williams & Williams, manufactured the framework for the walls and the production of the asbestos cement roof covering was carried out by Turners' Asbestos Cement Ltd. Joinery was distributed amongst sixty firms under the aegis of Taylor Woodrow which joined the group in 1945 to co-ordinate the subcontractors and erect the bungalows on site. By 1946 Imperial Chemical Industries (industrially manufactured boards and plastics), The United Steel Co. (steel) and Williams & Williams (steel) had been added to the list of contributors to the project. An example of the Arcon bungalow now stands at the Avoncroft Museum of Building in West Bromwich.

The aircraft industry

An unlikely, but remarkably successful, diversification was also carried out by the aircraft industry. It manufactured 54,000 aluminium bungalows as part of the Temporary Housing Programme and over 17,000 permanent dwellings.

As early as 1942 members of the industry had begun to prepare for the collapse of aircraft manufacture by establishing the Aluminium Development Association "to find and develop markets which will spread the products of the industry".[32] For this purpose, a number of aircraft manufacturers combined to form the Aircraft Industries Research Organisation for Housing (AIROH). Of the total cost of the design eventually produced, 77 per cent was absorbed in the purchase, fabrication and assembly of aluminium components and in 1948 the production of the bungalow absorbed 32 per cent of the entire aluminium industry's output of semi-fabrications. Due to the relatively high cost of aluminium, the bungalow proved expensive and, although considerably smaller than the two-storey houses promoted by other sponsors, in its permanent form received by far the largest subsidy of any non-traditional method of construction. Indeed, the government supported the AIROH house because it *too* wished to preserve aircraft manufacture from total collapse. Had this been allowed, not only would it have threatened the future of a major industry but would have seriously affected the nation's ability to rearm quickly for any future conflict.[33] As the Minister of Reconstruction pointed out in 1945, the issues which eventually led to government support for the aluminium house were less concerned with housing need than "with broader grounds of national policy".[34]

In terms of permanent house construction the BISF was the most successful engineering producer. By 1945 it had established a Housing Committee and was promoting three systems of construction, each of which required substantial quantities of steel. What is interesting about these designs is the way in which they displayed the range of old and new techniques. The type "A" departed little from methods used in the Dorlonco House, consisting of short lengths of hot-rolled steel section bolted together on site. Type "B" accorded more with the general trend in having a structural frame made of lightweight cold-formed composite members, while type "C" utilised two-storey pressed steel wall panels in the most technically innovative design of the three. In the event Type "A" was chosen for production and, in addition to the steel frame, included steel floor beams and roof trusses, rolled sheet steel roof cladding and pressed steel eaves and skirtings.[35] It is significant that the Type "A" was the heaviest user of steel. Although the reasons are not clear, this choice would certainly have accorded with the Federation's desire to maximise the use of its products. The Federation eventually formed a company, British Steel Houses Ltd, comprising member firms involved in the scheme, to manufacture the houses which were erected on site by building contractors. By 1950 over 38,000 local authority dwellings had been built in steel systems and of these 31,320 were accounted for by the BISF which in 1947 completed more than half of all non-traditional housing (*see* Appendix 4).

Rapid decline

The late 1940s brought a hasty end to engineering industry's housing diversification. In 1948 the government withdrew subsidies to non-traditional producers in general, thereby disadvantaging the more expensive steel systems. Later in the year this was followed by restrictions on the use of steel in house construction. By then engineering industry had converted to peacetime production and the government intended that the nation's supply of steel should be reserved for manufactured products which could assist in the government's export drive. Indeed, it was in this direction that many of the diversifying firms turned their production for a number of years.[36] In 1950 fewer than 1,000 steel frame houses were built for the home market (*see* Appendix 4).

Ideology: the Prefabrication Movement

Previous sections of this chapter have described the economic processes which led to the use of non-traditional houses. It is evident, however, that underlying these motives was the continuing belief that housing could be mass produced with all the benefits this entailed in terms of cost, improved quality and, above all considering post-war demand, rapid production. Indeed, by the end of the War, prefabrication, as the attempt to mass produce housing had become known, was accepted as the means to achieve post-war rebuilding programmes. As the Royal Institute of Architects of Ireland commented in 1945: "Unquestionably prefabrication, more than any other aspect of building has excited public interest in recent years".[37] The Prefabrication Movement, enjoined by politicians of the newly-moulded Welfare State and Modernist architects alike, was one of the most intriguing characteristics of the "emergency" period.

Trans-Atlantic influences

The popularisation of prefabrication was as much the result of images of American industrial success as it was the product of European architectural theory. Alliance in war and the stationing of millions of American troops in Britain, focussed attention on economic achievements across the Atlantic.

The role Germany and France as pre-war centres of modern architectural theory was stopped by the conflict and the resulting shift of interest to recent developments in the States was encouraged as a matter of policy by the War Cabinet. In a report, *British Ignorance of America*, prepared by the Committee on Reconstruction Problems, it was pointed out that a lack of awareness of American achievements – bred by the popular press concentrating on Vaudeville and the antics of prohibition gangsters – fostered "mutual misunderstanding and suspicions which tend to hamper a co-operative war effort".[38] As a result, propaganda was proposed, utilising the avenues of popular communication including radio, the press, cinema and school education, to concentrate attention on American contributions to cultural, scientific and industrial progress. The government's intentions were fulfilled by journalists such as Alistair Cooke, who took up his highly successful career in broadcasting the "passions, the manners, the flavour" of the American way of life to an eager British audience as Special Correspondent to the BBC on American affairs in 1938. Cook later launched his famous "Letter from America" in 1946.[39]

One American development focussed on by the British architectural press was the use of prefabricated timber housing in the welfare programmes of the Tennessee Valley Authority (TVA). An early example of many articles on this subject appeared in the September 1941 edition of *Architectural Design* which reported on the "cottages" produced in the TVA's workshops assembled from four prefabricated sections taken to site by road.[40] Indeed, if a precedent is to be sought for the Temporary Housing Programme then this was it. The AIROH bungalow translated the same principle into aluminium: it too was manufactured in four complete sections in the factory and transported to site on derequisitioned aircraft trailers. In 1942, the *Builder* rightly concluded that the "panel and caravan" types of temporary prefabricated house, produced under the American government's Defense Housing Programme "will most probably be the prototypes for any adopted over here".[41]

The interest excited by American building techniques prompted the dispatch of two missions to observe developments at first hand. The earlier of these reported directly to the Minister of Works in 1944,[42] and the second was sent in 1949 by the Anglo-American Productivity Council, itself a product of British interest in American industrial organisation.[43] Indeed, the first years of peace saw the establishment of the Urwick Committee headed by Lyndale Urwick, a propagandist of Taylorism in Britain and eventually Chair of the British Institute of Management. In 1947 the Committee established a national syllabus for the teaching of management theory.[44] While Urwick had complained that there was little real understanding and adoption of Scientific Management by industry in Britain before the war, the late 1940s saw the beginning of a process whereby American business theories permeated management techniques at every level of British industry and public administration.

Accelerated industrial development

A belief that the era of mass produced housing had arrived was encouraged by the rapid development of industrial methods to increase munitions output. The manufacture of complex engineering products, previously carried out by craft processes, grew to a massive scale with the adoption of advanced forms of industrial organisation.

Aircraft manufacture was typical of the many expanded industries forced to adopt assembly line techniques. Whereas before the war, aeroplanes were hand-made in timber and canvas, the early 1940s saw steel and aluminium fighters and bombers rolling off production lines in vast numbers – the product of industrial co-operation relying on the assembly of standard components manufactured by a multiplicity of subcontractors. Indeed, this was the method of organisation adopted in the Temporary Housing Programme which brought together separate industrial interests in the large-scale manufacture of a single product.

According to Alfred Bossom MP in 1944, prefabrication had reduced the assembly of American Liberty Ships to four days. He therefore proposed that similar methods should be used to tackle the post-war housing problem at home.[45] Indeed, the principles adopted in manufacturing Liberty Ships were widely used for the British war effort in which prefabrication became a familiar technique. Belman demountable hangers and transportable Bailey Bridges all relied on the use of structural units manufactured away from the point of assembly. To increase the anti-submarine fleet, 110 frigates and 200 tugs were "mass produced" by 76 firms contributing large, prefabricated parts.[46]

"Standardisation", "mass production" and "prefabrication" became everyday terms in the prosecution of the war effort and in the vocabulary of those, including architects and policy makers, who looked on. Such was the interest aroused in this subject that the formation of CISPH was welcomed by *Architectural Design* as the translation of "ceaseless talk, talk, talk on prefabrication into positive action".[47] Small wonder that by June 1943 the *Architects' Journal* proposed its remedy for wartime destruction in singular terms: "There is one solution only to the problems of post-war housing. It can be expressed in three words – use the machine".[48]

Prefabrication mythology and the reality of non-traditional housing

The extensive use of non-traditional techniques in post-war housing engendered the belief that mass production was here to stay. However, an examination of the systems used suggests that the resemblance to mass production was superficial only. Nevertheless, in as much as it validated faith in technology, this myth was extensively promoted by Modern Movement architects and housing politicians.

By 1944 the Burt Committee had vetted 101 of the non-traditional systems intended to expand housing supply. While all of these departed from conventional construction, very few utilised prefabrication extensively. Indeed, many were of *in situ* poured concrete. Prefabrication was used to a greater degree in the Temporary Housing Programme, but only the AIROH bungalow actually consisted of large factory made units. Nevertheless, the majority of non-traditional dwellings used materials new to housing such as concrete, steel and laminates and familiar materials such as timber in new ways to replace labour intensive craft processes. While the houses themselves were not prefabricated, prefabrication was used to a larger extent in the preparation of the parts and materials of which they were built. This was particularly the case with the steel frame systems which used the latest techniques in lightweight steel fabrication. Of more impact than the real extent of mechanised production was the innovative nature of the materials and methods of construction used. The fact that many of the houses were sponsored by engineering firms and appeared as standard models in the manner of automobiles made them very distinct from traditional construction in the minds of enthusiastic onlookers.

Although not mass produced in any true sense of the word, new methods of building were promoted by ideologists as beginning the major change in techniques forecast by the Modern Movement. In 1946 a spate of

44

publications appeared devoted to prefabrication. These were characterised by two features: the assertion that factory made houses had arrived and a conviction that they were here to stay. In a survey of systems produced in America and latterly in Britain, Richard Sheppard, later to become a noted post-war architect, introduced his readers to the subject by emphasising that the book would not consider the feasibility of prefabrication as this was no longer necessary: "such a discussion is now largely academic, for it has been amply demonstrated that efficient buildings can be constructed from mass produced factory units. Prefabrication is no longer a possibility but a fact".[49] J. Madge, editor of a "practical book written for practical men", commented of the AIROH bungalow that although it did not have the lines of the Spitfire

> the minds which have created the modern aircraft have turned their attention to the solution of an almost equally urgent problem. In so doing they have produced a design which is more completely prefabricated than any which has so far appeared . . . the substance of the method may equally well be applied in the future to the provision of permanent homes.[50]

Mechanisation and the Welfare State

A tendency to eulogise non-traditional housing and, by implication, draw attention to the progressiveness of social policy was displayed by politicians on several occasions. As well as expressing current beliefs in the role of technology, the state enthused new building methods in a way which can only have been intended to aid acceptance of its policies by reluctant local authorities and a possibly apprehensive working class. Furthermore, it could be suggested that the newly emerged and, as yet, insecure Welfare State had a vested interest in promoting the belief that it had found an answer to society's housing needs.

Politicians focussed on the temporary bungalow as the embodiment of the state's ideal of scientific progress wedded to the "tasks of peace". In 1944 Winston Churchill described the proposed houses as "far superior to the ordinary cottage"[51] even though it was considerably smaller in size and designed to last only for five years.

Similar sentiments were expressed in the House of Commons by the Secretary of State for Scotland of the highly equipped, if cramped, kitchen of the prototype bungalow erected outside the Tate: "I have been inside the house which struck me as splendid. The gadgets, the health conditions – everything splendid".[52] Dr Reginald Stradling, formerly the Director of the Building Research Station, pointed out to Parliament that "this bungalow has had more attention in matters of detail than any house or bungalow has ever had before. It is probably more scientifically correct than any house has ever been".[53] When displaying the progress made in domestic design since the war at the Ideal Home Exhibition in 1948, the Ministry of Health described its bungalows as "luxury flats on the ground", and proudly announced that "in prefabrication Britain now leads the world".[54]

The affection of politicians for non-traditional housing was undoubtedly fuelled by a sincere recognition of the role played by scientific research in the war effort. According to N. Vig, the Second World War constituted "the great turning point in government—science relations".[55] Scientific and technical developments had been seen to make a crucial contribution to the war's outcome and scientists and engineers came to play a major part in operational strategy and tactics. In 1945 Herbert Morrison, Lord President of the Council, proclaimed that

> The Government attach the very greatest importance to science. We recognise the contribution which science made to the prosecution of the war and the achievement of victory, and we are no less desirous that science shall play its part in the constructive tasks of peace and of economic advancement and progress.[56]

The Second World War firmly placed scientific invention in the minds of politicians as a means of ensuring the economic growth necessary to maintain high levels of welfare expenditure on measures such as state housing. It could be suggested that if technology was believed to have ensured the survival of the nation in war, then, harnessed to the Welfare State, it would strengthen the system in peace by creating the wealth necessary to ensure unity in an unequal society. A sure belief in the benefits of scientific invention for the embryonic Welfare State prompted Aneurin Bevan, on taking office as Minister of Health in 1945, to embark upon his search for a method of mass producing working-class housing. Soon after, he was forced to admit that he was, as yet, unsuccessful. However, armed with a certain belief in science and the practical example of so many completed prefabricated houses, he optimistically reassured those among his electorate who were unconvinced that the Welfare State could satisfy their housing needs: "The age we live in will surely be known as the age of invention . . . the skill and ingenuity of our technicians can revolutionise housing as they have revolutionised so many other undertakings".[57]

Chapter 3
HOUSING RECORDS: 1948–56

Having weathered the "emergency" period, the Welfare State went on to provide the majority of working-class housing throughout the late 1940s. Indeed, while the economy adjusted to peace time, the building of private housing was curtailed. No longer in crisis, however, the state lessened its interest in the ideological aspects of housing construction and allowed system building to assist in local authority programmes more quietly. Nevertheless, improved methods of production were always under consideration by government agencies involved in building and state funded research continued. As a major housing producer, the Welfare State did not ignore the efficiency of building methods.

During the late 1940s the use of non-traditional housing declined as demobilised building workers returned to pre-war trades and the brunt of demand was absorbed. In April 1948, the Labour Cabinet resolved to stabilise the national housing programme at 200,000 completions per year until 1952 and, at the same time, removed the subsidies from non-traditional construction.[1] Furthermore, by the end of 1946, Rosenburg estimated that, with the exception of a number of the materials – producing industries with poor pay and conditions, the building industry had regained approximately 80 per cent of its pre-war labour force.[2] In 1950 Parliament was advised that the load on the building industry had been steady for the past three years and the building industry labour force constant at one million operatives.[3] Although by no means under utilised, at a national scale, building demand seemed to be in line with the industry's capacity and in the early 1950s system building fell to around fifteen per cent per annum of all local authority housing (*see* Appendix 2).

This state of affairs changed after the Conservative election victory in 1951. The new Minister of Housing and Local Government, Harold MacMillan, considered it his first priority to ensure a well-housed working population:

> The People need more houses. They need them quickly. This is the most urgent of all social services. For the home is the basis of the family, just as the family is the basis of the nation.[4]

In order to fulfil its election promise, the Conservative government built up to 300,000 houses a year during the early 1950s (*see* Appendix 1). As well as by reducing space standards and retaining the system of building controls developed at the end of the war, targets were met by using system building on a large scale. Like the previous Labour administration, the Conservatives took an active role in the promotion of non-traditional housing, by both assisting sponsors and coercing local government. In 1954, 26 per cent of local authority housing was completed in system building (*see* Appendix 2).

3 Housing, Coventry (No-Fines, Geo. Wimpey, 1950s)
Stretching as far as the eye can see, systems such as this were a major contributor to the 1950s housing drives concentrated in areas of industrial growth

Local authorities: facing facts

With the removal of government grants to non-traditional housing in 1948, the initiative in using new methods moved to local authorities. Encouraged by central government, many of the larger urban and rural authorities had powerful incentives to use system building as it had became obvious that housing programmes could not be completed by relying on local firms using traditional methods. The early 1950s saw an increasing number of local authorities with large housing programmes turning to system building. In some cases successful sponsors achieved virtual monopolies of municipal housing programmes.

Geographical distribution

A particularly significant feature of system building was the marked variation in use by individual local authorities. This was attributable to two factors: unequal demands for housing by different regions and the ability of those regions to meet this demand through traditional building resources. Both factors were largely the result of changes in the structure and distribution of industry occasioned by the war.

By 1945 major new industrial centres had formed in the Southern and Midland towns which had swelled with the expansion of munitions manufacture. Within these areas of rapid growth there were few incentives for workers to take jobs in building. As the Ministry of Health noted in 1946: "we are losing labour which is badly needed because men are being attracted away from the building industry to other industries where they can —earn more".[5]

In 1951 C.H.H. Smith, Regional Production Officer for the Ministry of Housing and Local Government, described recent changes in the industrial structure of his South West region.

In this region there is a general shortage of bricklayers. Moreover in certain areas . . . the building labour situation is much less satisfactory than before the war. The retention of new factories, established for armament production, has not only tempted many of the skilled craftsmen to leave the building industry for better paid and more congenial work in modern factories, but factory maintenance and extension work have thrown heavy burdens on the depleted industry. At the same time an influx of population has created exceptionally heavy demands for new houses.[6]

The problems described by Smith could be largely overcome through the use of system building due to its reduced requirement for skilled labour. The areas which had experienced the most dramatic growth in engineering industry were those which relied most heavily on system building. This lead to the heaviest concentration, from the end of the war to the mid 1950s, in the Midlands and South. The highest user was Smith's South-West Region (46.7 per cent of completions), followed by Wales (32.2 per cent), North Midlands (24.8 per cent) and the Midlands (23.5 per cent). The four lowest users were Northern, Eastern, South East and London each with less than 15 per cent. In addition to shortages of skilled building labour Marian Bowley cites the absence of brickworks as a significant factor encouraging the high usage of systems in the South West. Furthermore, the lack of a developed building industry in rural areas influenced the high percentages in the South West, Scotland and Wales.[7] (*See* Appendix 3.)

Coventry: new technology and necessity

Changes in the distribution of industry and population were major factors accounting for the exceptionally high use of system building in Coventry. This created a remarkable but by no means unique situation whereby the major part of a city's housing programme was carried out by one sponsor using a single system of construction. Indeed, a visit to Coventry reveals entire landscapes of uniformly finished roughcast concrete houses for, by 1958, George Wimpey had completed over 6,000 dwellings in their No-Fines system of construction.[8]

The Second World War left Coventry with an extensively bombed city centre and a burgeoning engineering industry which rapidly established it at the centre of British automobile manufacture. The dramatic expansion that had taken place in older industrial areas of Britain during the nineteenth century occurred in Coventry in the middle of the twentieth. In 1951 Councillor W. Callow stated that a population the size of Canterbury had been added to his city in the past six years generating a housing waiting list of 14,000.[9] The success of Coventry's engineering industry placed a double burden on housing supply. Not only did it increase the numbers to be housed but also, as the Ministry of Health noted, high wages earned in factories inhibited the growth of the local building industry. In 1959, 66.1 per cent of the city's employment was in engineering and vehicle manufacture with 6.2 per cent in building compared to national averages of 16.8 per cent and 8.9 per cent respectively.

Coventry Council first turned its attention to non-traditional building methods when, in September 1941, the Housing Committee approved the construction of experimental houses. In these projects it was anticipated that local engineering firms would participate in preparation for the reduced demand for munitions following the war. Coventry's early experiments with new methods of construction attracted the attention of protagonists of prefabrication and most probably influenced the invitation extended to its Housing Committee Chair, Harry Weston, and Chief Architect, Donald Gibson, to join CISPH. Three years later Gibson constructed an experimental house of tubular steel and pre-cast concrete in association with Messrs Gyproc. As well as pursuing its own prefabricated system, the Committee discussed a number of others, none of which were found to be satisfactory. By 1946 Gibson had failed to find producers or attract government support for his design and from this point on the city relied on the systems sponsored by commercial producers. If anything, Coventry's early experience illustrated the difficulty of a single local authority developing and sponsoring a housing system of its own no matter how progressive its lay members and professional staff. Nevertheless, the commitment which Coventry eventually made to commercially sponsored systems must in some part have been due to the early interest of its City Architect in new housing methods.

In March 1946 the Housing Committee ordered 2,000 of the BISF houses. Despite government subsidy, the BISF proved more expensive than traditional construction due to the cost of providing travelling expenses and subsistence allowances to labour imported by the erection contractors. In the face of government refusals to bear these costs, the Council reduced its allocation to the 506 already in contract. By 1948, as a result of the diversion of building labour to the rebuilding of the city centre and war damage repairs, problems encountered with the BISF and temporary curbs on local authority housebuilding during the balance of payments crisis, only 380 permanent houses had been completed by the Council.

In April 1949, the Housing Committee again considered reviving its ailing housing programme with new technology. A proposal to order a further 500 of the ill-fated BISF houses faltered, for with the government subsidy withdrawn, the cost of these was now £1,548 each. The Committee did, however, enter negotiations with Unity Structures for 100 houses at the (verbally) agreed price of £1,360. However, this project failed as the sponsors were unable to find a contractor willing to erect the dwellings. The third system under consideration was offered by Wimpey. A fixed price had been agreed with the firm who were prepared to bear the cost of importing labour necessary to complete the 100 No-Fines houses in eleven months. In January 1950, Gibson reported good progress on the No-Fines contract and the Committee approved the negotiation of an additional 252 flats. Six months later Gibson reported difficulties in the negotiation of the Tile Hill North Estate contract with traditional builders busy on other work and presented an offer made by Wimpey. Wimpey would provide the 1,636 houses in accordance with the architect's site layout providing the full range of house types envisaged. In September, with reassurance that Wimpey's price was lower than that of equivalent houses recently completed in traditional construction, the Committee accepted a contract price of £1,149,576. In June 1952, at the same time progress on Coventry's traditionally built estates was found to be less than hoped for, work on Tile Hill North was ahead of programme. As a result, the Housing Committee considered awarding further contracts to Wimpey with the following aim in mind:

> If their labour force is to be retained . . . it will be necessary to allocate to them a further contract on another estate, to which their labour force can be transferred without interruption in house building progress.

By this time it had become apparent to the Committee that its housing programme was dependent on the commitment of labour resources brought in by a national contractor sponsoring its own system. In September 1952 the Housing Committee approved a proposal by Gibson to reserve a portion of each of the Willenhall, Tile Hill, Bell Green and Stoke Aldemore Neighbourhood Units for non-traditional construction in order to maintain the housing programme at a satisfactory level. Eventually the Council agreed a five-year programme of 5,000 non-traditional houses for the City, the first instalment of which were to be 848 dwellings in No-Fines at Tile Hill North and Bell Green.

Coventry's growing dependence on one system of construction developed in spite of its pursuit of alternatives. In February 1951 Gibson opened discussions with Wates on the use of their pre-cast concrete house and three months later the Housing Committee invited Costain to its June meeting to discuss its Schindler Goehner system. At this time the Committee also considered a system by Redifice and were still pursuing the Unity project. However, with the exception of the latter, which was used for a contract of 126 dwellings at Bell Green, discussions fell through on each of these alternative projects due to difficulties in negotiating satisfactory prices and specifications. The site set aside for Costain's system predictably went to No-Fines and, although the Committee eventually built in the Unity system, it took five years from the opening of nëotiations in 1949 to finally approve the project in 1954. In contrast with the other systems, No-Fines was tried and tested, competitive in price and readily available from a large building firm able to bring its own labour to the area.

A further fillip to the use of No-Fines in Coventry came with the de-licencing of speculative housebuilding in 1953. This placed a further strain on the city's inadequate local building industry and prompted yet more increases in the non-traditional programme. In mid-1955, by which time private completions had out-stripped public housing, the Council had 3,791 No-Fines houses in contract, with 909 by other contractors using traditional methods. Two years later, towards the end of Coventry's general needs programme, these figures were 2,142 and 235 respectively – Wimpey were building nearly 90 per cent of local authority housing in the city.[10]

The relationship which developed between Coventry Council and the contractor which was building, almost single-handedly, its municipal housing programme was celebrated by the ceremony held to open the 6,000th No-Fines house in 1958. At this the Mayoress presented a bouquet to the management of George Wimpey & Co. in recognition of their contribution to rehousing the City.

Sponsors: adjusting to new markets

The post-war diversification of non-building firms into housing was dramatic but short-lived. The construction industry itself eventually completed the majority of system built houses as they adjusted to conditions created by the newly emerged Welfare State. The firms most affected by government policy in the immediate post-war years were the pre-war speculative house builders; it was these firms that produced the bulk of non-traditional housing after 1948.

Speculative housebuilding before the Second World War

The adoption of system building by speculative contractors seems the more unexpected, considering the success with which they built traditional houses before the war and the degree to which technical change had remained absent from their operations. The bulk of pre-war housing was produced by small and medium-sized firms producing for local markets. However, this period also saw rapid growth for a number of housing developers building in and around the larger southern towns, in particular London. By the mid-1930s both Taylor Woodrow and Wates were each building more than 2,000 houses a year.[11] Nevertheless, despite the outstanding success of these firms the majority of housing developers remained moderate in size. According to Richardson and Aldcroft this arose from the absence of major technical developments in domestic construction which presented benefits to large-scale operations.[12] Furthermore, it could also be said that the archetypal brick-built detached or paired villa was so successful with private purchasers that fundamental changes to its character through new building methods were precluded. Although the inter-war period witnessed the adoption of a range of new techniques by contractors, including reinforced concrete and steel, their use was confined mainly to the construction of commercial and industrial buildings, offices and some flats, having little impact on the process of housebuilding which stayed as it had been in the nineteenth century; a craft-based, labour-intensive operation.

While it is true that the technical basis of house construction remained the same, the erection of large speculative estates by major developers bore resemblances to system building in the post-war years. These estates were characterised by the repetition of standard house-types in which the designer and builder were one and the same. This enabled a closer relationship between design and construction than was usual in general contracting and encouraged speculating firms to invest in new methods of production – albeit on a modest scale. Standardisation and prefabrication of joinery components such as kitchen fittings and windows are well-known features of inter-war speculative housing.

By early 1944 government plans for the introduction of new technology to housebuilding were well known and had prompted responses from the established and apprehensive organs of the traditional housebuilding industry. In April the Minister of Reconstruction received a memo from the National Federation of Registered Housebuilders criticising the government's plans. Jealous of work traditionally its own, the Federation extolled the merits of brickwork and poured scorn on intentions to introduce new industries and their methods to house building.[13] The Federation also claimed that its members could readily produce half-a-million houses each year were it freed from government control. This proposal was considered by Sir Hugh Beaver, at the time Controller General of the Ministry of Works, as "unrealistic" and he recalled "how few were the builders who supported the intensive efforts of the Ministry to develop alternative methods".[14]

The building industry and the War

Although excluded from temporary house construction, other than as erection contractors, a number of large building firms made a substantial contribution to the provision of permanent non-traditional housing despite the protests of their Federation. The Second World War changed both the building industry and market, giving considerable impetus to large firms and stopping the construction of speculative housing.

By 1942, ten firms, many of which were pre-war speculative housebuilders such as Wimpey, John Laing and Taylor Woodrow were employing over 10,000 operatives each.[15] Individuals such as John Laing, Frank Taylor and G.W. Mitchel (Wimpey), became significant figures in the war effort which relied heavily on massive construction programmes suited to large firms with the requisite organisational capability.[16] Indeed, both Laing and Mitchel participated in the development of post-war housing production policy and sat on the Burt Committee considering new methods of construction. In the case of Wates, another pre-war speculative housebuilder, participation in the Mulberry project (whereby massive pre-cast concrete caissons were constructed for use as a floating dock in the Normandy landings) furnished it with technical and organisational experience in a new technique which it harnessed directly to the development of a housing system. By 1945, through involvement with the state war machine, a new breed of large contractor had emerged, unprecedented in size, organisational and technical expertise.[17]

While the building industry could not complain that there was a shortage of work in immediate post-war years, government policy forced the speculative housing developer into a bespoke builder for government departments and local authorities. This state of affairs was preserved until private housebuilding was decontrolled in 1956. Marian Bowley has noted that of the five most prolific system builders to the end of 1950, Smiths, Building Systems, the Unit Construction Company and Woolaway, were previously "moderate or small builders based on local markets".[18] The other building firms, who produced the largest numbers of non-traditional housing were, she notes, the large pre-war speculative house-builders attracted to system building because: "At a time when normal building was expected to be limited by a lack of traditional resources, it offered the prospect of a market." Essentially, non-traditional housing enlarged a market otherwise limited by lack of skilled labour. To this straightforward explanation, however, must be added the proposition that system building was a natural approach to the large-scale production of social housing by firms which had designed and built their own speculative estates before the war. Instead of tendering against local contractors for individual schemes and competing for scarce local craft labour, they were able to sell complete dwellings of their own design to the extensive and comparatively standardised local authority market. System building made use of their ability to integrate the design and construction of housing on a national scale. Furthermore, instead of investing in speculative development, the resources of these firms could be invested in large-scale methods of production for forthcoming and assured state housing programmes. This must have been an important consideration for firms looking at ways of using assets previously required for speculative development. In post-war local authority housing, given the general shortage of building labour, system building offered large contractors a potentially more extensive market with greater control over the product than traditional construction.

Laing: success through system building

Laing, in particular, proved very successful in sponsoring a building system after the war.[19] In ten years of local authority house building, the company erected 47,000 Easiform dwellings for local authorities (*see* Appendix 4).

Laing's involvement in system building originated with the Addison housing programme for which it developed the Easiform method of construction. This system featured the use of standardised shutters for the erection of poured concrete walls, thereby replacing skilled bricklayers with substantial investment in the many sets of shutters necessary for large-scale production. With the initial investment made, considerable numbers of houses could be produced with relatively small amounts of skilled labour.

Towards the end of the Second World War, Easiform was modified by a foresightful John Laing who had the "specifications re-examined, had seconded a major manager to work on improvements and refinements, and had spent considerable sums on formwork" in anticipation of post-war housing demand. Laing were first into the market with a system competitive in cost with traditional construction, fully developed and tested, and supported by the plant necessary for large-scale production. By December 1946 the house magazine, *Team Spirit*, was able to report that one-third of the dwellings constructed for housing authorities in England and Wales were Easiform. Such was demand that the company licensed the system to eight other contractors, including John Mowlem and Gilbert Ash. In December 1947 Laing had 6,842 Easiform houses in contract while its licensees had a further 2,220. Government policy was a major contributor to this success as the house magazine acknowledged: "When our present programme of Easiform houses was started . . . the business of getting people interested was comparatively uphill". Vigorous promotion of the system and the erection of demonstration houses helped, but:

> the trickle turned into a flood when the Ministry of Health "blessed" Easiform . . . [Circular 56/46] Then came the "National Price" and the Government Subsidy, just at a time when we could be proud of our progress, and the river became a flood.

Although overtaken by Wimpey's No-Fines in 1953, Easiform provided Laing, who claimed to have built one-twentieth of the private dwellings in London during the 1930s, with a market in housing denied it by the curtailment of speculative construction. In 1947 half the company's labour force of 7,000 were engaged in Easiform construction and by December 1950 this fiure had risen to 5,267. In addition to this, it should be remembered that Laing also played a major role in the erection and production of the BISF house. In 1950 the company erected 4,394 Easiform houses, reaching a production peak at the height of Macmillan's drive of 8,300 completions in 1954. The proportion of Laing's labour force which these latter figures represent is not known but they suggest an increasing commitment of company resources to Easiform construction throughout the late 1940s and early 1950s.

What is particularly noticeable of Easiform was the concentration of contracts in particular locations. By means of system building, Laing's were able to bring powerful housebuilding resources to areas with an inadequate building industry and thereby monopolise a number of local authority markets in a similar manner to Wimpey at Coventry. This can only have been a significant factor in Laing's wholehearted commitment to new technology in these and later years. In November

1951 *Team Spirit* noted that "one of the most satisfying factors during the six year period [since the end of the war] has been the number of repeat contracts placed with us by local authorities". Of the 170 Easiform contracts by this time, seven each had been placed by Cambridge, Carlisle and Plymouth and five by Swindon. By 1952 Easiform had accounted for 33 per cent of Bristol's 9,000 houses and by 1960 it had built 7,000 houses for Leicester, 5,000 for Bristol and 2,000 for Carlisle, Bradford and Plymouth. Together with its involvement in the BISF programme, these figures illustrated the centrality of system building to the post-war fortunes of a firm whose pre-war development had been concerned with traditionally built speculative housing. Even though the mid-1950s saw a change of direction in Laing's application of new technology to social housing, Easiform production continued, reaching 100,000 by 1968. The system was eventually withdrawn in 1971. Although it continued to work in the fields of civil engineering and general contracting, rather than a speculative housing developer, the early post-war years saw Laing taking on the new commercial form of a system building sponsor.

State policy: economic management and coercion

The state continued to promote non-traditional housing throughout the late 1940s and early 1950s, although it did not offer subsidies as it had during the post-war "emergency" period. As well as offering a solution to hard pressed local authorities attempting to achieve centrally determined targets, system building seemed a possible means of both reducing housebuilding costs and making more labour available to industries engaged in export manufacture. Feeling compelled to encourage the use of new technology in local authority housing to meet social and economic goals, the state eventually adopted more coercive policies toward local authorities.

High costs and reduced efficiency

The realisation that a dramatic increase had taken place in the cost of local authority housing re-awakened the state's concern with building technology. New methods of construction, utilising the techniques of manufacturing industry, it was hoped, might overcome the inefficiencies of traditional construction and yield savings in the enormous burden social housing was placing on the Exchequer.

In 1948 the government Committee of Inquiry Into the Cost of Housebuilding found that the post-war house was three-and-a-quarter times more expensive than its pre-war counterpart. The report stated that the increase was largely due to a 45 per cent higher labour requirement which was "equivalent to a 31 per cent decline in output".[20] Aside from the exceptional conditions of recent years, the causes of lowered productivity were, in the Committee's view, twofold; the deskilling effect of the war and a "lack of individual effort" occasioned by the less coercive labour market under conditions of full employment. This dramatic decline in the efficiency of the building industry was discussed twice by the Cabinet during the post-war Labour administration[21] and in April 1950 the Ad Hoc Cabinet Committee on Future Policy Towards the Building Industry stated that "the economic future is largely dependent on the ability of such a large and important industry to achieve a really high standard of efficiency and to reduce its costs".[22] To this end, the Committee reviewed the means by which efficiency in housebuilding could be promoted by the government, noting that prefabrication had not yet provided a solution but that further experiments were proceeding in this respect both in housing and schoolbuilding which might prove beneficial in the future.

The perceived lowering of productivity in building had two results. On the one hand, fierce criticisms were made of the British building worker: for instance, in 1950 the Rt Hon. G.P. Stevens berated workers who were not "pulling their weight" and thereby depriving the nation "of that marginal productivity" which would not only build more houses but build them more cheaply.[23] A second reaction was the retention by employers of the payment by results scheme introduced in 1941 by the War Cabinet. The extent to which the scheme operated and its contribution to lower labour costs is not known. However, in 1950 it was estimated that only one in ten operatives worked under such schemes although this was to grow in the form of labour only subcontracting in later years.[24]

Ministry policy during the late 1940s

In order to encourage efficiency in housebuilding and
alleviate regional building labour shortages, the government continued to promote system building after withdrawing subsidies in 1947. Without fiscal incentives, the
Ministry of Health relied on encouraging local authorities
to use system building and assisted sponsors in relating
production to local authority requirements.

The types of measure used to encourage system
building were outlined in 1948 by the Ministry of Health
which noted that a number of systems had developed "on
economic lines" through the subsidies and encouragement
offered over the past two years to a point whereby they
could compete with traditional construction. As these
formed a supplement to traditional resources and a
stimulus to increased efficiency, a policy was adopted
which enabled sponsors "to plan their production ahead
on the basis of estimates of the probable demand".[25]
Local authorities were therefore asked to give early
intimation to the Ministry of the number and types of
systems they wished to use before applying for approval
of their housing programmes: "The information supplied
in this way would then be collated and transmitted to the
firms involved".

The economics of state housing

The enlargement of housing programmes after 1951
renewed discussion of the implications of housebuilding
on the economy as a whole. The result of these
discussions was the development of a positive policy
toward system building at Cabinet level.

Unprecedented housing targets were discussed by the
Conservative Cabinet in December 1951. During the
course of debate the Chancellor of the Exchequer, R.A.
Butler, stated the conditions on which he would consider
the new programme of 300,000 houses a year. As well as
demanding that steel consumption should not be increased
until supplies became more plentiful and that a limit
should be set to softwood consumption, he insisted "that
the labour force engaged on house building should not be
increased above its present level".[26] These stipulations
were agreed by the Cabinet who still licensed the use of

basic building materials and retained some influence over the employment of labour under Defence Regulation 56(A).

The production of more houses with the same amount of building labour could only be achieved by increasing productivity or by removing work from the site to the factory. While it had yet to be shown that system building could fulfil the former, it was certainly known to achieve the latter. In 1952 The Ministry of Housing and Local Government instructed its Regional Production Officers to increase the use of non-traditional housing systems "in areas of good as well as bad [building] labour supply".[27]

The object of Butler's policy was to prevent the construction of houses taking labour away from manufacturing industry, thereby jeopardising the nation's ability to earn foreign currency through the export of manufactured goods. As the Cabinet noted in July 1952 "more of the available building resources must be transferred to the development of the engineering industries, which were capable of expanding their exports".[28] The fact that house building was now thought to be highly inefficient accentuated this concern. These factors assumed increasing importance in policy towards the building industry as future administrations sought to enlarge housing construction programmes. A climate was thus created in which any technical improvement to building efficiency would be warmly greeted and promoted by the state and although it never again provided direct financial subsidies, from 1952 onwards central government used its powers to vigorously promote system building by local authorities.

Assisting sponsors and coercing local authorities

The means by which the government attempted to implement its Keynesian policies in the building industry after 1951 were twofold. First, it continued to assist sponsors in planning production and second, it became more open in the means by which local authorities were coerced into implementing technical policies.

In January 1952 the Ministry of Housing and Local Government conducted extensive interviews with producers who were asked to state "their maximum possible expansion", and where they would find it easiest to build.

Government enthusiasm to assist sponsors caused it to approach Costain, the single largest building firm without a system, with the suggestion that it should sponsor one and erect a factory in the Stoke-on-Trent area to build a major portion of the miners' housing programme: "Mr Costain felt they might well do that if they had some assurance of, say, two years output being taken up and they've now gone away to think about this". Clearly, Costain's response was favourable for, in December 1953, his firm was erecting 1,000 dwellings for the government-sponsored Coal Industry Housing Association in the West Midlands using the Swiss Schindler Goehner system.[29]

Assisting sponsors was one way of increasing the use of new methods; of equal significance were attempts by the government to encourage the many local authorities less than willing to use system building in their housing programmes. These attempts are described in an exchange of memos between C.H.H. Smith and his superiors in London. According to Smith, by 1951 the larger authorities in his region, such as Bristol, Plymouth, Cheltenham, Gloucester and Swindon, had realised that system building was essential to their housing programmes. However, persuading them of this had not been easy:

> The methods of encouragement have been various, and have covered a period of several years. In the early post-war period, every opportunity was taken of inviting local authorities, at individual interviews, zonal conferences and group meetings, to examine the labour situation and to assess the output potential. . . . This process of general education was long and difficult: and it was pursued in the face of strong opposition and prejudice which, even today, has by no means been overcome.

Although emphasising that local authorities had not been forced to use non-traditional housing he admitted that "we may sometimes go rather near the line" by refusing applications for loan sanction for traditional methods on the grounds that the necessary skilled labour was unavailable, whereas, he added, care was taken never to penalise an authority if it included non-traditional houses in its programme. Other measures included exploiting the desire of many councils to maximise their allocations of licenses for private housing development, in which case the Regional Office had "dangled extra licenses before their eyes, with non-traditional allocations attached to the other ends of the strings". Although admitting that his policies seemed a little "underhanded", Smith felt the use of coercion justified by circumstances: "local authorities refuse to face the facts unless they are led to them".

Despite his best efforts, Smith was finding it increasingly difficult to ensure that non-traditional housing was exploited as widely as he thought it should. Resistance was focused on the expense of building and maintaining non-traditional houses, their unattractive and monotonous appearance, the unsatisfactory performance of some contractors and "constant pressure from interested parties" such as councillors with financial interests in traditional building firms. The job of ensuring the use of new methods had been made all the more difficult with the withdrawal of the government subsidy in 1947. Summing up, Smith feared "a severe risk of non-traditional houses fading from the picture". If the Conservative administration was to realise the increase in non-traditional methods they sought, Smith urged that "special measures" would have to be adopted.

After discussion at the Ministry, the following course of action was agreed. The Ministry would write at once to local authorities stating the "merits" of non-traditional systems (that they offered a 30–50 per cent saving in labour and allowed much faster construction) and offer authorities a 50 per cent increase in approvals on any part of their housing programme which included non-traditional houses. Councils were to be instructed to encourage private building of housing systems through the issue of block licenses to speculative developers prepared to use system building (there is no evidence that this was taken advantage of) and Regional Officers were to be instructed to "increase their popularity and remove prejudice". Although the general policy would be to achieve willing acceptance, the possibility that in areas of acute labour shortage specific quotas might have to be allocated was not ruled out. Despite these preparations, Smith once again contributed to the development of Ministry policy in February 1952 by suggesting that a circular should be sent to local authorities emphasising that the policy on new methods of construction had originated with the Minister. Furthermore, he considered that a circular "will receive publicity, and be regarded as an issue of real importance". Such a circular was indeed prepared and, as well as stressing the advantages to be gained from new methods of construction, stated quite plainly that the more local authorities used system building, the more the government would be prepared to give them in the way of subsidies:

> The Minister feels quite justified in offering increased programme installments to those authorities who employ in their current or future programmes the new methods of building for some or all of the houses they had intended to build by traditional methods. Authorities will thus be able to get more houses under contract.[30]

This direct measure demonstrated the extent to which the government was prepared to pursue its social and economic policies through the use of system building.

Chapter 4
A REVOLUTION IN BUILDING: 1959–75

In the 1960s system building reached its highest levels. Between 1966 and 1972, completions averaged 30 per cent of all local authority housing and reached a peak of 41 per cent in 1970 (*see* Appendix 2). As in the late 1940s, system building was associated with the implementation of enormous social housing programmes at times of strained building resources.

Despite the potent but short-lived Prefabrication Movement, non-traditional housing during the late 1940s and early 1950s had been regarded as a temporary measure to overcome immediate housing shortages. During the 1960s a different attitude prevailed: system building was seen as part of a larger process in which building methods would change permanently and irrevocably. The reasons for this widely held view extended beyond the purely practical aspects of building and arose from a broader set of economic and social factors.

At the practical level, the types of dwelling required by local authorities, and their methods of construction, had definitely changed by the 1960s. Although not exclusively, the major housebuilding authorities built multi-storey housing on confined sites. The 1960s was the era of the tower block: a building type indisputably suited to system building. Furthermore, as local authorities faced the prospect of increases in housing targets, they began to rely on large contractors sponsoring specialised systems of construction. The demands placed upon the economy by housing programmes also meant that policies were developed by central government to encourage building methods using less skilled labour.

The view that technology would resolve social pressures played an important part in the continuing development of system building. Two goals of the Welfare State were to satisfy immediate demands for improved living standards from all social classes and export sufficient goods to maintain Britain's position in the world economy. The pressure for increased consumption at home while maintaining output for export could only be resolved (in the view of contemporary opinion) through technology. This imperative brought about the Modernisation of Britain Movement which, as its title suggests, proposed improving industrial efficiency through new technology, be it managerial or mechanical. An aspect of this programme involved system building. The degree to which architectural theory was able to influence government policy arose from the fact that, by the 1960s, Modern Movement architects occupied the highest positions within the state building apparatus. No longer a rising generation with new ideas, as they had been a decade previously, these architects were able to formulate Modern Movement building policies, centred on technology and mass production. A role was, therefore, created for system building in social housing whereby it would serve as the mechanism for modernising the construction industry to realise the goal of progressive architectural theory.

4 Aylesbury Estate, London (Jespersen, Laing, 1967)
In its day the largest system built contract in Europe. System building was crucial to the "Modernisation of Britain"

Affluence, new social pressures and housing

Whereas during the late 1950s, social housing programmes fell, targets began to rise dramatically in the early 1960s. The reasons for this expansion lay in the Welfare State's perception that new policies were required if housing provision was to keep pace with general standards of living. The pressure for new construction resulting from these policies coincided with a quicker rate of expansion in the economy as a whole and posed new pressures on the building industry.

In 1954 the Conservative Government abolished controls over private housebuilding and curbed the output of local authorities. Although this rapidly produced a fall in state housing, total numbers built remained high as private developers increased their share of the market to 67 per cent in 1959 (*see* Appendix 1). The Conservative Party was firmly entrenched in government and, while it had no intention of abolishing the Welfare State, was determined to restore greater autonomy to the market. Even so, local authority housebuilding dipped below 100,000 in only three years during the Conservative hegemony. There was no speech on housing at the 1961 Conservative Annual Conference but its provision on a major scale was still considered a necessary and appropriate activity of the state.

As social housing programmes fell, they no longer exerted intense pressure on the building industry as they had during the first post-war decade. While the late 1950s saw the continued use of systems by local authorities and considerable technical development in building methods by the construction industry, system building did not occupy a central role in housing policy as it had done previously.

A further aspect of 1950s housing policy had a major effect on system building both at the time and in later years. In 1955 policy moved away from general needs (new houses to increase overall numbers) to redevelopment (the replacement of substandard housing). As a result, the focus of local authority housebuilding shifted from suburban estates to inner cities with their confined sites, resulting in higher densities and, in particular, taller buildings – or "high-rise". It was a number of years before sponsors were able to develop new systems to exploit this policy which also encouraged the fall in system building.

Housing policy changed dramatically in the early 1960s as the result of a redirection of economic and social policies. Living standards were rising but, in the opinion of many commentators, not fast enough by comparison with the rest of the Western World. According to Michael Shanks, Economic Advisor to the 1964 Labour Government, the system was simply not producing the goods fast enough: "if existing productivity trends in the various countries were to continue, by the early 1970s the average Briton would find himself worse off than almost all his Continental cousins, and on a roughly comparable level with the average Russian, Venezuelan or Israeli".[1] Despite frequent references to the "affluent society", living standards in Britain were not rising as fast as in other countries. During the 1960s the state attempted to address this situation by accelerating economic growth and increasing welfare expenditure.

Within this, social housing once again played a major role. In 1961 the Parker Morris Committee published *Homes For Today and Tomorrow*, the first major review of social housing standards since the Second World War. The report concluded that the quality of social housing was not keeping pace with living standards and advised greater space and more amenities.[2] Successive governments recommended (and for a short period compelled) local authorities to adopt Parker Morris recommendations, establishing a hitherto unknown standard of state housing which has not been exceeded since. In response to pressures for improved welfare provision, Conservative governments of the late 1950s promised not only higher standards but more houses. From 1958, overall completions began to rise again and from 1962 so did those built by the state.

As housing programmes rose in hand with the expanding economy, so did demands on the building industry. Anxiety over the shortage of labour and bricks first appeared in the *Report of the Ministry of Housing and Local Government 1961*: "this disappointing turn-out was the result of a further slowing in the pace of construction, due mainly to the shortage of craftsmen".[3] The value of new work carried out by the building industry rose 30 per cent in money terms between 1958 and 1962[4] and it was apparent that, even before major housing drives later in the decade, building outputs associated with increased rates of economic growth and welfare expenditure were once again straining the capacity of the construction industry.

Housing issues played a major role in the 1964 election debate. In May 1963 the Conservatives raised their housing target to 350,000 and in the run up to the election again to 400,000.[5] In the event, Labour was elected with policies promising more vigorous activity by the government in housing and in the managed expansion of the economy. 1965 saw publication of the *National Plan* which proposed an annual programme of half-a-million dwellings by 1970.[6] Housing production was to rise to its highest levels ever, a major proportion of this to be built by local authorities.

Local authorities: moving with the times

As in earlier years, local government carried the burden of state house building. Throughout the 1960s local authorities increasingly used systems of construction sponsored by large contractors for two reasons. First, it was seen as the only way of meeting housing targets within the limited building resources available and second, it was considered the most suitable approach to the administrative and technical peculiarities of social housing, particularly with the introduction of multi-storey building types.

Early redevelopment programmes

From the mid-1950s uban authorities began the clearance and redevelopment of slum housing. In taking on this task, they adopted the systems of construction available not only in Britain but in other European countries.

By 1954 Birmingham was building on four major redevelopment sites[7] and in March 1957 Glasgow gained ministerial approval of a 16,000 dwelling clearance plan (the largest yet) for its Hutchesontown and Gorbals districts.[8] By 1962 Glasgow City Architects had already decided to use prefabricated components in place of brickwork for the Pollokshaws redevelopment area[9] and in the same year Liverpool, having sent a delegation to Paris to inspect three pre-cast concrete systems, placed a contract with the Unit Construction Co. for 2,500 dwellings in the Camus system.[10] So it can be seen that the use of industrialised systems by urban authorities with large clearance programmes began well before the major housing drives of the mid 1960s. This suggests that some local authorities were originally drawn to system building because of its suitability for large redevelopment schemes. A trend was set in which the major urban authorities were looking to new building methods in the hands of large construction firms to carry out their redevelopment programmes. In 1963 the Civic Trust "Industrialised Building" conference noted that "The first twelve system constructed schemes in Great Britain are all in cities of more than 3,000,000".[11]

Geographical distribution

Immediately after the war, system built housing was concentrated in specific regions but, during the 1960s, it was focussed on the larger urban areas with redevelopment programmes.

The regional distribution of system built housing between 1965 (before which figures are not available) and 1972 displays a more even pattern than between 1945 and 1955. With the exception of East Anglia and the North – predominantly rural areas with few urban concentrations – system building by local authorities in England and Wales varied between 27 per cent and 44 per cent of total housing starts. Again, two of the three largest users were the East and West Midlands, with the North-West industrial region the second largest (*see* Appendix 3).

The analysis of system building completions by different types of local government administrative unit reveals considerable variations. By far the largest users were the County Boroughs and the New Towns with averages of 44 per cent and 43 per cent respectively. Greater London proved to be the third largest user (34 per cent) with Urban Districts coming third (28.7 per cent) and Rural Districts last at 15 per cent. Between 1945 and 1955 the use of housing systems was focussed on specific regions, whereas, during the 1960s it was concentrated on major cities and new towns. By 1967 Manchester, Liverpool, Leeds and Swansea were all using systems for over 60 per cent of their municipal housing.[12]

The London County Council (LCC)[13] developed a policy towards new building technology earlier than most authorities and, during the 1950s, carried out a number of experiments applying prefabrication to redevelopment schemes. However, during the early 1960s, pressures on building resources forced the Council to put this process to one side and to adopt continental systems of construction.

Estimated in 1953 to be the largest producer of housing in the world, with an annual output of 10,000 homes,[14] the LCC's influence spread far and wide. This occurred, both through the practical example of its building projects, which were extensively visited by other authorities, and through the web formed by LCC architects taking senior posts elsewhere in the public service. Three LCC architects: J. Foreshaw, H.J. Whitfield Lewis and A.W. Cleeve Barr later became Chief Architects to the Ministry of Housing and Local Government and four others became city architects or planners for large cities: Arthur Ling (Coventry), D. Jenkins (Hull), J.A. Maudsley (Birmingham) and Walter Bor (Liverpool).[15] Because the LCC served as a model for other authorities, its policies illustrate many of the issues involved in system building.

The LCC used system building extensively in its post-war general needs programme, completing 12,000 non-traditional houses out of a total of 54,000 by 1953.[16] With the shift to redevelopment, the LCC made a concerted effort to apply new techniques to high-rise housing, carrying out a number of experiments with large contractors. A tradition of "close collaboration" with building firms began on the multi-storey Minerva Street project built by Holland Hannen and Cubitts in 1947. In this scheme Cubitts and the Council co-operated in the design of standardised details to maximise the use of mechanical aids and reusable shuttering.[17] In 1953 the Architect to the Council, Robert Mathew, prepared a report for the Housing Committee which proposed a practical building experiment in high-rise construction with the aim of saving costs and speeding construction. The contractor, chosen fourteen months before the site start of what eventually became known as the Picton Street Experiment, was Laing. In December 1956,

Mathew's successor, Hubert Bennett, reported the findings of the experiment. Although the first phase had cost more and taken longer than planned, it was expected that phase two would show savings in time, and cost the same as traditional construction. To follow this success Bennett proposed further experimental schemes on the same basis. One of these modified the Reema system, originally developed for two-storey housing but adapted for flats in 1959, to an LCC slab-block maisonette design. The first block of the Aegis Grove scheme in Battersea, now demolished, was completed in 1962, and as a result Reema continued to market the modified system to other authorities. As with Picton Street, Bennett estimated there to have been savings in time and marginal savings in cost.[18]

In the early 1960s the LCC's use of new technology took on a new character. Rather than conducting experiments in which the Architect's Department and innovative contractors developed and tested new designs and methods of construction, increased housing programmes and the "overheating" of the building industry prompted the LCC to turn to foreign systems operated by British contracting firms. In November 1961, Bennett reported to the Housing Committee on a recent visit by his colleagues to view the "large scale" prefabrication methods currently in use on the continent but little studied in Britain. As a result of the group's findings Bennett informed the Committee that:

the possibilities in terms of increased housing output appear on the information available to be so promising that I propose to make a thorough investigation with the object of submitting detailed proposals for supplementing the present output by large scale industrialised prefabrication.

In 1962 the increasing workload of the building industry added a note of urgency to the Council's consideration of foreign systems. Before having a chance to report further on his experiments Bennett prepared a report on serious staff shortages which were threatening the execution of the housing programme. Between 1959 and 1961 the workload of the department had grown by 11 per cent while the numbers of architectural staff had fallen by 13 per cent. In Bennett's view this was the result of demands on the industry inflating salaries in the private sector above those offered by the Council. As well as improving recruitment, in order to keep abreast of the building programme the report stated that the architectural department would have to "increase productivity per man".

Five days later Bennett unveiled his proposal for improved staff productivity and greater speed in building by bringing the Danish Larsen Nielsen system to London. Preliminary discussions with the sponsors revealed that the system could be rapidly adapted to a number of the Council's approved dwelling plans. Furthermore, Larsen Nielsen were prepared to grant a manufacturing license to Taylor Woodrow Anglian, a company established to operate the system by the fusion of a subsidiary of Taylor Woodrow, Myton, with the precast concrete specialists, Anglian Building Products. With these necessary preliminaries underway, Bennett reported that he was investigating the development of a number of sites on the basis of placing a contract for 1,000 dwellings in the system. In August a delegation from the Housing Committee visited the parent Larsen Nielsen plant in Copenhagen and a number of completed projects concluding "that this system of industrialised building was capable of . . . an effective contribution to the Housing effort of the LCC".

The Morris Walk development, in which 562 dwellings were built in Greenwich, was the first scheme chosen for Larsen Nielsen. If the system's performance proved satisfactory, the Council intended to enter into continuation contracts for another 438 dwellings, in which case half the cost of the moulds would be discounted by the sponsors. In September 1962 Bennett notified the Council that its building programme was being held up by labour shortages, particularly in the finishing trades, and that the year's programme would not be met. Soon after, in April 1963, the Housing Committee accepted an tender of £2,179,086 for the Morris Walk scheme although the Valuer to the Council pointed out that this would exceed traditional construction costs by 3–3.5 per cent. However, as the Valuer also pointed out, the great saving would be in time for, even with the construction of the pre-casting factory in Norwich, the contract would take only twenty-seven months – nine months less than traditional methods. Aside from other factors, this would bring forward the time at which rents could be collected. In the event, the contract at Morris Walk was completed to the Committee's satisfaction and followed not only by continuity contracts discussed at the outset (eventually built in Brixton, Fulham and Peckham) but also a further 850 dwellings by January 1968.[19]

Although 182 Larsen Nielsen blocks were eventually built for the LCC, it was not the Council's policy to rely on one system: by 1968 several were in use on its extensive housing programme. As Bennett pointed out, it "would be unwise to assign the whole programme to a single manufacturer; there must be some diversity". This enabled the Council to compare the costs and performance of different systems and maintain an element of competition between sponsors. Between 1959 and 1965 the Council let fifteen industrialised housing contracts using seven systems (including a low-rise system which it developed in association with Taylor Woodrow Anglian to complement the Larsen Nielsen high-rise system)[20] totalling 3,192 dwellings. The LCC's policies reflected the growing willingness of larger authorities to use new technology in redevelopment programmes. Furthermore, in using a range of systems these authorities maintained a degree of competition between sponsors preventing the monopolistic position that had taken place in Coventry during the 1950s.

Coventry: the rejection of traditional building

The policies pursued by Coventry during the 1960s illustrated the choice by many urban authorities to use system building in place of traditional methods. This was sometimes the case even where local building resources might have proved adequate.

From 1959 Coventry expanded its redevelopment schemes in the city centre, however, municipal completions never again matched those of previous years: between 1961 and 1965 completions remained below 2,000 dwellings per annum in contrast to 3,500 in both 1955 and 1956.[21] Coventry selected large system building firms in the first place for these programmes as a result of their ability to contribute design experience to high-rise projects. This was explained to the Council by the City Architect, Arthur Ling, who had succeeded Donald Gibson in 1955:

If local firms were to be seriously considered it would

mean that full tender drawings, together with bills of quantities, would have to be prepared in this department, which would mean that the start of work on the ground would be delayed. On the other hand were authority given for the negotiation with a national contractor, experienced in this form of development, advantage could be taken of his technical design services and a start could be made earlier.[22]

By 1966 four national system building firms were building 71 per cent of Coventry's 2,368 houses. Furthermore, an additional 16 per cent were being carried out by the Council's Direct Works Department using its own system of construction. This left only 13 per cent of the programme for local builders. The exclusion of local builders was assisted by large contracts, which, for the major part of the programme, varied between 100 to 250 dwellings.[23] In 1965 this state of affairs prompted the Coventry and District Association of Building Trades Employers to form a grouping of small contractors hoping to negotiate some of the city's large housing contracts and "heal the rift" it felt had arisen between itself and the Council. In response to this overture, Ling pointed out to the Housing Committee that future programmes had been planned on the basis of negotiated contracts with national firms using system building. Of the sites unaccounted for in the 1966–8 programme the majority were earmarked as continuity contracts for system builders already committed to the City. In response to the Association's assertion that they would be easier to deal with than national contractors with remotely situated headquarters, Ling responded: "there is no reason to believe that out-of-town firms are difficult to contact or negotiate with" and that it was common practice for any contractor dealing with a large contract to establish locally "an efficient management team".[24] On this basis Coventry continued to use a range of national contractors for its redevelopment projects despite the presence of willing local builders.

Birmingham: a river of productivity

Birmingham was the heaviest user of system building during the 1960s, repeatedly employing a small number of selected sponsors for low and high-rise housing. Once they had proved their ability, these firms were apportioned major chunks of the City's programme.

This policy was viewed as essential to secure the massive expansion of Birmingham's housing programme from 2,506 dwellings in 1964 to 9,034 in 1967. Eighty-three per cent of this peak output was system built. According to the City Architect in 1968: "There is no doubt that without [system building] . . . last years figures would have been impossible".[25] By 1967 the city was concentrating on only three systems: No-Fines (1,660 completions in 1967) and Bryant (1,044 completions in 1966) for its low-rise housing and Bison for its high-rise flats (1,530 completions in 1967). In addition to these, 1,030 houses had been completed in 1967 by four rationalised traditional systems.

The policy which lay behind the heavy use of three systems was described by Birmingham's Chief Quantity Surveyor to a conference on new contracting procedures. In particular, the Surveyor stressed the way in which the many forms of contract now available were used to identify and then retain the most efficient firms:

> they should all have efficiency as the common denominator of their organisations and they should be rewarded with continuity of production by one of the many methods of negotiation now open to us. . . . So the pattern emerges: a section of the programme set aside for competitive tenders invited from firms selected from the authority's lists and thus providing a means of testing the market and giving an opportunity for firms to show their worth; and at the same time a trickle of schemes running through the programme set aside for negotiated continuity for the efficient: a trickle that could become a steady river of productivity for the authority.(1968)[26]

Within such a policy there was little room for traditional construction.

The package deal

By the mid-1960s the "package deal" had made it far easier for smaller authorities with modestly sized professional departments and inexperienced officers to use system building.

With this type of contract, the sponsor of the system (many of whom had their own architectural staff or used consultants) designed the building and undertook all professional duties as well as construction. A further attraction to this type of contract was the provision of a total service for a fixed price, greatly easing the burden of financial management on the authority. The approvals of package deals increased to 39 per cent of industrialised building contracts by 1970.[27] In the form of a package deal, system building became a comparatively straight-forward solution to the resourcing problems facing local authorities at times of peak building demand. It alleviated the pressures posed by shortages of skilled building labour and professional staff, and the problems of the additional technical complexity of high-rise construction and large, long-term housing programmes. A pleased Town Clerk of a modest-sized Midland town found overwhelming advantages in the Bison blocks they had bought from Concrete Ltd.: "the tender for the three blocks at Kidderminster by Concrete Ltd., and Bryant & Co. was the lowest, completion date offered was the earliest, approval by the Ministry was automatic." (1964)[28] It appears there was no easier way to build.

State policy: the management of resources

As important to the government as the knowledge that labour shortages were hampering the expansion of building programmes, was the fear that low efficiency in construction, coupled with enlarged housing programmes, would pose an obstacle to faster economic growth. Together, these concerns led to an ambitious industrialised building drive mounted by the state in 1965. This was to take the proportion of system built housing to its highest since 1946.

Indicative Planning

The early 1960s saw a new type of government economic policy making: Indicative Planning, which involved identification of the factors involved in maximising economic growth. One crucial factor was acknowledged to be the efficiency of the construction industry.

The outcome of state commitment Indicative Planning

was the National Economic Development Council (NEDC).[29] Formed in March 1962, its members, drawn from government, industry and the unions, jointly considered obstacles to quicker growth and what could be done to use the nation's resources more efficiently. In February 1963 the Council published the *Growth of the UK Economy to 1966* which set out the targets and the conditions that would have to be met for their fulfillment by individual industries. Technology was a major feature of the plan: "A key factor in achieving a 4 per cent growth rate will be the degree to which new investment embodies the results of up-to-date technical advance".[30] In the section on construction the report saw manpower as the principle problem inhibiting a rapid rise in output. This could only be overcome by improved productivity through investment in new building methods and to aid this the NEDC urged that the technological changes which were now under way should proceed at a faster rate than they had in the past.

At the core of newly stimulated government interest in building technology was a concern that low productivity posed an obstacle to the expansion of manufacturing industry, which also required more labour to meet its growth targets. In September 1963, the Minister of Works, Geoffrey Rippon, pointed out that, within the context of full employment, the labour force was "our most precious national asset".[31] Later in the year a government White Paper stated that construction demands would rise by 50 per cent over the next decade and that "This will have to be done without any great increase in the demand on the Nation's limited labour resources".[32] The solution, the Paper continued, was higher productivity, to be gained through the "industrialisation" of the industry's methods by investment in labour saving building systems for housing. In 1964 a NEDC report forecast a regressive effect on the economy as a whole were demand to exceed the capacity of the industry to produce: "What is clear is that there is no certainty, in present conditions, that the industry will be able to meet the demands upon it. And the possibility cannot be ruled out that by falling short it may hold back the expansion of the economy as a whole."[33]

The 1964 Labour Government was elected on a platform which promised more vigorous management of the economy. The *National Plan* was the means by which this would be achieved, posing greater targets than ever before and relying on massive investment in new technology both in building and industry generally.

The first task of the new Labour Government was to establish the Department of Economic Affairs, described by its head, George Brown, as "the greatest contribution of the Labour Party to the recasting of the machinery of government to meet the needs of the twentieth century".[34] One year later the Department published its proposal for the managed growth of the economy over the following five years, the *National Plan*, which relied heavily on improving the productivity of British industry to achieve a 4.6 per cent increase in the output of the economy with only a 0.9 per cent rise in employment. In particular, the Plan envisaged an increased rate of capital investment in new technology by the building industry, largely in the form of system building, second to none. As had been anticipated with temporary bungalows in 1942, new technology would vastly increase the output of homes with a "relatively small" increase in labour:

> with large scale production, selected system houses built by industrialised systems should become competitive in cost and in design with those built by traditional methods. The number of industrialised dwellings in tenders approved is likely to be 38,000 in 1965 rising to about 100,000 in 1970. The use of industrialised systems should enable the larger building programme envisaged to be carried out with a relatively small addition to the labour force.[35]

The crucial role system building played in Labour's housing policy resulted not only from current labour shortages in construction and the economy in general, but also from an anticipation that the building labour force engaged on *new* construction would start to *decline*. In 1965 the Ministry of Labour forecasted that soon

> the numbers of young persons entering employment will decline: construction may not continue to receive

81

a net gain through transfers between it and other industries and it may be that in the future the industry will gain fewer workers than in the past from migration[36]

Furthermore, it was anticipated that such new workers as there were, would be committed to the repair of the growing stock of existing buildings. This area of building work, absorbing up to 40 per cent of the construction labour force, had become a major source of concern. In March 1965 P.A. Stone drew attention to its effect on the building economy as a whole, pointing out that, as the stock of existing buildings was increasing, "there seems to be little doubt that expenditure on maintenance work will rise in the future". Due to the difficulty of applying new techniques to this type of work, its relative efficiency could not be expected to rise significantly with the result that "a growing proportion of labour will need to be devoted to it".[37] With such an outlook, increased productivity in new building was seen to be essential.

The Emmerson Report

Throughout the 1960s government attempts to improve construction efficiency included a number of measures designed, in particular, to increase the use of system building in state housing. Many of these policies resulted from publication, in 1962, of the *Survey of Problems Before the Construction Industry*, by the Ministry of Works. Known as the Emmerson Report, this document urged a greater involvement by government in the activities of the construction industry.

Some of the measures by which the state encouraged system building anticipated the Emmerson Report. The 1961 Public Health Act made provisions for replacing building bye-laws with a national system of building regulations. The bye-laws had long been considered an obstacle to new technology and had been suspended where necessary by the government to allow the use of non-traditional building during the late 1940s. In reporting on the principles to be adopted for a national system, the government advisory committee advocated requirements which would be tailored to "the economic importance of preserving flexibility or an incentive to new methods".[38] Commenting on the introduction of the new regulations in 1964, Geoffrey Rippon, Minister of Public Buildings and Works, described them as making "it possible to approve once and for all for use anywhere in England and Wales a new building method or design".[39]

The central message of the Emmerson Report was that there was no single remedy to the efficiency of the building industry: what was needed was a new relationship with its major customer, the state. In particular the report proposed greater co-operation between industry and government:

> the government needs to exercise a more powerful influence on the general efficiency of the industry. This is not a question of imposing controls, but simply of creating a new relationship between government departments and the industries, and of trying to establish conditions in which all of those engaged in construction can themselves increase their efficiency.[40]

One of the conditions stressed by Emmerson was the implementation of longer-term and assured government building programmes in contrast to using public building output as a short-term regulator of the economy. This issue was considered to be a major restraint on investment in new technology. Between 1945 and 1954 local authority housing programmes were approved by central government on an annual basis. After this, authorities were free to build as many houses as they wished until the economic crisis of 1957 caused the government to return to the annual approvals system. The effect of such a system was that programmes were known only one year in advance and, furthermore, were always subject to cuts at short notice. The "stop-go" policies exercised in the late 1950s were implemented through a series of credit squeezes and drastic cuts in public building programmes, the outcome of which led to considerable uncertainty within the industry. The absence of a stable and foreseeable demand, the Emmerson Report claimed, along with many building firms, produced a general reluctance to invest in techniques which might take years of full utilisation to adequately return expenditure.

When addressing the National Federation of Building Trades Employers on new technology in 1962, the Minister of Works proposed that he would "help by securing a balanced long-term construction programme".[41]

This eventually took the form of assurances of steady growth in building programmes and modifications to the Ministry of Housing and Local Government approvals process. By May 1963 the Ministry reported that it was encouraging large authorities to plan their programmes five years ahead to allow them to "let big forward programmes",[42] and had approved for six years hence the programmes of the major northern authorities.[43] The most definite advice came in Circular 21/65 when local authorities were instructed to submit housing programme forecasts for the years 1965–8, after which "it is intended to repeat this request for four year programmes each year".[44] In 1965 the programmes of the 34 London authorities were guaranteed and in 1966 this was extended to cover another 106 authorities with the effect that 60 per cent of state housing output was guaranteed for four years. While the precise impact of this policy on system building cannot be measured, there is no doubt that it alleviated a major objection to investment in new technology.

The National Building Agency

Perhaps the most conspicuous result of Emmerson's plea for a new relationship between government and industry was the formation of a National Building Agency (NBA) in 1963. For a generation to come, this quango had as its official role the development of building technology. In practice, however, it served as a government agent for the promotion of system building in local authority housing.

A government White Paper described the role to be fulfilled:

> Most clients, public and private also, need help in the choice and use of industrialised methods. Those local authorities which lack whole-time highly qualified professional staffs cannot be expected to evaluate and employ the new methods unless they have access to expert objective advice . . . a new source of independent advice drawn from the available pool of specialised professional expertise appears to be essential.[45]

The Agency offered many services each intended to adapt local authority building policies to the use of system building. These included:

– helping individual authorities to group their requirements and create enlarged programmes for system building,

– advice on administrative procedures related to system building,

– a full system building design and planning service,

– advice on the suitability of individual sponsors,

– assistance in forming "sound working relationships" with sponsors,

– advice to sponsors on the development and modification of their products to suit local authority requirements.

The Agency took the form of a limited company managed by a board of government appointed directors, including representatives from local and central government and the building industry. The aim was that the NBA should be staffed by professionals drawn from the public sector who would resume their posts after a limited period: "in this way increasing numbers of professional officers could gain knowledge of the new techniques".

Two years after its creation in 1964 the Agency described itself as:

three well organised divisions – administrative, architectural and operational – with multi-professional teams serving local authorities and a wide variety of other building clients, a consultancy service, close links with government departments and professional and trade associations, a first class library and information centre, a London headquarters housed in a new office block, regional offices in Edinburgh, Newcastle and Manchester.[46]

In 1968 the Agency employed 208 staff promoting industrialised building. In 1967 the NBA received £157,772 in fees and expended £704,110, the balance being made up by government grant.[47] In 1968 *Official Architecture* reported that the intention to secure a high turnover of staff had succeeded and that the Agency was engaged on a number of demonstration projects; developing brick construction techniques for Crawley New

Town, providing design services for a large housing development in Sunderland, developing the Surebuilt system for Harlow New Town, and working on three systems in Glenrothes.[48] Published information on the number of interventions made by the NBA into building programmes of local authorities is not available, however, in 1965 it was called in by Liverpool to review its ailing housing programme and advised the clearance of larger sites in order to extend the use of system building – advice duly taken by the Council.[49]

The industrialised building drive

By the time Labour replaced the Conservative government in 1964, the groundwork for the boom that took place in system building between 1965 and 1969 had been carried out. What followed was a concerted effort to centrally direct local government building policies on a scale not attempted since the Temporary Housing Programme of 1945.

Reporting on the impending explosion of system building *The Economist* commented in May 1965 that "if Mr Crossman will be able to say that he set it off, he ought to recognise that the laying of the powder and the trailing of the fuses was the energetic work of two Tory ministers fortunate in their civil servants: Mr Geoffrey Rippon and Sir Keith Joseph".[50] By this time the industry was marketing a plethora of systems and had carried out the investment necessary to fulfil Labour's pledge of half a million houses a year by 1970.

Crossman's drive began in earnest in April 1965, with Circular 21/65 instructing local authorities to begin planning their housing programmes with particular attention to system building.[51] Seven months later this was followed by Circular 76/65 which dwelt on the advantages of system building and described the procedure to be adopted for the immediate drive "aimed at giving the industrialised building programme the best possible conditions to get on its feet".[52]

Many of the measures involved were reminiscent of earlier attempts by government to promote system building and were characterised by increased intervention in the housing programmes of local government. The larger authorities, on whom the drive was to be concentrated, were instructed to discuss their programmes with the Ministry of Housing and Local Government's regional officers who would assess the proportion to be carried out in system building, the individual sites to be used, the density range, the general form of development and the family sizes to be housed. The NBA would then make its contribution by recommending the system most suited to an individual programme ensuring "a satisfactory flow of work" for sponsors. To give local authorities added confidence, the NBA would also issue appraisal certificates for systems "considered by them to be suitable for local authority use". A further aspect of policy was the negotiation with sponsors of national prices for a range of systems to allow authorities to choose "in the confidence that the resulting contract sum is likely to be acceptable for loan sanction when application is made to the ministry". This gave sponsors a degree of certainty denied to the purveyors of traditional building methods.

Selective Employment Tax

A later measure to encourage system building was the exemption of off-site construction labour from Selective Employment Tax (SET). This policy clearly illustrated the relationship seen between construction and manufacturing industry in the mind of government.

Levied on "service" industry in 1966, SET was intended to encourage the transfer of employment from service to manufacturing industry, thereby encouraging the use of scarce labour resources in the manufacture of goods for export. Significantly, an anomaly to the broad classification of "service" and "non-service" industry was the inclusion of building in the former to encourage economy in the use of site labour. Off-site labour (such as that working in system building component and plant manufacture) was exempt. Coincidentally, the pill was sweetened by bringing the entire building industry within the government investment grants scheme. This unpopular tax levied £80 million a year according to the *National Builder*, increasing the cost of traditional houses by £70[53] and costing in 1969 £6 "to get an operative on site before he even does a stroke of work".[54] As with many government measures it is impossible to determine the effect of SET, however, the tax can only have served to demonstrate the government's intent to encourage new building methods.

The new relationship sought between government and industry was undoubtedly cemented by informal contacts between building firms, government officials and politicians. However, this should not necessarily be seen as evidence of widespread corruption, but the product of a common aim that government and industry should pull together to achieve greater national prosperity.

High level politicians with financial interests in system building companies included Keith Joseph (Bovis), Reginald Maudling (Open Systems Building) and Geoffrey Rippon (Cubitts Construction Systems).[55] To this list should be added the Permanent Secretary to the Ministry of Housing and Local Government, Dame Evelyn Sharp.[56] However, the view that sectional interests of a particular class of capital, or indeed corruption, as popular accounts of system building have suggested, played a significant part in the adoption of new building methods implies a more passive position on the part of the state than was the case. While well known cases of corruption took place in Birmingham and Newcastle, these were exceptions. If anything it was the government which made the effort to persuade industry to invest in system building.

In 1962 the Ministry of Housing and Local Government convened a meeting to which it invited sixty to seventy representatives of the largest building firms, and by July 1964 had held over 700 interviews with various contractors during which it discussed its building policies.[57] It was a department of government that appointed T.V. Prosser, an ex-director of the system building firm W.M. Thorntons, to Chair the NBA and Crossman who consummated the new relationship between government and industry by persuading Peter Lederer, a director of Costains, to join his ministry and be responsible "for pushing and shoving and getting industrialised building off the launching pad".[58] Indeed, when Crossman met Maurice Laing, McAlpine and others at "the club" in December 1964, he found them apprehensive rather than bullish for the prospects of system building. This apprehension was founded on a suspicion that the government's intention to secure the steady growth of housing programmes would not be carried through – a suspicion later acknowledged by Crossman to have been well founded.

Sponsors: optimism and investment

The late 1950s saw building firms tentatively adopting foreign systems for the newly expanding redevelopment and high-rise housing markets. As housing programmes grew and the commitment to system building by local authorities and central government became more evident, the building industry invested in new technology with increasing confidence. This led to a mid-1960s bonanza in which foreign and home grown systems flooded onto the local authority housing market.

Systems from home and abroad

During the late 1950s the building industry's investment in system building aimed at multi-storey housing was modest and concentrated on site-based poured concrete techniques. Such methods were rapidly overtaken, however, in the early 1960s, by the purchase of expensive pre-cast panel systems (with their far greater production capabilities) from Scandinavia and France.

Robert M. Douglas, bought a licence to use the American Lift slab system of *in situ* concrete frame construction which it marketed through a specially formed subsidiary, British Lift Slab. By 1960 this firm was working on a nine storey block of flats in Birmingham.[59] At the same time W.M. Thorntons, a Liverpool building firm, was using the Swedish Prometo sliding shutter system for high-rise blocks at the Birkenhead docks[60] and Wimpey was adapting its No-Fines system to 11-storey flats on the Tile Hill estate for Coventry City Council.[61]

The early 1960s saw a major drive by the building industry to adopt high production multi-storey continental housing systems. There can be little doubt that this was linked to the government's intention to secure an ambitious increase in social housing by encouraging system building. Government intervention in building efficiency was warmly welcomed by the National Federation of Building Trades Employers (NFBTE) in its annual report of 1962 and again in 1963 when the Federation's President said: "let me say here that this new-found participation in the affairs of industry generally and of the building industry in particular is not resented".[62] Following the Cement and Concrete Association's 1962 Conference, Housing From the Factory, during which a multitude of central and local government politicians, architects and building scientists spoke favourably on system building, *Interbuild* noted frenzied activity as contractors rushed to licence foreign systems or bring their older ones up to date.[63]

By 1963 system builders were beginning to distinguish themselves from mainstream general contracting. In September the NFBTE formed a System Builders' Section with two classes of membership; the first for members of the Federation who produced their own or marketed foreign systems, and a second for non-Federation members involved in system building as sponsors or component producers.[64] An early task addressed by the emergent system building industry was the promotion of its products. The theme of the 1963 International Building Exhibition was Industrialised Building and this was followed a year later by the staging of a one-million square feet exhibition devoted to the subject by Industrialised Building Systems and Components (IBSAC), a company formed especially for the event by the NFBTE in association with Industrial and Trade Fairs Ltd. 1964 also saw the industry launch a vigorous advertising campaign, discussed in some detail by P. Dunleavy, to persuade local authorities that system building was the only solution to the problems of modern-day building.[65]

Laing: acquiring additional capacity

With other firms, Laing continued to apply new techniques to house construction during the 1950s and, to keep ahead of developments, the firm invested heavily in two foreign systems of construction as part of an ambitious system building policy.[66]

In 1951 J.M. Laing reported that "Work was going ahead on other forms of construction in addition to Easiform . . . [and] prophesied interesting developments in the next few months". In the same year *Team Spirit* reported that extensive work was being carried out on pre-cast concrete units for housing. However, neither initiative produced an alternative to Easiform for several years. In 1956 Laing experimented with the application of Easiform shuttering to the crosswalls of an estate of six storey flats at Duddleston in Birmingham, and in 1957 introduced Storiform for high-rise flats using sliding shutters.

Laing developed early expertise in applying limited prefabrication to multi-storey housing in the Picton Street scheme for the LCC. The initiative for this experiment came from the Council but Laing took a financial risk in agreeing that any losses compared with traditional construction would be shared equally between both parties. As a result of the experiment, by 1957 Laing were marketing the Picton Street design as a system called High Structure. However, the degree of pre-casting in High Structure was limited to the cladding panels, balconies, party floor planks and horizontal beams. The main structural element of the design, the crosswalls, were cast *in situ* and in this sense the design was less advanced than pre-casting developments on the continent.

In January 1960 *Team Spirit's* review of the previous year announced that the economic gloom and stringent credit squeezes of the past had ended and that the company stood on the edge of an period of unprecedented building activity. In September 1962 Laing acquired, after "extensive studies", the sole rights to M. Lucien Quentin's Sectra system. Designed for up to 25 stories, Sectra was a more sophisticated version of Storiform and represented the first prong of Laing's strategy for an early entry into the system building market as they had done with Easiform a generation earlier. The system was *in situ* and, therefore, did not depend on the proximity of casting factories to construction sites, making it suitable for widely dispersed smaller contracts. According to *Team Spirit* the largest contract on which it was used was 188 flats.

The second prong of Laing's strategy was the purchase of sole rights for the Jespersen system in April 1963. The subsequent development of Jespersen for use in Britain was carried out in collaboration with the government who, together with Laing and Ove Arup, intended that it should represent the ultimate in the state of the art of industrialised building: "it is a highly mechanised process in which a variety of pre-cast concrete components are produced under highly controlled conditions in a semi-automated factory".[67] Jespersen was the opposite to Sectra in being a high volume, completely pre-cast system suited to large contracts near to casting factories which were, therefore, built close to urban concentrations with large redevelopment programmes. The first factory at Livingstone was reckoned to have cost the company half a million pounds,[68] and two further factories were built at Andover and Heywood near Manchester, at between £600,000 and £750,000 each.[69] By January 1967 *IBSAC* estimated Laing's investment in Jespersen to be £2m in permanent casting factories, a further £1m in research and development "and they back this up with a continuing investment of £250,000 each year".[70]

The economics of excess capacity

What became evident to observers of new technology was that the number of systems adopted far exceeded the size of the state housing market (*see* Appendix 5). It soon became apparent that only a proportion of sponsors would be successful in making a significant profit on their investment.

The factors which gave firms such as Laing the confidence to continue to invest so heavily in system building were various but amounted to a compelling incentive. Primarily, the experience of previous years had shown that where the demand for social housing exceeded the ability of the traditional industry to supply, system building made the best use of scarce labour resources and enabled sponsors to maximise their output with a given workforce. Furthermore, many large urban authorities were showing themselves very willing to use system building in the hands of large firms rather than traditional construction for redevelopment projects. New social housing types, such as high-rise, encouraged the development of specialised systems of construction and, as had also been demonstrated in previous years, enormous orders rewarded the firm which could combine the right system with the requisite management and organisation capability. Each of these reasons were underpinned by the development of firm government policies to encourage system building. Undoubtedly, the industry's conception was that state housing was a sector of the building market which was very amenable to capital investment in highly productive building methods: "Public sector housing is without question the ideal market for industrialised building, meeting as it does all the basic requirements of large contracts and continuity of orders from land-owning clients".[71] The ongoing tendency for contracts to increase in size was also important as system building was better suited to large projects: between 1960 (before which official figures are not available) and 1963 the proportion of contracts for over 250 dwellings doubled from 12.2 per cent to 24.4 per cent.[72]

A very noticeable feature of the sophisticated systems bought by firms such as Laing was their enormous production capability. The three Jespersen factories between them could produce 12,000 dwellings a year if required – or the equivalent of 10 per cent of the entire local authority housing market. Attempting to explain the tendency for sponsors to introduce far more capacity to the market than could be absorbed, the editor of *Industrialised Building Systems and Components* concluded in April 1966 that the industry was playing a waiting game. The rewards of this, he speculated, would be considerable for the victor once the system building market had settled down to the boom ahead:

> This does not imply that those techniques due to go to the wall will be technically, qualitatively or aesthetically inferior to those which survive, indeed endurance and stamina in the form of capital and the capacity to operate initially at a loss may well be the deciding factors in this building Armageddon, for the harvest to be reaped in the field of local authority housing is worth a long-term policy of financial outlay.[73]

A survey of system building completions in 1966 indicated that a small number of sponsors with successful systems, were already reaping a bountiful harvest in local authority housing orders: in particular these included Wimpey (No-Fines – 12,085 completions), Laing (Easiform – 2,763), Concrete Ltd. (Bison – 2,733), Wates (Wates' High Rise – 1,980). System building was a growing portion of state housing and more than 50 per cent of this was produced by four firms. With No-Fines alone, Wimpey were themselves taking 8 per cent of the entire local authority housing market. It may well have been the success of No-Fines and Easiform a decade earlier which encouraged firms to make such a substantial investment in new technology. The desire to monopolise a major share of the building market, in the manner of automobile manufacture, was expressed by Maurice

Laing in 1972 when he complained of the British Building Industry that: "The top ten contractors carry out less than 20 per cent of new work, and not one contractor carries out as much as 4 per cent. By comparison it is quite normal in other major industries for one firm to have over 40 per cent of the market."[74]

Diversification

A further feature of the 1960s system building boom was a second post-war attempt by engineering industry to diversify into state housing. However, in the absence of substantial government subsidies, as had been provided in earlier years, this attempt was largely unsuccessful.

In May 1963 the Minister of Works reported that he and the Minister of Housing and Local Government "were receiving a flood of enquiries about industrialised building, not only from local authorities but from building firms, building component manufacturers and many other industries which would like to diversify".[75] The ailing fortunes of the British engineering and steel producing industries once again prompted government to encourage its use in building. In 1963 the government published a report, *Production of Building Components in Shipyards* which considered both the practicalities of the shipbuilding industry diversifying into building and the means by which it could do so.[76] The Ministry of Works assisted this by setting up a number of enquiry centres to help shipyards divert their resources towards social housing. Two shipbuilders which sponsored housing systems were Blyth Dry Dock & Shipbuilding and the Duxford and Sunderland Shipbuilding and Engineering Group.

Events in Britain encouraged Arcon, which since the late 1940s had been producing building systems for export to the Commonwealth, to once again consider the home market. After an initial period of research, the group was joined by Hawthorne Leslie, a diversifying shipbuilder, and together development work began on a low-rise steel frame system for local authority housing. Of their attempt to re-enter housing, Jim Gear, Arcon's architectural consultant, realistically recognised that "The cheapest or local authority kind of 'system' house usually relies a good deal on timber, concrete and brick to keep the cost down. Group members are more interested in steel, aluminium, gypsum, plastics, asbestos, etc."[77] The group's difficulty in promoting a suitable system was compounded in 1963 when the building member of Arcon, Taylor Woodrow, purchased a continental pre-cast concrete system. In 1967 Hawthorne Leslie withdrew from system building altogether and with the failure of their housing initiative, the Group was disbanded in the same year. Williams & Williams, a steel firm member of Arcon, eventually sponsored the Roften steel frame system, 600 of which were built (*see* Appendix 5).

The most ambitious project, rivalling the earlier BISF house in scope and ambition, was mounted by Richard Thomas & Baldwin and the Pressed Steel Company, who in 1963 unveiled plans to manufacture the Industrialised Building in Steel (IBIS) house. Pressed steel sheet was to be used for the structural frame, internal and external wall panels, doors, windows, floor and roof decks, staircases and bathroom and kitchen units – the utilisation of a single material to a degree preceded only by the aluminium bungalow. By 1967 two prototypes had been erected and the company was confident that with "mass production" of components, IBIS would compete easily with traditional construction in cost.[78] However, this confidence did not endure to the stage of production and development was eventually dropped. The firm also attempted to introduce a partition system into educational building programmes.

The latter movement of engineering industry into housing was far less successful than immediately following the war as government financial support, to offset the high cost of using steel in house construction, was not forthcoming. Those systems which were successful used steel for the structural frame only rather than for non structural components and cladding elements. At the peak of steel frame construction during the 1960s, only 3,759 dwellings were completed (1967): rather less than 10 per cent of all system built housing (*see* Appendix 6).

Ideology: the Modernisation of Britain

During the 1960s mass produced housing once again excited the minds of politicians and housing experts who felt themselves to be on the verge of a veritable "revolution" in construction methods. Indeed, this transformation of the building industry was to be part of a larger process known as the Modernisation of Britain in which technology would propel the British economy to new levels of production. This revitalisation of the Welfare State was intended to strengthen the social system by meeting the demands placed on it for new levels of material consumption. Within this, system building was a crucial element.

Science in politics

After the post-war "emergency period", popular discussion of prefabrication waned as the nation busied itself with reconstruction projects. Nevertheless, although reduced in the popular consciousness, prefabrication continued to arouse interest within the building professions. In 1951 the Building Research Congress was named The Influence of Mechanisation and Prefabrication on Techniques and Costs of Building. Prefabrication also possessed as intellectual attraction to the post-war generation of newly trained architects. As the Principal of the Architectural Association, M. Pattric, pointed out in 1956, "Generally speaking, the idea of prefabricated building appeals to students and they find it difficult to understand how a system of construction which is so obviously cheaper in theory is not more used".[79]

Although the 1950s saw fewer references to mass produced buildings in the speeches of politicians, it is evident that state interest in science and technology continued to grow. Indeed, according to A. King, this took place on an international scale resulting from the relatively recent appraisal of the role of science in economic development and a tendency to make international comparisons of research expenditure which "provided an international ranking order somewhat like a football league table . . . the United States, at the top, was the pacemaker".[80] The culmination of state interest in science and technology was the appointment of Quentin Hogg (Lord Hailsham) as Minister for Science, a post created by the MacMillan Government in 1959. In *Science and Politics*, Hogg described the process by which "this development of the political interest in the scientific, has rested upon the clear demonstration that a nation's power to prosper in peace, survive in war, and command the respect of its neighbours, depends very

96

largely on its degree of scientific and technological advance."[81]

During the 1960s the state identified a crucial role for technology in The Modernisation of Britain. This radical programme, in which indicative planning played its part, was intended to accelerate economic growth to levels enjoyed by Britain's neighbours on the Continent and halt the nation's relative decline as a world economic power. The attempt to reform the character and ethos of the British economy and culture has been described by writers such as N. Vig as little more than an electoral manoeuvre, "an element of style rather than substance".[82] However, while undoubtedly exploited to this end, it is evident that The Modernisation of Britain resulted from a genuine belief by the twentieth century political and intellectual establishment that technology was the panacea to economic and social problems. As a result, the 1960s saw the birth of science policy journals such as *Minerva* and the formation of the Science of Science group on the lines of the inter-war Social Relations of Science movement.

Party politics and the rhetoric of "revolution"

Technology and its relationship with house building was referred to by both political parties in the years leading up to and immediately following the hotly contested 1964 election. For the Conservatives it gave credence to their newly initiated system building policies and for Labour it broadened their appeal beyond sectional class interests.

In considering the discussion of system building during the 1960s it is important to bear in mind that it was identified as "revolutionary", rather than as a trend in the construction of social housing which had developed continuously since the Second World War. Whether or not the intention of politicians, this gave greater weight to attempts to promote system building policies than a more cautious terminology. In the early 1960s Geoffrey Rippon, for instance, displayed a degree of enthusiasm for system building which was more the product of faith in techniques as yet unproven than a realistic assessment of the increased tempo of technical development in housing. Nevertheless, by focusing on the "miraculous" qualities of system building, Rippon at once espoused current beliefs in the virtues of technology and gave credibility to reforming the production methods of social

housing. Furthermore, he drew attention to the progressiveness of Conservative technical policy adding weight
to his claim to be vigorously pursuing the Modernisation
of Britain. Thus, in 1963, Rippon enthusiastically announced to Parliament that the gradual evolution of
traditional building technology would not do for Conservative policy:

> progress in increasing output which has been made so
> far has been achieved without any major change in the
> characteristic methods of work of the construction
> industries. If these methods of work could be trans-
> formed, we might get increases of output which at this
> moment would appear to be almost miraculous. What
> is needed is something of the nature of an industrial
> revolution in building.[83]

The rhetoric of a "revolution" in building methods was
no less energetically promoted by the Labour Party. As
Harold Wilson pointed out of Britain's relative industrial
decline in 1964, the long-term social stability of the
nation was at stake: "Without a quickening of innovation
and productivity in Britain, the very basis of our social
fabric would be endangered".[84] The role of technology in
post-war Labour Party policy was defined in Wilson's
equation of socialism with science: "In a recent newspaper
interview I was asked what, above all, I associated with
socialism in this modern age. I answered that if there was
one word I would use to identify modern socialism it was
science". Indeed, Wilson's biographer, Paul Foot, has
noted the way in which "technologism" gradually removed
overtly socialist policies from Labour Party policy in the
early 1960s: "Perhaps the main change in Labour's home
and economic policies between 1959 and 1964 was a shift
in emphasis away from traditional welfare demands
towards economic growth, efficiency and technocracy".[85]
Technology played a major role in Labour's election
campaign, minimising the party's identification with
working-class interests and broadening its appeal to all
classes concerned with economic reform. Wilson claimed
that "the cities of the future, cities worthy of our people"
were to be constructed by "a great breakthrough in
science and technology",[86] rather than through a fundamental restructuring of the social and economic system as
Labour Party orthodoxy had earlier enshrined in Clause
Four of its constitution.

References to "revolution" by politicians were mostly vague and therefore without technical detail. Elaboration was left to senior architects in the public service. In conference papers and in the press they detailed the processes by which the industry would be transformed through system building and the improvement this would allow in standards of social housing.

When speaking in public, politicians were inclined to hedge their often dramatic statements of intent regarding the construction industry by pointing out that future demands would more than keep traditional builders fully occupied.[87] However, senior architects in the public service were less concerned that the interests of established industry should be challenged openly. As K.J. Campbell, Housing Architect to the LCC pointed out, the "real" reason why systems were being introduced was that traditional building had "run its course" and as a method of housebuilding was now obsolete.[88] A.W. Cleeve Barr, Chief Architect to the Ministry of Housing and Local Government, thought that advances in social housing technology would have implications beyond this immediate sector of the building market, serving as an example for the industry as a whole: "There are unique opportunities in housing, which if matched with good design and good quality in building, could act as a catalyst for transforming the industry generally".[89] Given that state housing in 1967 accounted for 20 per cent of new building,[90] the catalytic role identified by Cleeve Barr had an air of plausibility.

Having accepted the inevitability of a "revolution" in building, the state set out to promote this idea among the population at large and in particular local authority housing committees, architects and the building industry, without whose support the industrialisation of building policy could not be carried through. The fervour of this was noted by *Interbuild* in July 1964:

A widespread propaganda campaign had been carried out in which the national press, television and even the glossy women's magazines have played their part. The aim was to get the concept of industrialised building accepted by potential clients and the general public and to encourage the building industry to participate joyfully in the increase in industrialised building.[91]

A major event in this process of persuasion was the Cement & Concrete Association conference Houses From the Factory, held at the Royal Institute of British Architects in October 1962. So great was the interest in system building that the main lecture theatre was filled to capacity and an overflow audience watched the proceedings on closed circuit television. At the conference, Cleeve Barr elaborated the rationale of prefabrication, ignoring practical complexities and setting a style of official argument which dominated lectures and conferences for the remainder of the decade. Rather than promoting system building as the means to compensate for shortages in building labour, with several aspects as yet poorly understood and many problems unsolved, Cleeve Barr promoted it as a means of improving standards of social housing in line with *Homes for Today and Tomorrow*. Underlying Cleeve Barr's argument was the proposition that, due to the supposedly small labour content in manufacturing prefabricated components, larger wall and floor panels could only incur extra costs in terms of materials. As concrete was relatively cheap, this led to the conclusion that system building could provide more space at possibly a third to a half of the cost of traditional construction.[92] In later lectures, Cleeve Barr simplified this proposition by stating that "standardisation can give greater space for very little extra money".[93]

System building and the era of welfare building

Despite what we may feel today, it was never suggested at the time that system building would produce architecturally inferior dwellings. Aside from the belief of many architects that system building could equal the aesthetic qualities of traditional construction, to have cast doubts on its architectural merits would have undermined the very purpose of the Modernisation of Britain: namely that technology was capable of meeting society's material aspirations. Thus, Cleeve Barr and government ministers, promoted the aesthetic qualities of system building, claiming that it would produce an architecture worthy of the Welfare State.

At the "Houses From the Factory" Conference Cleeve Barr pointed out that concrete panels came in 23 varieties of finish and 57 different colours: it would not be difficult, therefore, to improve on the appearance of traditional building. Furthermore the contribution of the machine would automatically ensure a superior finish:

> You only have to think for a moment about the quality of factory made goods, which are standardised and produced in large numbers, particularly the standard of finish, to realise this – television sets, motorcars, furniture, office equipment and so on.[94]

In the 1963 Civic Trust Conference "Industrialised Building", Geoffrey Rippon extolled the architecture of system building evoking images of eighteenth century neo-classical town planning:

> industrialised building is perfectly capable of making a proper contribution to the beauty of our towns and villages . . . you have only to look at a terrace of Georgian or Regency houses to see that uniformity of design and architectural merit can go together. What we have done before we can do again. We are a rich country. We must afford to bring a new deal to those who still live in conditions of dreary squalor; and we can afford good design.[95]

Rather than relying solely on economic arguments for system building, political expediency required that the state should promote it as a superior form of architecture with higher amenity standards. This was essential if system building was to be accepted as a believable part of policies for a more affluent and contented society. The words Modernisation of Britain would have rung hollow were it thought they would be characterised by ugly rows of badly built concrete housing blocks.

The conviction that system building was at least as good, if not better, than traditional construction became a significant theme in official government advice to local authorities. Acknowledging only the advantages of system building, rather than a more rounded appraisal of its qualities, had always been a feature of Ministry policy. When Brigadier Barraclough, Chair of the Regional (Midland) Housing Production Board, referred in 1952 to "admitted disadvantages" in non-traditional building he received a curt response from Whitehall: "we do not admit any disadvantages in the current models other than the prejudice we have to wear down!"[96] At the very least, as the Ministry of Housing and Local Government Circular 59/63 impressed upon local housing committees, system building would allow current design standards to be maintained: "There is, in fact, no reason why houses built by industrialised building methods need be more standardised than houses built by traditional methods . . . the use of these components . . . opens up new opportunities for skilled and imaginative design". (1963)[93] By 1965, the proposition had been elaborated to suggest that system building would allow authorities to achieve *higher* standards of design. The logic behind this argument was described in the Ministry Circular 76/65 which proposed, as had Cleeve Barr, that a better quality of finish would be achieved and also that:

> the use of carefully prepared standard designs will release scarce professional time to concentrate on raising the quality of layouts both for industralised and traditional building . . . the aim of all authorities should be careful attention to groupings, layouts and landscaping to use industrialised building to improve the environment.[98]

The same circular also gave an incentive for councils to preserve the drive, despite reservations they might still have as to the quality and cost of system building, by suggesting that the methods currently available were a stepping stone to improved generations of system which would follow transformation of the industry. The circular pointed out that "there is a continuing need for industralisation but the immediate drive is a short term effort aimed at giving the industrialised building pro-gramme the best possible conditions to get off its feet". Once there, the Ministry suggested, system building would eventually become cheaper, in the manner of general industrial advance, as larger quantities of increas-ingly standardised components were produced. Initially production would be by the "batch" only but the ultimate aim was to secure "flow" production in order to gain the full benefits of "industrialisation". Authorities were assured that the Ministry and the NBA were working on improved techniques, although, it was also pointed out, their realisation was "not the kind of development in which quick solutions can be expected". The message was clear: if authorities ignored their reservations and played their part in the government's industrialised building drive, they would be the eventual beneficiaries of the "revolution" in building methods.

Visions of the future

To suggest the idea that industrialised building would lead to new heights of architectural civility while solving housing shortages was conceived and promoted solely by politicians and bureaucrats to implement system building policies denies the wider influence it had.

The technical and administrative developments that were taking place in social housing inspired architectural journalists to envisage Orwellian building economies of future years in which unproductive traditional firms were "swallowed up" by giant corporations using the full benefits of automated production.[99] In 1965 J. Carter, journalist and Architectural Advisor to the *RIBA Journal*, described a future building site devoid of mud and of such clinical precision that it would fully merit a place in the era that lay ahead. In years to come Carter envisaged a technocratic society of abundant provision for all classes where "worker and architect, builder and occupant then go back to their ample comfortable homes, to their ample culture-filled, well organised leisure time". The contribution to this vision of wealth focused on by Carter was building technology: "a group of (almost) white coated, well paid workers, slotting and clipping standard components into place in rhythmic sequence on an orderly, networked and mechanised site to a faultless programme without mud, mess, sweat or swearing".[100] By 1965 there were few in the building establishment who did not carry the lamp of a "revolution" in building.

Reluctant customers and economic crisis

In 1970 41.3 per cent of local authority housing was completed in system building (*see* Appendix 2). High though this figure was, it is evident that local authorities were slower to adopt new methods than the government and industry desired. Furthermore, no sooner had this figure been achieved than the economic crisis of the late 1960s dried up what remained of the system building boom leaving sponsors with redundant factories yet to show a return on investments.

Local Authority resistance

There is no doubt that while many of the larger authorities committed themselves to system building wholeheartedly, the smaller ones ignored its use until absolutely necessary, and were unreceptive to the many arguments presented for new technology. As in previous years, this led to pressure from central government aimed at increasing the proportion of local authority programmes awarded to system building sponsors.

The tendency for local authorities to make insufficient use of system building brought frequent rebukes from government ministers. In February 1965 Charlie Pannel, Minister of Public Buildings and Works, addressed a Council Meeting of the Association of Municipal Corporations complaining that too many councils "leave their neighbours to make use of industrialised systems of building while they proceed with traditional methods".[101] By July 1965 the capacity of the industrialised building industry was estimated to be 50,000 units per year while government forecasts expected only two-thirds of this to be used. As Pannel stated in the House of Commons in response to a demand for the state to set up system building factories of its own, "the principal obstacle to greater use of industrialised building is the need to organise the demand, not to supplement the supply".[102] In April 1965, Circular 21/65 departed from the Ministerial policy hitherto of seeking to increase the use of systems through persuasion by threatening, as it had in 1952, to withhold loan sanction: "in deciding what programmes to approve the Minister will be influenced by the extent of the proposed use of industrialised methods".[103] This intention was restated in *The Housing Programme 1965–7* White Paper published later in the year.[104]

Opposition to system building by individual local authorities was conspicuously absent from building industry and professional journals which unanimously upheld the prevailing orthodoxy that new technology was desirable and should be encouraged whenever possible. Nevertheless, objections occasionally surfaced in conference reports carried by *Municipal Journal*. Throughout the 1960s an often stated opinion of Rural District Councils was that "problems of planning for dense urban areas should be separated from planning for rural areas . . . this division would save rural districts endless talk on industrialised building and housing".[105] The Housing Centre Trust conference in July 1964 found a number of delegates from both urban and rural councils sceptical of the benefits of the large system building contracts that were being let by "pioneering" urban councils such as Liverpool and the LCC.[106]

The 1966 Annual Conference of the Association of Municipal Corporations saw the most sustained public criticism of system building by lay committee members. By this time many of those present had actually seen system building at first hand and had not liked it. The controversy was undoubtedly fuelled by a paper delivered by W.S. Jones, managing director of a sponsoring firm, who criticised local authorities for not making the fullest and most efficient use of system building and, in a particularly partisan manner, attacked direct labour organisations. The "counter attack" was led by a Wigan Alderman, H.R. Hancock, who stated that his authority had actually used system building and not found it to be cheaper or superior in any way to traditional methods. The representative from Reading pointed out that councils had a "justifiable" fear of the possible future maintenance costs of industrialised housing which was not allayed by the apparent refusal of private housing developers to depart from traditional methods. However, it was left to the Lord Mayor of Norwich, H. Derry, to ask when the building industry was going to rationalise itself and reduce the number of systems available to a reasonable number which were proven and economic:

How can we evaluate all 240 systems and know which is the most economic . . . it is not in this year 1966 economical at all to go in for industrialised systems. In my authority we can build traditional homes and traditional flats in very nearly the same time as it takes to put up industrialised buildings at something of the order of 600 or 700 cheaper for two-bedroomed accommodation . . . I am suggesting to the building industry it ought to rationalise itself and it ought to decide which are the best systems . . . because until costs are reduced considerably my authority is prepared to fight the Ministry in relation to the threat in the White Paper.[107]

The relationship between the costs of system building and traditional construction varied according to many factors, including the number of storeys and the types of system used. Furthermore, costs were not documented nationally until 1964 and it was not until 1970 that the available statistics suggested that system building was cheaper than traditional construction for all housing types (see Appendix 7). The economic case for system building was yet to be proven and until it was, Alderman Derry would not be coerced by government policies into choosing from a bewildering variety of unproven methods.

Whimsy and procrastination

Although the use of system building eventually approached government targets, local authorities were frequently accused of using it inefficiently, preventing those sponsors who were able to obtain orders from profiting from their investments. This in turn led to the loss of many of the claimed productivity benefits of system building under-mining government policies for increased building efficiency.

A source of particular concern was the general refusal to offer contracts of a sufficient size. As Cleeve Barr pointed out to local government: "they cannot be run economically on the basis of one order for 300 houses here, 30 different houses in another part of the country, 20 elsewhere and infinitely protracted negotiations for a few dozen again-different types elsewhere".[108] Circular 76/65, published in December 1965, advised authorities that contracts for system building should be for at least 100 dwellings and that a string of different systems should not be used.[109] Although the letting of contracts for over 100 dwellings increased from 39.5 per cent in 1960 to 66 per cent in 1966,[110] the bulk of contracts for system building remained below 100 dwellings despite ministerial advice. In late 1966 the National Federation of Building Trades Employers found that of a survey of 87 current industrialised building contracts 51 were for less than 100 units.[111]

As regards government advice that only a few systems should be used by any one authority, in 1966 Crossman described as one of his greatest problems the tendency of councils to "flit from one building system to another according to the whim of fashion".[112] Indeed the "whimsy" of local government caused one sponsor of a "carefully designed" system to withdraw from the market in 1965, having gained contracts for over 500 dwellings, with the complaint that "In the municipal housing market one is dealing with laymen. . . . I have been shocked at some of the questions . . . all we get from the biggest potential market is procrastination and a lot of waste of time."[113]

In common with fellow sponsors, Laing experienced major problems with its local authority clients. By January 1966 Jespersen had been used on a number of large contracts worth £15m. In 1967 these were followed by a huge, 1,957 dwelling, contract for the London Borough of Southwark. Despite the magnitude of these orders, variations from the standard design played havoc with the economics of system building production. At the Oldham development the Council insisted on having 13 different house types which, together with the undulating site, prevented standardisation of the concrete units and slowed erection. At Hulme No.2 the council insisted on implementing its favoured 8ft 9ins floor to floor height, instead of the 8ft 4ins dimension to which the system was designed, again increasing the number of non-standard components. The effect of such deviations was to render the system more complicated to manufacture and erect.[114] In the opinion of W. Kirby Laing, central government was at fault in allowing this situation to continue. Despite all it had said to the contrary, Laing complained, government seemed unprepared to bring authorities into line: "We have the ridiculous situation where each authority is still able to ask for a completely different basis of design, even in such simple matters as the dimension to be used for the distance from floor to ceiling".[115]

Empty order books

Government and industry complained that local authority policies were the cause of distress in the system building industry. However, it is evident that no matter how co-operative councils might have been, the industry sealed its own fate by sponsoring too many systems requiring vast production runs to be operated profitably. The result was too many empty order books.

The precarious position of the system building market was noted in 1965 by *IBSAC* which claimed that no other country in the world

> possessed such a variety of systems from so many building firms. . . . A superabundance of systems, too many of which are inefficient and hastily designed, all confusedly jostling and crowding each other in the market, could well hoist industrialised building on the petard of its own success.[116]

In a survey of low-rise system building in 1967 L.W. Madden noted that, while some firms were doing exceptionally well, the majority of sponsors had very few orders. Thirty-three firms were sharing only 10,145 houses with six having orders for less than 40 and three for less than 20. A similar analysis later in the year exposed a similar situation.[117] Indeed, it cannot escape attention that, had local authorities resisted the desire to flit from system to system, as the government wished, there would have been even more sponsors with empty order books.

In 1967 a spate of reports appeared in *Building* indicating difficulties faced by the system building industry with larger firms, such as Bryant, the Fram Group and Trollop & Colls, announcing losses in profits directly attributable to system building and a number of smaller specialists, Dorrans and Hawthorne Leslie, closing down.[118] While the condition of the economy was known at this point to be worsening, its effect was not yet apparent in housing programmes: these problems were the result of the system building market being spread too thinly and unevenly for more than a very few sponsors to justify the investment involved.

By 1967 empty order books had caused Jespersen to become an expensive liability. In March 1967 *Building* reported that Laing were in severe difficulties "in the industrialised building field".[119] Indeed, completions of Jespersen dwellings for that year – four years after introduction of the system – were only 765, considerably less than 10 per cent of its capacity. This figure rose to 1,588 in the next year but fell again to 702 in 1969 and dwindled to zero in 1975 (these figures do not include Scotland where Jespersen had one of its four plants). The company was having even less success with Sectra, which in nine years of production completed little more than 2,500 dwellings (*see* Appendix 5). In 1963 company profits stood at £1.1m[120] and this rose to £2.5m in 1965. However, by 1966, despite the success of Easiform and the company's other building activities, profits had fallen to £64,000 and the relative loss which these figures represented was attributed by the company to its problems with system building.[121]

The death of system building

Despite difficulties which the majority of sponsors faced, a number did well throughout the 1960s. It was fundamental changes to the economy as a whole which eventually sealed the fate of system building.

The clouds of economic gloom were already gathering in 1965 as the National Federation of Building Trades Employers noted growing uncertainty within the industry and a steady improvement in the availability of brick-layers.[122] In 1966 the growth in overall construction output slowed and completions of private housing fell. In the same year came the first credit squeeze and on 18 November 1967 the pound was devalued as economic targets in the National Plan were abandoned. Between 1966 and 1967 the growth of world trade fell from 10 per cent per annum to 5 per cent – the long post-war boom was drawing to an end.[123] By 1968 the single undisputed factor in system building's favour disappeared as the building industry noted that "the availability of labour has generally been adequate".[124]

By 1969 Laing's Scottish factory had turned over to the production of various non-system pre-cast concrete units and in 1975 the Heywood factory closed followed a year later by the Andover plant which was turned into an industrial estate. The same year found the Princess Risborough factory producing the last few panels for the final stages of the huge Aylesbury estate in Southwark.[125]

Even though sponsors closed down their pre-casting plants in the early 1970s, the government was reluctant to give up its aim of improving productivity within the industry. In February 1970 unemployment stood at 10.2 per cent but in response to demands that this should be addressed the Parliamentary Secretary to the Minister of Public Buildings and Works responded that the industry still needed "a highly skilled and compact labour force to match the best of world practice".[126] It was not until 1978 that Peter Shore, Secretary of State for the Environment, stated that, as well as building efficiency, his concern was with "maintaining as high a level of employment in the industry as we possibly can. We shall always be prepared to consider measures which promote these ends"[127] By this time 15 per cent of job creation schemes were in building. In contrast to the building policy of previous years, government was by this time seeking to increase employment in construction rather than reduce it.

The seriousness of the 1967 economic crisis in Britain was matched by the speed with which the vision of a "revolution" in building evaporated. As the recession brought about cuts in housing and welfare expenditure it broke the simple faith that technology was a means to uninhibited economic growth. Science and technology played minor roles in Labour's re-election programme of 1966 as the difficulty of achieving the Modernisation of Britain subdued optimistic forecasts of a scientific revolution. Despite the support government still professed towards system building, popular discussion of the subject waned. Between 1967 and 1969 the two journals devoted to system building, *Interbuild* and *IBSAC*, ceased publication without a word of explanation to their readers. 1967 saw the highest proportion of new housing tenders approved in system building: thereafter, despite a brief resurgence in the early 1970s, discussion of system building, which had dominated editions for the four years between the creation of the NBA in 1963 and the economic crisis in 1967, is scarcely to be found in the architectural press. Six years later a rare mention in *Building Design* declared the completion of the last stages of the Thamesmeade Development to be industrialised building's "death rattle".[128]

Chapter 5
WORKERS BY HAND AND
BY BRAIN

It was seen to be inevitable that mass production would have a major effect on two of the largest areas of building labour: operatives and architects. Indeed, the literature indicates that their respective institutions discussed building technology in relation to economic interests and developed policies to cope with the threat posed by system building. But, while building labour found little comfort in the use of system building, the architectural profession adapted to changes with considerable success. Indeed, under the peculiar conditions created by post-war social policy, architects were able to develop a new role in the building economy, helped considerably by the very conspicuous promotion of system building.

Operatives

Skilled labour had much to fear from the mechanisation of building operations: it threatened to eliminate craft content from their work, undermine basic rates of pay and, in turn, to overthrow trade union structures built up over many years. Indeed, these aspects of system building were the cause of dispute in inter-war years. However, due to the weakness of post-war organised building labour, opposition was effectively prevented. Furthermore, throughout the 1960s, when changes in building technology seemed most radical and permanent, the building industry operated a policy of consultation to diffuse conflicts which might arise during the "industrialisation of building". Furthermore, the ideology of the Welfare State, where science and technology were equated with social progress, rendered the defence of sectional class interests all the more problematic. This was particularly so in system building which promised to achieve so much in terms of working-class housing. The result was that the use of system building in post-war housing was accompanied by relative industrial harmony.

In the spirit of social harmony

During the later years of the war, the National Federation of Building Trades Operatives (NFBTO) viewed with apprehension the effect prefabrication would have on their trade union structure. However, industrial action was thought inappropriate due to the spirit of social unity which accompanied early welfare policies.

Industrial harmony was not always a feature of system building. During the 1920s a serious dispute followed introduction of the Weir House. Although Weir's system was no more than "a timber-framed house faced externally with steel sheeting",[1] its economic viability was based on the use of engineering workers at

5 Steel houses under construction in Banbury (BISF, late 1940s) The introduction of engineering techniques to housing could not but have an effect on the work of operatives and the architectural profession

engineering rates of pay. These were lower than for building work which was paid in accordance with nationally agreed "flat" rates. In response, the NFBTO warned local authorities that the erection of Weir houses with labour paid at anything other than the agreed building trade rates would result in stoppages on all municipal sites. Although a government court of enquiry found against the Federation, local authority fears of dispute helped to undermine the market for Weir's house which was later withdrawn. A precedent had been established: while the unions had not sought to control rates of pay within factories, they had made it clear that the site erection of building systems was to be their work paid under established rates. Both Telford and Braithwaite, also promoting steel systems before the war, observed this practice.[2]

In order to avoid a recurrence of the conflict associated with Weir's house, the government carefully involved union leaders in wartime deliberations on future building policy. As well as being approached to sit on CISPH (an offer he declined) Richard Coppock, Secretary of the NFBTO, sat on both the subcommittee of the Central Housing Advisory Committee considering temporary housing and the Burt Committee considering new methods of construction. Despite involvement in policy preparation, Coppock harboured few illusions on the significance of system building to craft labour. In a memorandum prepared for his Federation in 1944, Coppock concluded that, as well as introducing non-building labour controlled by other unions, prefabrication threatened to undermine the craft structure of the building industry:

> unless we are prepared boldly to face up to the question we may find our craft processes broken down to small units of such simplicity and specialisation, that the entire fabric of our organisation . . . and our economic position is placed in jeopardy.[3]

However, as Coppock also pointed out, any initiative by government to expand housing supply would receive the acclamation of the nation and, were the Federation to hinder this, it would attract the "most caustic criticism". The ability of welfare measures to encourage social harmony was already apparent: no matter how injurious, building unions felt unable to oppose new methods of

113

construction if used for socially progressive projects such as working class housing. Under these circumstances, a more effective approach, reasoned Coppock, would be to seek to influence the development of system building so that new processes and the labour involved would be brought within the "control" of the NFBTO. In 1945, the Federation's annual conference passed a motion accepting non-traditional methods of construction on the basis that "whatever type of prefabricated house may be invented, it should be regarded as normal building trade practice, and that building trade rates and conditions should apply".[4]

While the unions may have seen prefabrication, both within and without the factory, as building work deserving the proper demarcation of skills and rates of pay, sponsors did not. For instance, when Weir launched a post-war housing system he accepted the Amalgamated Society of Woodworkers' demand that site labour should consist of gangs consisting of a high proportion of skilled labour paid at current rates. However, within his workshops Weir used unskilled workers in tasks such as pipe bending, paint spraying and the preparation of wall and floor units, claiming that "scientific methods of efficient industrial production" obviated the need for craft skills. The Federation was disturbed to hear that trade work was being carried out by "girls" and men, all on a labourer's rate of 1s 8d. per hour. The absence of a dispute over this breach of NFBTO policy indicated that, as in the case of Weir's earlier house, the unions were prepared to insist on a high degree of control on the building site but not in the factories.

In March 1946, the Minister of Labour and National Service and the Permanent Secretaries from the Ministry of Works and Ministry of Health visited the General Council of the NFBTO to discuss future building policy. Arguing that building demands over the next decade would more than absorb the planned increase in the labour force and that prefabrication was a temporary expedient only, they found a Council very sympathetic to government housing policy:

> The meeting pledged itself to support all the Ministers in all steps necessary to expand the housing programme . . . and appreciated the vital importance of supporting the present government in such a way that there should be no failure of the housing programme.[5]

Building unions subordinated sectional interests to those of their class as a whole and chose neither to jeopardise the survival of a Labour Government pledged to social reform nor hinder the welfare measures it pursued. This was a recurrent theme in building union policy throughout the post-war period. A year later, the Ministry of Works was able to report that, with the careful consultation of the unions, on non-traditional building sites for which they had been responsible, "The co-operation of the workmen has been as wholehearted as could have been wished".[6]

While generally co-operative, by no means all building workers welcomed new methods of construction. At the NFBTO Conference in 1950, the Midland Counties proposed a motion opposing system building which it felt was causing not only a "deterioration of craftsmanship" but unnecessary expense and a reduction in working-class housing quality. As the delegate from the plasterers' union not unreasonably pointed out: "it is the people of our class who have to pay for all the experiments and all the stunts that have been introduced in the name of housing since 1945".[7] In the ensuing debate opinions ranged from support for the motion to a fear that the Federation might be branded as "people not prepared to face up to new developments in the industry". As a result of the quandary raised by the debate, no vote was taken and the motion was referred to the Executive Committee for further consideration.

Full employment and the "lump"

Post-war union policy toward system building was undoubtedly affected by high levels of employment and the growth of labour-only subcontracting. Together, the two created a climate which worked against policies opposing new building methods.

Although it varied according to different regions, high levels of post-war employment had a major effect in reducing the potential for conflict: workers made redundant by labour-saving or skill-eliminating methods were able to find employment elsewhere. A more fundamental dampening of union activity, however, began with the wartime introduction of "payment by results" in an attempt to improve productivity in military building programmes.[8] Initiated by the War Cabinet, this early example of state intervention in building efficiency was retained after the war by employers eager to introduce pieceworking. According to L.W. Wood, the local negotiation of wage payments opened the door to "labour only" subcontracting (the lump). The seemingly generous premium (untaxed wage) offered under the lump reduced the incentive for workers to join trade unions which negotiated the hitherto universally applied national flat rates.[9] From 1947 building union membership began to fall and by the late 1960s a number of craft unions were considering amalgamation to overcome financial difficulties.[10] This was eventually achieved in 1968 when individual unions, previously federated under the NFBTO, combined to form the Union of Construction and Allied Trades Technicians. The combination of building unions into a stronger whole and greater militancy provoked by declining wage rates and increasing use of the lump, culminated in the first ever national building strike in 1972, bringing to an end the relative tranquillity covered by this account.

A virtue of necessity

Despite weakened union structures, the growth of system building in the 1960s was accompanied by careful negotiation to defuse industrial conflict. The aim of these consultations was to give unions some control over the balance of skills used in system building. However, it is apparent that more general developments in post-war building were having a fundamental affect on the skill structure of the industry, outweighing any concessions negotiated by unions in respect of system building. The building industry was changing irrevocably and unions were powerless to prevent this. With the election of a Labour government in 1964 committed to even larger social housing programmes, the National Federation gave up any semblance of opposition and even advocated the introduction of nationalised system building factories.

The introduction of continental large panel systems in the early 1960s was thought to herald the greatest change in building methods so far. On this occasion government and industry made no attempt to obscure departures from tradition with assurances that they were only temporary. The prevalent ideology was that a revolution in building methods was taking place and this by its very nature would be permanent. One delegate at the 1962 NFBTO conference described his visit to a system building factory in East Germany and the threat that large panel systems held for his class of labour:

> Here were complete wall units manufactured in a factory without one skilled operative having to touch that work. They were transported to site and joined together like a pack of cards. . . . This is what we are going to face, this is industrialised building.[11]

Still unwilling to resist new methods which severely diminished the skilled labour content of building operations, the Federation reiterated its previous position demanding in 1963 that, not only should it be informed of government policies on the use of system building, but also that:

> The labour engaged in the production and erection of new materials should be that trained within the construction industry and controlled by the unions affiliated to the NFBTO.

This policy was endorsed by the National Joint Council for the Building Industry, on which representatives of the unions and employers sat. Significantly, the National Joint Council for the pre-cast concrete industry, under which many pre-casting firms worked, did not accept the agreement as their workers belonged to non-building unions eager to take the new work for themselves.[12] Nevertheless, building firms sponsoring systems had, for the first time as a body, formally agreed to observe the application of building rates of pay and conditions both *within* factories manufacturing components and on the sites where they were erected. It would appear that the industry had no intention of allowing confrontations with labour to hamper the use of system building in forthcoming state housing programmes. Indeed, it could be said that, in light of the "miraculous" productivity claims made for system building, the payment of slightly higher rates in factories was a light enough burden in relation to the overall reductions anticipated in skilled labour.

To heighten the atmosphere of industrial co-operation, building firms were meticulous about involving unions in early negotiations. In 1962 Laing approached the NFBTO with an invitation to view the Sectra system it was about to import from France and, in consultation with the Federation, devised an erection gang made up of a mix of skilled and unskilled labour.[13] Unit Construction undertook a similar process with the Camus system agreeing an erection team of 7 trade operatives, 3 steel fixers and 16 labourers.[14] In April 1964 the National Federation of Building Trades Employers set up a committee, comprising both employer's and operative's representatives, to settle any disputes that arose on the composition of gangs for specific systems.

An exception to this seemingly conciliatory process was Taylor Woodrow who introduced the Larsen Nielsen system without consulting the Federation, intending that building conditions and rates of pay would not be extended to their factory workforce. In response to this, the Federation "told the firm quite frankly" that if it did not toe the line and observe the national agreement in the manufacture of their panels "it was quite likely there would be considerable difficulty in getting them erected".[15] Having flexed its muscles, the Federation noted the following year that not only were facilities and working conditions in Taylor Woodrow's factory excellent, but that the firm was also employing a large number of craft operatives who were to be paid according to the National Agreement.

In assessing the impact of system building on craft skills, and the degree to which unions were successful in realising their aim of controlling the labour involved, it is necessary to appreciate the wider developments that were taking place in post-war building methods. In 1958 the NFBTO noted that a recent £1.5 million non-system building contract in Swindon had been completed in ten months by only 40–50 labourers and 14 craft operatives. At a conference called in the following year to examine new technology, Coppock reviewed general changes that had taken place in architectural form and techniques of construction, concluding that "our industry is bound to become more simplified and part of the craftsmanship may be eliminated".[16] By 1959, well before the major system building drives of later years, it is evident that the proportion of work carried out by bricklayers and plasterers was declining significantly while that of carpenters was increasing as a result of the widespread use of factory-finished components. Indeed, the effect of this redistribution of trade work on union organisation was a subject for much discussion at the 1959 conference.

Demands by the weakened bricklaying union for a more even distribution of work created by new technology were firmly opposed by the Amalgamated Society of Woodworkers. The tendency for bricklaying and plastering to suffer to the advantage of carpentry, painting and decorating was accentuated by the wider use of system building in later years.[17]

One of the most noticeable effects of new trends in building was the increased numbers of semi-skilled workers. Rather than assigning new techniques to an existing craft, they were often carried out by quickly trained unskilled labour paid at a higher or "plus" rate for the time spent on the new job. Again, although general to the industry as a whole, this was particularly evident in the use of pre-cast concrete building systems. For instance, of the twenty-six operatives in the unit gang, the twelve responsible for erecting and sealing the concrete panels were plus-rated labourers, and the number of bricklayers was reduced to two. Such occurrences brought the complaint that "this prefabrication work is being based on the labourer, and not on the craftsman".[18] As H.J.O. Weaver noted in 1964, so far "the big problem had been the desire of most of the firms to use as high a ratio as possible of non-craft labour in the balanced gangs erecting the systems".[19] The figure aimed for by the Federation was a 50 per cent mix, corresponding to labour levels in traditional construction. The feeling that this was not generally achieved caused a Conference on New Techniques to be convened in 1964 to discuss the problem.

While it might be consulted by system building firms and was able to flex its muscles if ignored, craft unions were effectively powerless in the face of fundamental changes to the building economy. Indeed, if anything, consultations over system building were red herrings diffusing opposition to larger processes. In the midst of irrevocable change, the National Federation made a virtue of necessity in adopting the ideology of the Modernisation of Britain as the route to improving working-class living conditions. This position was consolidated with the return of the Labour Government in 1964.

The putting aside of sectional class interests could be observed at the 1963 Annual Conference of the Amalgamated Union of Building Trades Workers, where a delegate pointed out that unions could hardly criticise the government for building too few homes at the same time as opposing the new methods of construction which, it was believed, would allow increased housing targets to be met. Furthermore, "they could not condemn the lack of high investment in the industry and the lack of scientific planning without some responsibility in participation in methods of building".[20] Labour ideology, convinced that its social goals could only be gained through the scientific revolution, made it difficult for progressive union members to resist system building. The contradiction posed by a belief that "socialism equals science" was heightened with the return of the Labour Government in 1964. At the NFBTO conference of that year Coppock urged support for the new government in its housebuilding programme while another speaker suggested that sectional interests should be set aside "in the wider interests of the economy of the country".[21] The consideration of "wider" issues culminated in the 1966 NFBTO conference calling for the setting up of state-owned factories to manufacture prefabricated components for houses, flats, schools and hospitals, to be supplied to local authorities at cost price on long term loans.[22] In the space of twenty years, the erstwhile opponents of system building had joined its many advocates.

Architects

Like building workers, architects too initially feared new technology. However, it soon became apparent that conspicuous participation in system building was contributing to the adoption of a newly identified social role. While the next chapter looks in more detail at the way in which architects attempted to implement their social role through system building, this section deals with the profession's adaptation to the post-war Welfare State at a broader level. Indeed, the incorporation of a major part of professional practice within the government machine created opportunities for architects to pioneer in the application of system building to welfare policy. As a result, public sector architects began to overshadow their private practice colleagues, enhancing the post-war status of their profession.

Descending into parasitism

The eve of the Second World War saw architects fearful towards new methods of building. In its wartime statements, the Royal Institute of British Architects (RIBA) displayed an evident desire to denigrate prefabrication, prompting severe criticism from more progressive members of the profession.

The early fears of architects arose from a belief that increased mechanisation, relying as it did on standardisation and uniformity in buildings and their components, would inevitably reduce the scope for design. Design was the principle skill of the architect and the means by which the profession retained its pre-eminence in the building economy. The deskilling potential of prefabrication was readily appreciated by one practitioner:

> If one's house was produced as a motorcar was produced, and one received with it a book of words showing the spare parts that could be bought, where was the need of the architect?[23]

The profession's reluctance to accept new methods of construction was illustrated by the wartime statements of the RIBA. In its submission to the government committee considering temporary housing, the Institute stated that it "would regard with regret the creation of a body of labour unskilled in any craft but the assembly of ready made houses by means of the spanner".[24] No doubt concerned by its deskilling implications, the RIBA stigmatised factory produced housing in 1943 as fit only for temporary construction. This attitude was greeted with dismay by *Architectural Design* on behalf of "the more active and forward-looking members of the profession".[25] The profession's conservatism was severely criticised by the Chief Scientific Advisor to the Ministry of Works, Reginald Stradling, who concluded that the profession might well descend into "parasitism" which only a radical reappraisal of its training and outlook could arrest.[26]

Architects and the Welfare State

Although not as wholehearted as the advocates of mass production wished, the Second World War saw areas of the architectural profession not only adapting to changes in technology but also attempting to find a new role in society.

P. Malpass has argued that the identification of a social role by the architectural profession began before the war and involved two themes: the notion of the profession as the purveyor of a broad range of distinct technical skills and the view that architects could be of "quintessential value to society".[27] In 1936, the President of the RIBA, Percy Thomas, set out the profession's newly emerging self-view:

> it is on the technical ability of architects that the success or otherwise of rebuilding our towns and cities will depend . . . we exist solely to serve the community and we must bend our utmost power to that end.[28]

These ideas were greatly encouraged by the Modern Movement which, as well as arguing that mass-produced buildings were required to satisfy social needs, proposed that architects should verse themselves in science and technology to carry this task though. Within Modernist ideology, the architect was no longer a dilettante serving the artistic ideals of the few, but a technician serving the imperatives of mass society. The identification of a social role for the architect and technical expertise as the means to this end were dominant motifs in the profession's adjustment to conditions created by the Welfare State and may be seen as a major aspect of its eventual policy towards system building.

Architects undoubtedly saw in a mastery of science the means of enhancing their post-war status. By 1942 the RIBA had established the Architectural Science Board to educate members on technical developments in building. The purpose of this was to re-equip architects to maintain their central role in the building process. As *Architectural Design* pointed out in 1944, post-war building had become a multidisciplinary effort involving a number of technical specialists:

> Science has contributed much to practically every aspect of building and building organisation during the war years, and the professional standing of architects can be proportionally enhanced, provided they grasp the situation in a realistic spirit.[29]

The identification of a social role for architects was accompanied by their employment in growing numbers by the state. Whereas, before the war, architects worked predominantly in private practice, by 1967, 40 per cent were employed in local or central government; furthermore, the 50 per cent remaining in private practice found that, by then, more than half their work was awarded by the public sector. As Martin Pawley put it in 1971: "Thus within fifty years, the involvement of the architectural profession with the state has become almost as complete as that of the doctors or the teachers".[30]

Professional recognition and system building

The direction of building resources to social programmes through the licensing system relegated private practice to a subsidiary role in the development of early post-war architecture. Architects who gained greatest professional recognition were those in the public sector applying system building to housing and schoolbuilding programmes.

As the *Economist* noted, local authority architects were taking the interesting work while private architects had to make do with the overflow from public offices. Indeed, the profession's interest in new technology and belief in a social role was synthesised in the public sector office where many of the new systems of construction were developed. This was particularly so in schoolbuilding where they:

> have demonstrated a variety of non-traditional methods and materials – and even invented some – within a genre of architectural comeliness which has brought foreign architects flocking to these shores. A bitter pill this for the old school, whose efforts in the inter-war years hardly raised a flicker of interest among their questing overseas colleagues.[31]

By the mid 1950s local authority architects who had been promoting system building began to gain recognition and eminence within the profession. By 1954, the County Architect for Hertfordshire, C.H. Aslin, was elected President of the RIBA and his former deputy, Stirrat Johnson Marshall, was Chief Architect at the Ministry of Education. Perhaps the most singular public success of local authority architects was the award of a special prize to the system built school exhibited at an Italian design fair in 1960. The fame brought to its County Architect, Dan Lacey, was noted by Raynor Banham in "A Gong For the Welfare State":

> by the end of the month every thinking architect in Europe could of told you he was the titular designer of the *Schola Inglese* at the *Triennale di Milano*, which so far outdid all other exhibits that an unprecedented class of award – *Grand Premo con Menzione Speziale* – had to be created for it.[32]

Professional orthodoxy and industrialised building

During the 1960s the RIBA gave wholehearted support to government efforts to improve efficiency in the construction industry, cementing the bond between professionalism, system building and social purpose.

In an attempt to set its house in order, the RIBA published a survey on working practices in architect's offices, *The Architect and Productivity* (1962). A characteristic of the report, indicating the flavour of opinion by this time to be found within the profession, was the distinction between "good" and "bad" offices. The former tended to be the larger, more highly organised and efficient practices, while the latter were smaller, less profitable and less inclined to make use of modern organisational techniques. Both types of office were aware of the increasing trend towards industrialised building. While the "bad" offices "did not understand the effect it would have on the practice of architecture"[33] and felt it a threat to their professional position, not surprisingly, the "good" offices "welcomed the inevitability of increasing industrialisation in the building industry as an aid to higher productivity" and felt that the profession should become more involved to strengthen the architect's position.

In 1963, the RIBA's annual conference was held on the subject of "Architects and Productivity" and in his opening speech the President, Robert Mathew, re-emphasised the architect's social role. The foremost responsibility of the profession to its clients, whether individual or collective, was clearly to increase the output of buildings:

As architects we have to think first of our responsibility to our clients, and to the public at large, all of whom want a vast output of new buildings, and can't afford, or aren't prepared, to wait very long for them.[34]

Two years later the RIBA published its definitive statement on system building, *The Industrialisation of Building*, pointing out the benefits of system building to both architects and clients. If the system was properly designed, the report stated, architects would maintain high standards while, at the same time, handling up to sixty per cent more work. Interestingly, the report either overlooked or chose not to refer to the increased fee income that would accrue from larger workloads. To have laboured this point would have been to contradict the belief that architects were acting out of a sense of social responsibility in their promotion of system building. Instead, the report referred to the additional time that could be used to "analyse and solve users' requirements and tackle any particularly difficult problems".[35] The report left architects in little doubt of where their responsibility lay:

Many forms of industrialisation enable the architect to give . . . [the client] a better professional service, the manufacturer to produce better quality components at a more favourable price, and the contractor to maintain a more uniform and high standard of construction.

Rather than verging on "parasitism", as Reginald Stradling had feared, by 1963 the architectural profession could justifiably claim that it had adapted itself to the needs of the day.

Chapter 6
A QUESTION OF CONTROL

Architects played a major role in formulating building policies of the Welfare State. Indeed, the majority of post-war state housing was designed by architects directly employed by local and central government. Furthermore, the professional expertise of architects was highly prized by politicians. As a result, Modernist architects formulated state research and development policy and used their power within the government building process to design systems of their own. The post-war period saw the emergence of the state as sponsor of building systems and continuous efforts by public service architects to control the development of construction technology.

The license architects were given to exercise these policies arose from the status they were afforded by politicians only too keen to have beliefs in science and technology validated by professional expertise. On taking office, post-war ministers of housing and construction were, without exception, unversed in building economics and, therefore, reliant on professional advice. In 1954, Nigel Birch, the Minister of Works, unashamedly announced to the assembled architectural profession that he was "entirely unburdened by the slightest technical knowledge".[1] This state of affairs presented few problems to civil servants who were happy to continue with technical policies despite party political changes occurring about them. Pointing out that they usually stayed for less than two years, one senior civil servant found it understandable that a minister had "difficulty in getting to know the full extent of his responsibilities".[2] While they held the reins of overall political control, evidence suggests that ministers relied on advice from departmental experts who had a relatively free hand in formulating research and development policy. The common pursuit of welfare aims by different governments created a context in which the professional played a major role.

For as long as there was agreement on goals, professional expertise was needed to find the means by which they might be achieved. The Welfare State raised to high office a generation of Modernist architects committed to prefabrication in building.

The apparatus through which architects implemented their policies was extensive. As well as the Ministry of Housing and Local Government, the Ministry of Works existed to promote technical advance in methods of construction. Staffed by architects eager to implement their beliefs, it designed a succession of building systems, although few entered production. At local government level, the profession was more successful. Through the Consortia Movement, architects effectively controlled the application of system building to educational programmes and, at one stage, were seemingly about to do the same in housing.

Eventually, the direct intervention by state architects in the design and production of building systems led to a dispute with industry over which should control the development of new technology. So far as industry was concerned, system building was the province of commercial expertise organised on sound principles of competition. However, as the previous chapter has described, the architectural profession's post-war ideology was one of social purpose through science and technology. It was thereby committed to the guidance of system building in the direction of most benefit to society, even where this contrasted with commercial objectives. Furthermore, the architect's professional status as designer was at stake in the face of commercially developed building systems. The post-war history of social building programmes was, therefore, distinctively flavoured by the continuous attempts of public service architects to control the development of new technology and design building systems which reflected their theoretical beliefs.

Prefabrication and the Ministry of Works

The Second World War saw the creation of a new ministry of state charged with the efficiency of the building industry. One of the first tasks to which the Ministry of Works (MOW) addressed itself was experimentation in new methods of building. In order to establish prefabrication on the correct lines of mass production, ministry architects initiated a succession of building systems, displaying a clear preference for methods which most closely resembled factory manufacture. Although unsuccessful at this early stage, the state became a designer of building systems.

A ministry for the building industry

Created to oversee all aspects of building work during the war, the MOW's role was eventually narrowed to the purely technical aspects of construction. Ministry experts perceived in this role the opportunity to modernise what they regarded as a technically backward industry in need of radical change.

The transformation of the entire building industry into a part of the total war machine required the enlargement of the former Office of Works. By 1945 the new Ministry of Works had quadrupled in size, employing 22,000 staff. Responsible for administering all building resources, the Ministry was originally intended to oversee the post-war reconstruction of "towns and country" and in the latter years of the war played a major role in housing policy. However, housing and town planning functions were taken away with the creation of the Ministry of Town and Country Planning in 1943 and the reversion of all matters concerned with housing design and policy to the Ministry of Health in 1945. By the end of the war the MOW's role had been narrowed to the technical aspects of post-war reconstruction. Nevertheless, whereas previously the Office of Works had been concerned purely with administering government building requirements, 1945 saw the creation of a ministry with, in the words of the Prime Minister, "a general responsibility for the organisation and efficiency of the building industry as a whole".[3]

The first Chief Scientific Advisor to the Minister of Works was the former Director of the Building Research Station, Reginald Stradling. In 1940, in the same paper in which he castigated the architectural profession, he described the extent of work ahead and expressed his concern at the backwardness of the industry for which he was now responsible: "The building industry has not yet adjusted itself to modern conditions. Its personnel is largely ignorant of the basic principles of science upon which modern industry, and life itself has now come to depend".[4] In Stradling's view radical change was needed, and needed fast, if the nation's reconstruction plans were to be put to effect. As well as transforming the industry through basic research and education, Stradling suggested that the government itself should lead by example: "Nothing will be so effective in this education as the realisation that government can produce better, cheaper and quicker construction than anyone outside". Stradling thereby set out two principles on which government technical policy rested in future years: education through research, and experimental projects demonstrating the best in building practice. As well as publishing the influential series of "Post-war Building Studies", which dealt extensively with prefabrication, by 1946 the MOW had several divisions studying all forms of building operations, "the first time (in building) that any attempt has been made scientifically to deal with the question of human productive effort".[5] Indeed, it could be said that the analytical methods of Ford and Taylor were now being applied to the construction industry by this latest addition to the state machine. Characteristically, one of the Ministry's first publications was a time and motion study of men and plant in building and civil engineering.[6]

The MOW's involvement in the introduction of new systems was considerable. In 1943 the Minister of Works appointed a Controller of Experimental Building to assist "private enterprise and local authorities to develop new methods"[7] and if the Ministry felt a system to be of value it assisted promoters in development work and issued licenses for the erection of prototypes. These prototypes were then assessed by the Burt Committee and the Building Research Station and the more promising selected for further development. In the final stage, sites were found for a "development group" of one hundred and fifty houses, the construction of which was closely monitored to calculate a "definite figure" for labour content and therefore the labour saving contribution the system would make in the post-war period.

Putting theory into practice

As well as studying and analysing the products of industry, government experts concluded that they should involve themselves more actively in system building design. Indeed, they exceeded their brief for mere experimentation by attempting to design the very systems which would be used in post-war housing programmes.

The first prefabricated house designed by the MOW in 1944 was based on a lightweight steel frame manufactured by the Hills Patent Glazing Co. Encouraged by what it saw as favourable results, the Ministry claimed a range of advantages for prefabrication in line with Modern Movement theories of design and production. First, the Ministry maintained, components for the frame could be standardised, facilitating mass production, second, the cladding could be varied according to the availability of suitable materials and third, the rapid erection of the frame and its roofing protected the remaining works from bad weather, speeding the overall construction process.[8] The success of this first state designed system prompted the Minister of Works, Lord Portal, to advise the Cabinet that it should recommend the Northolt House, as it was named, to local authorities.[9]

Although nothing came of this initiative, Portal's architects were soon at work on a new project, the Pressed Steel Bungalow. Commonly referred to as the Portal House, the scheme was conceived as a part of the temporary housing programme. Portal's design was "based on mass production"[10], attempting to apply engineering industry methods to housing in the same manner as commercial organisations such as AIROH and the Arcon Group. The Portal House embodied the latest in lightweight steel technology and the name of the selected manufacturer, Briggs Motor Bodies, appropriately brings to mind the car as a source of design inspiration. The basic structure of the Portal House was ribbed pressed steel panels fixed to steel columns by spotwelded cleats. Joints in the external cladding were protected by pressed metal 'snap-on' cover pieces – a technique borrowed directly from automotive design. In May 1944 a prototype was exhibited outside the Tate Gallery. Reviewing the bungalow for *Architectural Design*, Edric Neel, one of Portal's acquaintances on CISPH, saw in it the most sophisticated application yet of engineering technology to housing: "this official solution to the problem of post-war emergency housing stands head and shoulders above anything yet attempted in this country or abroad".[11] However, the prolongation of the European war frustrated Portal's bold initiative delaying the diversion of engineering industry to housing production.[12] Eventually, the order placed with the Ministry of Supply for 50,000 bungalows was cancelled and contracts awarded to seven manufacturers who, unlike Portal, utilised materials less essential to war production.

Although the Portal bungalow was scrapped, a proposal to convert it to a permanent two-storey design capable of "real mass production"[13] was greeted enthusiastically by a MOW committee chaired by J.D. Bernal. This committee, charged to review current systems and "consider the practicality of designing an ideal type", was "strongly impressed" with Portal's design and recommended its energetic development. In August 1945 the new Minister of Works, Duncan Sandys, reported to the War Cabinet Housing Committee that he wished to place an order, again with Briggs Motor Bodies, for 25,000 Pressed Steel houses. While authorising Sandys to enter negotiations, the Cabinet refused to place the order without detailed costings and moved that the issue should be represented when these were available.[14] The production of the Pressed Steel House was not brought before the Cabinet again and it may be inferred that the scheme was abandoned when the likely cost became known.

6 Pressed Steel Bungalow (Ministry of Works, 1946)
Displaying the clean lines of automobile design, 50,000 of the first, state-developed, housing system were to be manufactured by Briggs Motor Bodies

The last attempt by the MOW to develop a prefabricated house was a proposal to blend the Arcon temporary bungalow and the Coventry House (designed by Donald Gibson and Edric Neel under the aegis of CISPH) to produce a hybrid design for local authorities. Two thousand of the blended houses were allocated to Coventry with production to start by the Arcon Group late in 1945. However, busy with its bungalow, Arcon was unable to produce components before 1947 causing the Ministry's project to fail once again.[15]

With the non-traditional housing programme underway and the disbanding of the "brilliant team of scientists and technologists brought together during the war"[16] the MOW abandoned the design of building systems. Under more scientific conditions than during the heyday of the Prefabrication Movement, the Building Research Station

7 Lord Portal (Minister of Works, 1944)
Seen in this publicity photograph testing taps in the prefabricated house designed by his architects, Lord Portal promoted state intervention in building methods

(BRS) collaborated in a series of experiments to measure the real benefits of system building. As early as 1943 the scientifically minded experts at the BRS had pointed out that the "remarkable dearth of systematic data"[17] made it impossible to form an objective opinion on the true merits of new methods of building. Contrary to the expectations of Modernist architects working in the MOW during the latter years of the war, these experiments indicated that under contemporary conditions, extensive prefabrication would not reduce the cost of house construction.[18] After further studies, in 1959 the Deputy Chief Scientific Officer to the BRS concluded that: "it seems for house building at least, economy is more to be sought in the evolution of traditional processes rather than by the introduction of radically different methods of construction".[19]

Research and development groups

After the MOW's wartime work, the state development of building systems was taken up by education architects working in local authorities and later in the Ministry of Education. Indeed, many of the Modernist architects who had previously worked at the MOW moved to local authorities implementing educational building programmes. Whereas architects had been unsuccessful in developing prefabricated systems for housing, they were very successful in schools design. Their achievements throughout the 1950s and early 1960s formed a model for the reorganisation of state research and development policy in all aspects of government building during the 1960s.

Early school building programmes

Like housing, the post-war implementation of a rapid school building programme relied heavily on new methods of construction to economise on scarce labour and traditional materials. Indeed, system building became as much a feature of school construction as it did housing.

In 1944 the Wood Committee, convened by the Minister of Works and comprising Modernist architects such as C.G. Stillman (W. Sussex County Architect) and Dennis Clarke Hall of CISPH, published *Standard*

Construction for Schools. The report concluded that "there is no reason in principle why the same plan should not serve for two or more schools of the same type and size"[20] and examined various methods of standardisation to speed the considerably enlarged educational building programme. The apparent success with which authorities such as Hertfordshire supplemented limited building labour through system building prompted the Ministry of Education to take a more active role in promoting these methods on a national scale. Towards the end of 1948 the Minister informed local authorities that he had "for some time encouraged the development of various new methods of building and their application to educational needs",[21] and, in order to carry this work, that further he intended to establish a small Development Group in the Architects and Building Branch. The duty of this group was to apply new building techniques to educational needs, and the choice of Head Architect was Stirrat Johnson Marshall, previously Deputy Architect for Hertfordshire County Council. Marshall's own purpose, quite simply, was to increase the use of prefabrication in school building and overcome the tendency of local authorities to regard it as a short term expedient.[22]

To achieve Marshall's aim, the Development Group embarked on a programme of building projects based on the principle of education by example.[23] In these, a number of systems were developed between 1950 and 1953 in conjunction with commercial sponsors using lightweight steel frames originally developed for housing and subsequently used by Hertfordshire in schools.[24] As well as developing systems, the group held meetings with education authorities to encourage their use in forthcoming programmes and published Building Bulletins publicising their work.[25] In the event, Marshall was successful and his systems entered commercial production. Unlike housing, prefabrication in school building was found to compare in cost with traditional methods and produced acceptable buildings at the same time economising on site labour. The state had become a designer of building systems.

The success with which the Development Group promoted system building in education was undoubtedly the outcome of, and to a large extent confused with, a number of administrative changes. The first was a requirement that programmes should be planned in advance to allow authorities to group projects for bulk ordering.[26] The second automatically gave Ministry approval for expenditure if an authority demonstrated that its schools met regulations on space standards and cost limits. As much as the systems of construction themselves, these procedures speeded programmes and improved cost control. More importantly, however, the Ministry of Education made a concerted effort to reduce the cost of school construction through more compact planning. By twice reducing cost limits between 1950 and 1951, schools radically changed from distended finger plans, with long corridors, to highly compact multi-storey forms minimising circulation areas. Between 1949 and 1954 the British school became 40 per cent smaller in plan area and correspondingly cheaper to build.[27]

Notably, the very building projects in which the Ministry designed new systems were also vehicles for developing space saving plans. Thus, the Research and Development Group was seen to combine new and rapid building techniques with dramatic space, and hence cost, savings to the Exchequer. Whether these savings were the result of prefabrication or of new planning and administrative techniques was never scientifically established and seems to have mattered little to inexpert politicians. In 1952 the economy conscious Cabinet Building Committee examined education policies and concluded they were "conducive to economy".[28] Taking the view that this was largely due to the Research and Development Group, the Committee advocated extending the principle to other government departments.

The ethos of R&D

Considered outstandingly successful in education, research and development groups were established in each of the government building ministries. A network of groups was thereby set up, charged with developing and experimenting in new forms of construction for the building programmes of their parent departments. The architects recruited to these groups were valued for their assertive policy making qualities rather than unquestioning servitude; their aspirations were those of the Modern Movement.

By 1961 nine government departments operated development groups. Describing the purpose and organisation of these, Roger Walters, Chief Architect to the War Office Development Group, stated that the parent organisation should be one with large building programmes

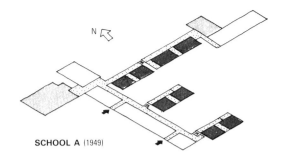

SCHOOL A (1949)

Throughout the 1950s, school planning changed radically to reduce circulation space. The economic benefits of this were frequently confused with new methods of construction

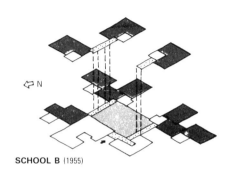

SCHOOL B (1955)

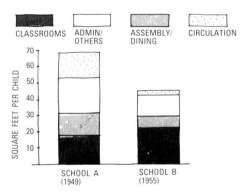

CLASSROOMS   ADMIN/ OTHERS   ASSEMBLY/ DINING   CIRCULATION

SPACE DISTRIBUTION

such as those of the Welfare State. Of the groups themselves, Walters stated that they should be "sensitive to future developments and should be ready to pioneer".[29] Walters also described quite specific attitudes which development architects should hold. Essentially, he felt they should be assertive policy makers in the Modernist mould rather than unquestioning public servants, who "will not ask the user what he wants, but what he wants to do, and how often he wants to do it: who believe that there is always a better answer to be found". Speaking for a parent department, W.D. Pile, administrative head of the Ministry of Education Architects and Building Branch, demonstrated the willingness with which policy makers accommodated the theories of their design professionals. Pile described the ideal public service architect in the following terms:

> The ability to make as well as to follow policy. There is no place in this dynamic organisation that the state needs for the slave . . . a perpetual discontent with the status quo, a revolutionary desire . . . to change the order of things . . . that revolutionary feeling must be guided by some systematic and scientific methodology . . . he has to be a business like character, I don't want any *prima donne* or little Corbs.[30]

More than any other, Donald Gibson personified the technocratic "public service" architect, basing a brilliant career on research and development work in welfare building. In 1938 Coventry City Council appointed Gibson as their first City Architect. Gibson's interest in new technology led to his wartime membership of CISPH and contributed to a number of experimental housing projects which were carried out in conjunction with local engineering firms. As well as redesigning Coventry's famous city centre according to Modern Movement principles of urban planning, it was Gibson who wrote the reports advising Coventry to concentrate its housing programme on No-Fines construction. While the leader of the Council, George Hodgkinson, displayed some anxiety over this "step into the dark",[31] Gibson's philosophy was more confident: "I find one ought to assume full responsibility for one's ideas" and if lay committees hesitate "do the job and take what comes".[32] Gibson's tendency to award municipal building contracts *en masse* to firms promoting new methods of construction applied also to education: in 1951 he proposed that for the next five years the city's schools should be awarded to the Bristol Aircraft Company for construction in their aluminium system.[33] Although the city eventually used four sponsors, the bulk of the programme was carried out in aluminium as Gibson envisaged. In 1957 Gibson became County Architect to Nottinghamshire and supervised the design and establishment of the CLASP system of school construction, an achievement which earned him considerable recognition by the profession.

Having identified a role for assertive policy makers within the state building machine, the early 1960s saw a number of organisational changes designed to make their work more effective. In 1958, the War Office became a civilian department and Donald Gibson was appointed head architect. Three years later, War Office architects were amalgamated with the Ministry of Works to become the Ministry of Public Buildings and Works. A major aspect of this reorganisation was the creation of the Directorate of Research and Development with Gibson at its head. The authority and status given Gibson in this new post, according to his Minister intended "to further the development and application of industrialised building techniques",[34] was considerable. Gibson was answerable only to the Permanent Secretary and received a salary of £7,000, larger than that of the Controller General for the entire Crown building programme and second only to his superior, the Permanent Secretary.[35] As a fitting tribute to the status he had achieved, the next year saw Gibson's name engraved on the marble walls of 66 Portland Place, alongside other acknowledged leaders of the profession, when he was made President of the RIBA. Later knighted, Gibson's career may be seen as perhaps the most remarkable of any post-war architect, illustrating the degree to which the practice of architecture had intertwined with the building policies of the Welfare State.

Gibson was by no means the only advocate of prefabrication to advance his career in the reorganisation of the public architectural service. In 1959 *Municipal Journal* reported that important changes were taking place at the Ministry of Housing and Local Government. The Ministry was forming a Development Group with a former Hertfordshire architect, Oliver Cox, at its head. In addition, J.H. Foreshaw, Chief Architect of the Ministry since 1945, was stepping down in the belief that a "younger man should take charge of the developments".[36] The new Chief Architect, A.W. Cleeve Barr, had, like Gibson, spent his life in the public service, previously with Hertfordshire and then the London County Council. Prefabrication had made an early impression on Barr. As a boy during the early 1920s he remembered "watching, fascinated [by] the erection of the first steel houses in my village",[37] and in 1958 he spoke of his time at the London County Council where he had "tried on a number of occasions . . . to evolve, for housing, systems of lightweight steel construction and of pre-cast concrete construction comparable to those which have made possible such notable advances in the field of school design".[38] The enlarged scope given to the "new men" at the Ministry of Housing and Local Government was commented on by Dame Evelyn Sharp, Permanent Secretary to the Minister. Between 1951 and 1969 the numbers of professional and technical staff in her ministry rose from 570 to 900. One of the largest contributors to this was the greater amount of research, development and promotional work carried out. Rather than performing a purely regulatory role, as previously, government architects became increasingly involved in

9 Sir Donald Gibson, Director General of Research and Development, Ministry of Public Buildings and Works
"I find one ought to take responsibility for one's ideas". Gibson personified the assertive postwar public service architect committed to Modern Movement ideals of technology harnessed to social purpose

the "formulation and dissemination among local author-ities of new ideas and new techniques".[39]

The fervour with which Donald Gibson and his colleagues approached their new jobs was indicated in 1961. Using the vocabulary of political revolution, Gibson observed that

> There is now a well established (although small) cadre of architects with the "know-how" of development work and its history and its possibilities.[40]

More importantly, this "cadre" was firmly lodged in the upper levels of the state building machine and poised in the attempt to set system building on a far more rational path than had hitherto been trod by commercial interests.

The control of design

The first post-war decade had seen architects designing building systems in the Ministry of Works and Ministry of Education. However, despite the involvement of education architects, the systems designed by Johnson Marshall's development group were still sponsored by building firms. Through an innovation in local authority administration, architects became sponsors of building systems, controlling their design, development and production. This innovation, more organisational than technical, was the Consortia Movement and had a fundamental effect on the character of local authority building.

Innovations in organisation

The school building requirements of most counties were too small to sponsor systems of their own design. From the mid-1950s, however, local authorities began to group together to overcome this problem.

Hertfordshire's school building programme had seen the architect's hand first come to the fore in designing and sponsoring a building system. C.H. Aslin, the County Architect, acknowledged the "vital" difference between his system and those marketed by commercial interests to be "that the various parts of the structure . . . have been designed by the architect".[41] However, the conditions under which Hertfordshire was able to design and operate its system were not enjoyed by other authorities. By the late 1940s, Hertfordshire's boundaries encompassed the new towns of Stevenage, Hemel Hempstead, Hatfield and Welwyn Garden City and was building up to twenty schools a year. Although other authorities had educational building requirements large enough to use commercially sponsored systems, programmes were too small to design their own.

A solution to this impasse was found in the mid-1950s at Nottinghamshire County Council. In 1955 Donald Gibson, formerly of Coventry, was appointed County Architect and a number of staff changes were made which included "the importation of new blood which had been subjected to the Hertfordshire experience".[42] Placing its 1956/7 school building programme with outside architects, Gibson set about developing a system of his own. However, Nottingham's most important contribution to the history of system building was less the system itself than the mechanism through which it was sponsored. By amalgamating a number of local authorities under the umbrella of the Consortium of Local Authorities Special Project (CLASP) a very much larger programme was made available for the new system than could be provided by any one of the individual authorities alone. Furthermore, members were not forced to commit all their schools to new methods of construction to enjoy a system designed and managed by their own architects. The 1957/8 CLASP programme included eleven schools worth £900,000: by 1959/60 this had grown to £3.4 million.

Much has been made of the ingenious structural joint (developed by Gibson's team) to overcome mining subsidence found in the north Midlands. However, it is important to emphasise that CLASP was not a technical innovation but an organisational one. Its major component, the modular steel frame, had been developed for Hertfordshire during the 1940s. Nor was the association of local authorities into larger buying units to increase their power in the market place originally the invention of Nottinghamshire's architects. In 1935 the Ministry of Health Committee on the Standardisation and Simplification of the Requirements of Local Authorities advocated the grouping of purchasers precisely for this reason. In its report the Committee urged first the standardisation of "innumerable articles" bought by local authorities and secondly that they should combine to "obtain for themselves the full benefits of bulk purchase".[43] Indeed, the architectural profession promoted consortia sponsored systems by drawing attention to the apparent savings made by purchasing standard components in bulk. Ultimately, however, the combination of local authorities into consortia provided a model by which architects could be designers of building systems. As one of the CLASP design team, Henry Swain, pointed out of commercially sponsored systems:

> The manufacturer of the system would generally control its development and it would tend to appear on the market for architects to take it or leave it, many of them would take it, but somewhat reluctantly. . . . The consortium formed by a number of public authorities was devised to overcome this disadvantage.[44]

10 West Bridgeford School, Notts (CLASP, mid-1950s)
By joining together to produce their own steel frame school systems, local authority architects regained the control they had lost over the building process

Once the principle of consortia was developed, it was promoted heavily in professional journals. In doing this architects emphasised benefits which consortia gave client organisations in terms of improved design and reduced costs: through consortia, system building could be designed and developed for the requirements of the "user" in place of commercial gain. Rather than protecting professional interests, architects argued that consortia were integral to fulfilling their social purpose.

As early as 1941 *Architects' Journal* urged that the profession should dominate prefabrication "in the interests of the community".[45] In his study of post-war school-building policy, Andrew Saint portrays the idealistic local authority architects who combined educational requirements and prefabrication in building systems intended to respond to social needs both functionally and architecturally.[46] The ideology of the Consortia Movement was summarised by *Architectural Review* in 1964 as the result of a "strong conviction . . . that user needs and not the exigencies of production should be the deciding factor".[47] There was no doubt in the minds of architects that they were best able to design systems in relation to client needs as they had always done with buildings constructed by traditional means.

Nevertheless, there is no evidence to suggest that the systems sponsored by consortia produced buildings superior to those of industry. Indeed, architects relied heavily on the technical expertise of steel fabricators to develop the modular frames on which their systems were based. The historic Hertfordshire system used a lightweight steel frame developed originally by Hills of West Bromwich for housing. After its further development for school construction in conjunction with Hertfordshire, the authority and Hills sponsored almost identical systems. The minimalist pre-cast concrete clad schools, which coined the phrase "light and dry", found in Hertfordshire were also built by Hills in Gloucestershire and South London. Hills and other commercial sponsors such as Gilbert Ash, the Bristol Aircraft Co. and Brockhouse willingly modified their systems in conjunction with government architects in the early 1950s to meet current educational requirements. Essentially, the issue was one of control and so far as the architectural profession was concerned, in designing and sponsoring systems of construction, commerce was "in fact usurping the function of the architect".

Consortia for housing

Having developed consortia for schools, it was only a matter of time before the principle was extended to housing. This opportunity came as housing programmes were enlarged in the early 1960s. Nevertheless, the sponsorship of systems for multi-storey housing was more complex than lightweight schools and number of years passed before architects achieved a similar level of control to education.

One of the first consortia for housing was initiated by Coventry. In December 1961, the Housing Committee considered a suggestion by its Architect, now Arthur Ling, to combine with neighbouring authorities to

> exchange information on designs, methods of construction and building costs and confer on the possibilities of standardising fittings and components and bulk purchase of such items for authorities in the group as a whole.[48]

By 1963 12 Midland authorities with a combined population of two million and housing capital expenditure in excess of £6.5 million had joined to form the Midland Housing Consortium (MHC). The first task tackled by the group was the organisation of bulk tendering programmes for components such as ironmongery, door-sets and rainwater goods. However, as Arthur Ling pointed out, this had been a preliminary step, for, "the real work" of the consortium began only with the design of its own system of house construction. In mid-1964 the MHC completed its first project of 129 houses at Woodway Lane in Coventry using the technically modest Mk.I system of blockwork crosswalls and tile hung timber infill panels. Like CLASP, MHC made little in the way of a technical contribution to building development, the novelty was in the promotion and control of a housing system by architects.

In 1964 the Yorkshire Development Group (YDG), consisting of Leeds, Sheffield, Nottingham and Hull, unveiled plans to sponsor a large panel concrete system for its own use. Up to this point, local authorities had concentrated on the less complex and capital intensive techniques of steel or timber frame and infill panel. This method of construction broke the building down to a number of elements involving several manufacturers. Although the steel frame was the most important component, the multiplicity of specialists, none of which originated from the contracting industry, was amenable to central control by the architect. Nevertheless, if they were to sponsor systems for urban redevelopment schemes, architects would have to control large panel pre-cast concrete. Systems of this type were generally sponsored by national contractors who brought together the expertise and capital to produce the heavy and complex structural elements. To gain control over this type of producer required complex tendering procedures.

YDG began the development of their system by designing a standard housing block, four to seven stories high, suited to construction in "a limited range of large simple components".[49] The project was tendered using a procedure developed by the MOW specifically to allow architects to sponsor building systems on behalf of their

11 Woodway Lane, Coventry (MHC, 1965)
Technically modest, the MHC housing system was nevertheless significant in being the first to be designed and controlled by local authority architects

clients. In the first stage, YDG examined the manufacturing techniques of 24 firms. Of these, four went on
to the next stage where they were required to submit
tenders on the basis of descriptive specifications, sketch
plans and elevations of the typical block designed by the
group's architects. The final details of construction were
worked out with the Shepherd Building Group who won
the contract to manufacture and erect the YDG system
for the first 440 dwellings in the programme at Leak
Street, Leeds. Eventually, Shepherd constructed the
remainder of the 3,734 dwelling programme. By combining
their requirements and using a new tendering procedure,
the members of YDG sponsored a complex building
system the parts for which were manufactured by a major
building firm. Rather than sponsor, Shepherd became
merely the supplier of components to a system designed
by local authority architects.

By 1968, 482 housing authorities had combined to
form forty consortia and, although most of these had not
designed their own systems, a trend was developing in
which local government architects were organising their
employers into larger buying units to exert more power
in the purchase of state housing.[50] In the field of
education, consortia were highly successful in using
systems of their own design and accounted for 75 per
cent of system built schools in 1971.[51] Through the local
authority Consortia Movement, the sponsorship and,
therefore, design of system building was coming
increasingly under the control of architects.

Modular co-ordination

The most consistently pursued strand of government
research and development work was modular co-
ordination, or the design of buildings to a common
dimensional framework. According to Modern Movement
theory, this was fundamental to any attempt at mass
production through prefabrication. Modular co-ordination
departed from traditional building by requiring the
standardisation of the previously arbitrary dimensions
applied independently to each building project. Furthermore, it was a concept ignored by commercial sponsors
in the systems they developed. The attempt to change
this state of affairs assumed increasing importance in
government building policies throughout the late 1950s.

Attempts to standardise the dimensions of building components were made before and during the Second World War. However, at this stage, official committees and central government showed a distinct lack of interest in theories of modular co-ordination despite the urgings of architects within the Ministry of Works and Building Research Station.

To assist the Addison Housing programme, the British Government set up a committee in 1921 to examine the standardisation of mass produced building components such as baths, water fittings, gutters and ironmongery. During the 1930s Modern Movement theorists, including Walter Gropius and Albert Farwell Bemis, also carried out work on modular co-ordination.[52] The attempt to standardise building products was continued by Lord Portal who appointed the Standards Committee in 1942 with the following terms of reference: "To study the application in building of standard plan elements, standard specifications and building components, and methods of prefabrication".[53] Conspicuous for failing to fulfill Portal's ambitious terms, the Committee restricted discussion to the interchange of fittings, thereby enabling manufacturers to stockpile prior to the onset of post-war house building without commenting on the standardisation of dimensions and specifications to facilitate pre-fabrication. In the event, the Committee made 260 recommendations to the British Standards Institute on fittings ranging from metal sinks to floor tiles and was happy to note that these changes, minor as they were, had been taken up by industry.

The conservatism of the Standards Committee did not satisfy the Building Research Station and MOW. Writing to the Burt Committee the Station urged that it should compile an encyclopedia of standard interchangeable components which could be manufactured in far greater numbers than parts for individual systems and selected freely by housing architects: "If a mass production system is adopted it is vital to ensure that the advantages of mass production are not thrown away".[54] Like the Standards Committee, the Burt Committee showed little desire to take such a radical approach. In 1945 D. Dex Harrison, an architect working for the MOW, described the implications of this lack of commitment to modular co-ordination.

5–10,000 off is [not] mass production as we know it today. Entrepreneurs tend to think rather in terms of 100,000 and we have to face the chance that the market may be collared by a few big scale producers who have broken into the market, achieved economy and gained control of the field. The alternative, equally disastrous, occurs if too many big interests try to participate in a programme too small to enable them all to mass produce on the requisite scale, for then the cost of housing will not fall and prefabrication will languish . . . we need to establish a common basis of dimensions to which sponsors of individual products can adhere and so that we get a range of standardised products that will fit together in different ways in the building, but, above all, that *will* fit together.[55]

In this passage Harrison described the problem inherent in commercial approaches to system building as it continued to be seen throughout the post-war period by official architects. Essentially, he felt a conflict existed between commercial sponsors, whose instinct was to design systems in which only their components could be used and scientific rationale which held that a common dimensional framework should be established to allow components to be interchanged between systems and manufactured in limitless numbers by however many producers the market could support. The conflict was summarised by the terms "closed" system (the outcome of commercial interests in the absence of modular co-ordination) and "open" system (the result of co-ordinating all building dimensions). The way to achieve a common dimensional basis, according to Harrison, was through a "*central body*" which could itself instigate standards both in dimensions and in the specification of components.

As well as facilitating true mass production, modular co-ordination was intended to promote flexibility in design as the architect of any single building could choose from a range of components and fit them together in a variety of ways to make the desired plan. The analogy frequently used was that of the Meccano sets that many Modernist architects had played with in former years. As Harrison stated, without the co-ordination of dimensions, the limited selection of fixed designs "achieves volume at the expense of variety and flexibility. . . . The predesigned house, which may be well or ill designed, is offered to the public by the

148

hundreds of thousands". So far as architects were concerned, modular co-ordination was essential in any effort to enhance the design of houses and schools to be built by new methods and axiomatic to achieving social aims through prefabrication. Furthermore, as the Bernal Committee noted in 1945, the monotony inherent in contemporary approaches threatened to engender "unjust-ified prejudice" against the appearance of prefabricated houses delaying "the acceptance of new and progressive methods of building".[56] There was, therefore, an added reason for the state to promote dimensional co-ordination aside from achieving mass production: if better designed and more flexible, architects and the public were more likely to accept new methods of construction.

Although state support for modular co-ordination was to be very evident in years to come, by 1947, with the work of the Burt and Standards committees complete, Harrison felt that Britain had missed its chance and that government had failed the cause of mass produced housing.[57] The Modular Society, formed in 1953, contin-ued to promote the co-ordination of dimensions on an unofficial basis but had little real impact on the building economy.

Design flexibility and school systems

The design of components that could be combined into varying forms underlay the development of school building systems during the 1950s. However, although these systems incorporated modular principles to a degree, they did not achieve the basic aim of interchang-ing components between each other.

Being much larger, the standardardisation of complete schools was less applicable or practical than in housing. The early development of prefabricated schools, such as that carried out C.G. Stillman in Sussex and discussed in *Standard Construction For Schools*, proposed classrooms of constant cross section which could be varied in length. Using standard structural frames, wall and window panels, these were joined together in different arrange-ments by long corridors connecting with a traditionally built central administration building. Indeed, in 1948 the Ministry of Education stated its aversion to the factory production of standard schools "in a sense comparable with totally prefabricated houses".[58] The schools system developed by Hertfordshire and Hills of West Bromwich was based on a 8ft 3ins planning grid which allowed any plan to be developed providing it adhered to the basic dimensional discipline. This grid was later reduced to 3ft 4ins to further increase planning flexibility. Variations in height were enabled by the development of multi-storey systems with vertical grids. Therefore, architects were able to vary not only the plans of their schools in any one system, but massing and elevational treatment. Nevertheless, despite longer-term aims and commitment to a philosophy of design which integrated architectural values with new technology, education architects made little headway in the struggle for dimensional co-ordination as none of their components could be used in

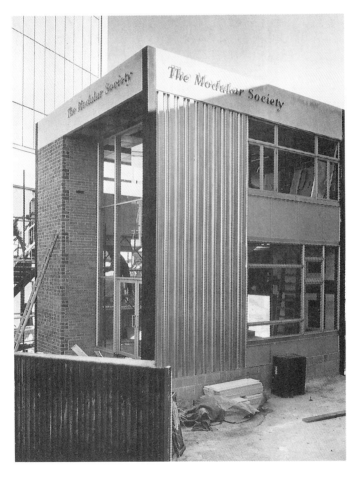

12 Modular Society exhibition building (1958)
Comprising different materials and techniques, each dimensional related to each other, this exhibition building was designed to promote modular theories developed by Modernist architects

150

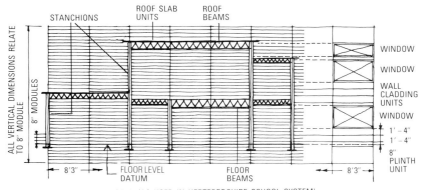

STANCHIONS
ROOF SLAB UNITS
ROOF BEAMS

ALL VERTICAL DIMENSIONS RELATE TO 8" MODULE

8" MODULES

WINDOW
WINDOW
WALL CLADDING UNITS
WINDOW

1'—4"
1'—4"
8"
PLINTH UNIT

8'3"
FLOOR LEVEL DATUM
FLOOR BEAMS
8'3"

VERTICAL GRID (AS USED IN HERTFORDSHIRE SCHOOL SYSTEM)

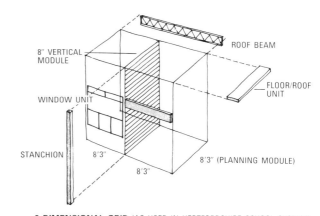

8" VERTICAL MODULE
ROOF BEAM
FLOOR/ROOF UNIT
WINDOW UNIT
STANCHION
8'3"
8'3"
8'3" (PLANNING MODULE)

3 DIMENSIONAL GRID (AS USED IN HERTFORDSHIRE SCHOOL SYSTEM)

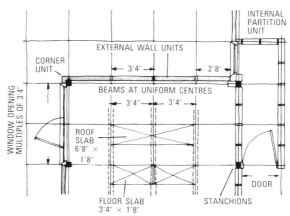

INTERNAL PARTITION UNIT
EXTERNAL WALL UNITS
CORNER UNIT
3'4"
2'8"
WINDOW OPENING MULTIPLES OF 3'4"
BEAMS AT UNIFORM CENTRES
3'4"
3'4"
ROOF SLAB 6'8" × 1'8"
DOOR
FLOOR SLAB 3'4" × 1'8"
STANCHIONS

PLANNING GRID (AS USED IN WOKINGHAM RESEARCH & DEVELOPMENT PROJECT)

13 Dimensional systems in prefabricated schools
Flexibility in school design was achieved through the use of horizontal and vertical grids. Nevertheless, the ambition of all systems conforming to a common grid so they could share components, was never achieved

151

more than one system. However, this failure was balanced by proof that a measure of flexibility in plan and elevation could be achieved within system building if these values were promoted strongly enough by the sponsor. This was to be the case with state designed housing systems in later years.

The adoption of modular co-ordination by the state

Whereas modular co-ordination had been ignored in state policy during the 1940s, the 1950s saw the beginning of a process whereby governments throughout Europe examined the subject. The finalisation of these studies co-incided with the onset of the building boom, rapidly bringing modular co-ordination to the fore in the state's industrialisation of building policy.

In 1954 the modular co-ordination initiative moved to an international forum when the European Productivity Agency of the Organisation of European Economic Co-operation began research on the subject. In 1961 the Agency produced its second report based on several years of negotiation and research recommending a 10cm module for metric countries and 4ins for imperial countries. This latter proposal was accepted and approved by the International Organisation for Standards.[59]

With a plea in the 1962 Emmerson Report that the state should finally adopt a modular framework, consistent policies were initiated on dimensional co-ordination by government departments. In May 1962 an Interdepartmental Committee was set up to agree a set of standard dimensions.[60] Between 1963 and 1968 the Ministry of Public Works and Buildings published several documents advocating horizontal and vertical dimensions for commercial, housing, educational, industrial and public buildings. In 1963 Parliament was informed that, from then on, all government buildings would be designed to these standards in the attempt to lead industry towards modular co-ordination.[61]

Research and development 1960–75

With the establishment of research and development groups in all building ministries, education by example was again taken up on a broad front. The government's industrialisation of building policy saw the state design of a number of systems, each of which incorporated latest theories on modular co-ordination. However, after the development of these systems, attention turned to initiating interchangeable components which would be available on a national basis and shared between a number of systems with standardised dimensions. The final element of government policy was the attempt to enforce the design of state housing to a prescribed set of dimensions, thereby allowing the use of the same set of components in all local authority programmes.

A new generation of building systems

In the early 1960s three systems of construction were designed or modified by government architects in an attempt to progress system building nearer the goal of modular co-ordination. In the event, none of these proved as successful as hoped.

The first of the new generation of state designed system was 5M CLASP, developed by the Ministry of Housing and Local Government Research and Development Group. The declared object of the Ministry in developing 5M was to provide a flexible low-rise system for small sites capable of being used by small builders. 5M directly applied to housing the modular steel frame developed by the most successful of the local authority schools consortia, CLASP, from which it partly borrowed its name. However, 5M also implemented recent international agreements on modular co-ordination. The designation "5M" referred to the planning grid which was a five-fold multiple of the International Standards Organisation 4ins module. This reduced the 3ft 4ins schools grid to 1ft 8ins, which was considered more suited to housing, allowing, in theory, the design of an endless range of different plan types and external treatments due to the use of different wall cladding panels ranging from concrete to tile hanging. The initial market for 5M was provided by the Crown barrack re-building programme of the 1960s when the system was used for a 370 house contract at Catterick. This project, undertaken by the Ministry of Public Buildings and Works Research and Development Group, was intended to establish the production of 5M components by individual manufacturers and represented a form of co-

153

operation that was to endure between the development groups of different ministries.[62] Indeed, most of the barrack rebuilding programme of the early 1960s conveniently served as an experimental vehicle for developing government building systems. By 1966, 5M, the first state designed housing system to enter production, was in use by 14 authorities and, as intended, 20 house types had been designed.[63]

Modular principles also underlay the Nenk system designed by the Ministry of Public Buildings and Works in 1963 as an all purpose building system. Like 5M, the system was based on the flexible steel frame and infill panel and its first project was a half million pound contract of communal buildings at the Invicta Park barrack complex, Maidstone. Although originally conceived for Crown use, Nenk was intended to further a national system of interchangeable components:

> In Nenk an effort has been made not only to devise a method of building which would allow the designer greater flexibility in planning . . . but it was also hoped that as it evolved, it might evolve in a more open manner. A key point for the future development of Nenk would be to ensure that new components could be introduced into it more readily than was possible with the existing systems.[64]

Indeed, the Research and Development Group intended that use of the system should extend beyond the Ministry and hoped that "in the national interest" it would be adopted by local authorities and "any architect public or private, who wants to use it".

The most ambitious state designed system was Jespersen 12M, developed in 1963 through an association with John Laing & Co. The first practical application of 12M was the Ministry of Housing and Local Government Research and Development project at Oldham in which the Group based its modifications to the Danish system on a twelve-fold multiple of the 4ins module. The choice of Jespersen for Ministerial support was quite deliberate: it was the only large panel concrete system whose components were based on a dimensional module rather than standard sizes. Wall panels were of three widths, 4ft, 6ft and 8ft while floor panels were 4ft wide and variable in length by 1ft increments. According to the designers, this feature made the system uniquely flexible as the internal plan

14 Nenk (Ministry of Public Works and Buildings Research and Development Group, 1963)
Intended to be a multi-purpose building system, Nenk achieved greater planning flexibility than any steel frame system previously. The roof frame units in the foreground related to the 1M module

was not fixed by an established range of room size panels, as in other systems, but could be derived from the module. Furthermore, the narrow panels made it possible to introduce staggers in section without departing from standard dimensions. While it did not possess the degree of planning versatility evident in schoolbuilding systems, Jespersen was a considerable advance in this sense on other pre-cast concrete housing systems. Variation in the external treatment was allowed by divorcing front and rear cladding panels from the structural system. These could be made by other manufacturers to varying designs in accordance with the policy of "opening" up the commercial systems.[65] The condition which the Ministry attached to carrying out development work on behalf of Laing was that the company should make the components available to

15 12M Jespersen,
typical floor plan
(Ministry of Housing and
Local Government/John
Laing, 1963)
Narrow panel widths of
varying length allowed a
degree of flexibility in
planning Jespersen flats
untypical of pre-cast
concrete systems

PANEL LAYOUT FOR TYPICAL FLAT

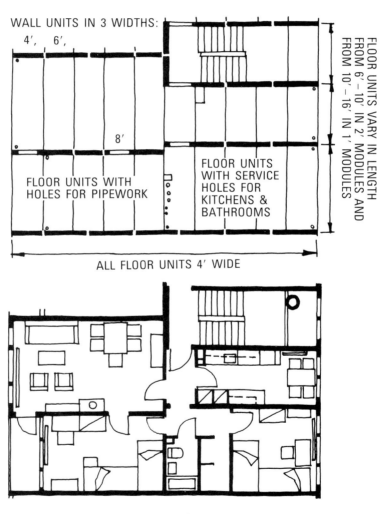

WALL UNITS IN 3 WIDTHS:
4', 6',

8'

FLOOR UNITS WITH
HOLES FOR PIPEWORK

FLOOR UNITS
WITH SERVICE
HOLES FOR
KITCHENS &
BATHROOMS

FLOOR UNITS VARY IN LENGTH
FROM 6' – 10' IN 2' MODULES AND
FROM 10' – 16' IN 1' MODULES

ALL FLOOR UNITS 4' WIDE

COMPLETED INTERNAL LAYOUT

outside contractors. This was duly done in November 1967. As with Nenk, the Ministry aimed to spread the use of its systems as widely as possible and to give Jespersen a secure foothold in the market. 2,252 barrack quarters in the Home Counties were awarded by the Ministry of Public Works and Buidings.

By 1965 "component building" had become commonly accepted as the next phase in industrialised building. In the same year the journal, *Interbuild*, opened a monthly section on the subject listing any product coming onto the market that might be described, however loosely, as a "component". By early 1966 the Ministry of Health had developed a range of standard components for use in hospital building which included complete doorsets, partitioning, storage units and window assemblies.[66] Indeed the words "component" and "open" became fashionable in the advertising copy of commercial firms. In 1966 Hawthorne Leslie named its modified low-rise system the "flexible component" system[67] and in the same year Cosmos launched an "open" housing system claiming that its components could be bought individually and, where desired, could be used in traditional construction or with other systems.[68]

16 Married Quarters, Gosport, Hants (12M Jespersen, 1965) Jespersen's flexibility allowed low and high-rise layouts to be developed. The narrow panels are evident on flank walls

Although technically sophisticated and attractive to adherents of dimensional co-ordination, the systems designed by government architects were unpopular with local authorities. The complexity of ordering 5M components from a large number of individual manufacturers made it less convenient than proprietary systems and required large contracts, contrary to the intention of the system, to make the effort worthwhile.[69] Ultimately only 3,468 houses were built (see Appendix 5). For Jespersen to be economical it demanded a rationality in design which belied its apparent flexibility. Nenk was only ever used on Crown projects, and did not survive the completion of the barrack rebuilding programme.

The IBIS partition

The design of building systems completed the first phase of government research and development policy during the 1960s. The second was more ambitious in attempting to directly initiate the national system of interchangeable components envisaged by D. Dex Harrison. As with their earlier systems, government research and development architects proved singularly unsuccessful in introducing the first of these, the IBIS partition.

In 1966 the government halted the development of further complete systems and concentrated on standard components. The way in which this was to be done was explained to Parliament by the Minister of Public Buildings and Works. Departmental professional staff, working in the Interdepartmental Component Co-ordination Group would provide potential producers with dimensional standards and performance requirements. When components satisfactory in design and price had been developed with industry it was intended that they should be used in public building programmes to stimulate large scale production before being marketed commercially.[70]

The first component to be developed by the state in this way was the Industrialised Building in Steel (IBIS) partition for schools. In 1966 the Department of Education and Science explained that it was hoping to promote the use of standard components in a number of the systems being sponsored by local authority consortia. Indeed, a number of educational consortia were currently considering sharing window units devised by the South East Architects Collaboration. However, the building element first chosen for development was an internal classroom partition system – a complex component which needed to be soundproof, lightweight and durable. This, it was hoped, would be the first component to be interchangeable and nationally used within a variety of systems.[71]

By July 1967 the Department of Education and Science had prepared the partition's performance and dimensional requirements and advertised for willing manufacturers in the press. Some firms dropped out in the early stages and only two of the remaining designs, IBIS and the Expanded Metal Partition System, were considered to have met the Department's requirements. On approval of a prototype, the Second Consortium of Local Authorities (SCOLA) undertook to enter negotiations with Richard Thomas & Baldwin for its inclusion in their schools programme.[72] However, it was not until 15 months later that agreement was reached on appearance, technical performance and – if half the consortium's programme was guaranteed – price also. In the ensuing debate it was pointed out that preparations for the partition's immediate adoption would prevent further development work from taking place on the system as a whole. Furthermore, as the Chief Architect from Leeds pointed out, the trend was moving towards open plan schools which might reduce the need for partitioning by up to 80 per cent. Already, the extensive lead-in time of the product threatened to render it obsolete before manufacture began. Arguments for adopting the partition concentrated on the "wider question of moral commitment" to support an attempt to develop open systems. To this end, the Department of Education and Science offered to guarantee consortia programmes using IBIS. Nevertheless, five members of SCOLA refused to commit themselves with the effect that the price once again rose. By March 1969 three other consortia groups had withdrawn from the project altogether. Later in that year, with the design of a cheaper version and the prospect of the component development programme grinding to a halt the Department of Education entreated SCOLA: "To consider the adverse reaction non-use of the partition in the next programme year might have on the industry as a whole . . . a modest use of the partition in 1970/71 may give a good impression".[73] The consortium resolved that use of IBIS should be left to individual members apparently sealing its fate as discussion was never minuted again.

The final thrust of official building research and development resulted in the Metric House Shells policy. Singularly unpopular, this attempted to standardise external wall dimensions in all local authority housing to enable the introduction of standard walling components on a national scale, as had been attempted with the IBIS partition in schools.

Early in 1969 Patricia Tindale, Principal Architect to the Ministry of Housing and Local Government since Cleeve Barr's departure to head the National Building Agency, announced the abandonment of 5M and, in line with government policy, the concentration of research and development on dimensional co-ordination.[74] To promote this, a working party of local authority architects started to prepare performance requirements for standard housing components. So far as practical building experiments were concerned, the initiative was taken by the National Building Agency which, under the Labour Administration, had been brought into the Ministry of Housing and Local Government in 1966.

In 1966 the National Building Agency carried out an experiment for the North-Eastern Major Authorities housing consortium. As it made clear, the Agency had "not produced yet another 'system'" but a "rational approach to repetitive building".[75] Essentially, the Agency developed a number of designs based on a 15ft structural span, dubbed the H1 house range. The object of the "basic shell approach", as it was called, was to allow the use of a standard wall component which could be constructed in a variety of techniques by different manufacturers. Initially the Agency designed a pilot scheme of seven houses at Sunderland and in 1968, 202 H1 house types were under construction in No-Fines for Newcastle and 273 in timber frame for Gateshead. This was truly a significant project as the Agency had established a series of dimensionally related house designs for which two commercial sponsors had adapted their systems. Although not given anything like the coverage by the architectural press of the technically conspicious 5M and 12M systems, this outwardly modest project was the biggest step towards modular co-ordination so far.

The next project undertaken by the state was to apply these principles on a national scale. In April 1968 the

National Building Agency published *Metric House Shell*, in which it proposed that the design of all housing should be standardised to a range of modular external wall dimensions.[76] As the journal *IBSAC* pointed out, this "would provide the greatest single impetus to date for developing industrialised building methods".[77] In the next year the adoption of Shell plans, in association with the metrication of housing dimensions, became official ministerial policy. Circular 69/69 pointed out to local authorities that:

> During the next three years local authorities will be changing the design of their dwellings to metric dimensions. . . . This provides an opportunity which may never recur for bringing about a significant reduction in the great variety of two storey house plans used by local authorities.[78]

Through Metric House Shells the Ministry intended to reduce dimensional variety and faciliate the greater use of standard components in housing. Furthermore, as well as encouraging modular co-ordination itself, it was hoped that the new policy would increase the ease with which existing types of system building could be applied to local authority housing generally. To give effect to the policy, from the end of 1969 the use of House Shell dimensions by local authorities was made a condition of loan sanction by the Minister. At a stroke, the government enforced a national system of modular co-ordination for public sector housing. Had it not coincided with the rapidly declining use of system building and the resurgence of traditional construction, the new policy might have made a more significant impact on the technical development of post-war building than any state initiative so far. As it was, the flurry of excitement caused by the introduction of House Shells soon subsided and they became little more than a source of complaint by architects at the increasingly centralised direction of housing design. There is no evidence to suggest that they were taken up on a large scale or that government attempted to enforce the policy outlined in its Circular.

The control of design

As a result of the success of the Consortia Movement and the efforts of government architects to promote modular co-ordination, the control of system building became an issue during the 1960s. While commercial interests had no choice but to concede a large portion of schoolbuilding to local authority consortia, in the event they had little to fear from attempts by Modernist architects to promote more fundamental changes to the building process.

Consortia in dispute

The division of sponsorship between industry and local authority architects, with the latter gaining ground through the Consortia Movement in the mid-1960s, was the cause of dispute over which of the two should control the use of system building and hence the production of a major portion of state building programmes.

The growth of consortia certainly conflicted with the efforts of large building firms, such as Laing, to monopolise local authority building markets by operating high capacity systems. The division between professional and commercial interests was evidenced by the alignment of the building journals: *RIBA Journal* and *Architects' Journal* gave considerable coverage to the growth of consortia while those representing building interests, such as *Interbuild* and the *The Builder*, did their best to ignore such crucial developments in the building world. In 1965 Concrete Ltd., the most successful of the pre-cast concrete sponsors, published *The Function of IB* which, as well as promoting system building generally, argued against the design of systems by client organisations in contrast to the greater efficiency of commercial experise.[79]

In 1963 the White Paper on the proposed National Building Agency described government intentions to assist the growth of consortia, provoking the most notable attack by *The Builder*. The journal, mindful of building industry interests, enlisted the services of a firm of industrial consultants hoping its prejudice against consortia would be born out by expert examination. O.W. Roskill's report, published in 1964, makes interesting reading, for it presents a sustained counter-argument against the many claims made for consortia despite the hail of indignation with which it was greeted by an affronted profession.[80]

Roskill confirmed that building interests had indeed much to fear from consortia which were already beginning to affect the structure and organisation of the industry:

If a significant number of powerful consortia are established, they are likely eventually to have a big impact on the building industry. Large contractors think that consortia may lead to the elimination of medium sized contractors some of whom are already seeking to avoid this fate by having themselves nominated as approved contractors for proprietary systems.[81]

Criticisms made of consortia, and CLASP in particular, included the following:

– low capital costs had been achieved at the expense of high maintenance costs,

– by not including development expenditure in published statistics, local authority architects were concealing the real costs of consortia schools,

– although costs may be lower than the national average, other authorities were building schools for less than CLASP, in traditional construction,

– manufacturers were now able to produce standard products as cheaply as the special items provided in bulk to CLASP,

– the monopolistic position of some of the consortia specialist suppliers, particularly the steel frame manufacturers, was contrary to cost efficiency.

Nonetheless, perhaps the greatest revelation was that there was no systematic statistical basis to support the many claims made by loyal CLASP architects: "in all cases they admitted that no detailed"nvestigation had ever been carried out to prove that their claims for CLASP designs could be firmly established by figures". Essentially, Roskill concluded that a myth had been ĉeated by participating architects which had then been transmitted widely throughout the public architectural profession by overlapping membership and the continuous interchange of staff between local authorities. Furthermore, the report claimed that recent government support for the movement was the result of policies framed by previous consortia architects now in senior ministry positions. The frequent movements of senior staff within the state architectural sector has been noted by other writers as an important factor in the growth of consortia.

Turning to the MHC, the report drew attention to the "impressive" anticipated £35,000 saving through bulk purchase in the 1964/5 programme which it felt

> has clearly been used tactically to reinforce the acceptability of the idea of the consortium with the elected representatives of the member authorities . . . [however] in two of the four cases there has been a change in the specification . . . there is a strong temptation to build up these advantages in the eyes of the elected representatives.

Indeed, an architect formerly employed by the Metropolitan Authorities Consortium for Education was later to maintain that in his experience "all the information is in the hands of the authorities and can be manipulated at will. The whole costing of schools is so fluid and obscure that statistics can be made to prove almost anything".[82]

Roskill's final conclusion was that the case for consortia designed and operated systems had yet to be proved. However, the one respect in which the report did approve of consortia was as a means of combining local authority programmes into larger units to make more effective use of proprietary systems. Indeed, in its eagerness to criticise consortia, the building industry overlooked this potential benefit. Despite the ideological aims of many architects, it was, in fact, the organisation of a market for contractor sponsored systems that lay at the heart of government support. The Ministry of Housing and Local Government were as concerned as the industry itself that numerous systems already in existence should not be added to by the many consortia they were fostering.[83] Indeed, many consortia, such as the London Housing Group which presented the largest of all combined programmes, used proprietary systems in conformity with government policy rather than devise systems of their own.

Commercial imperatives

Consortia were the most successful of architects many attempts to control the development of system building. So far as its larger aim of affecting a national system of interchangeable components, efforts were marked by a degree of idealism and optimism verging on naivete in the face of commercial influences and objectives. Ultimately, the innovatory zeal of government research and development policy was matched only by the completeness of its failure.

While the professional elite within the state architectural service was given the resources to experiment, it was not afforded the power to control the application of new technology by commercial interests. Forcing industry to adopt specific technical innovations had been dismissed by the Cabinet in 1948 as inappropriate to the political climate under which the Welfare State operated.[84] Furthermore, comparatively few resources were allocated to the more far reaching projects on which the experts embarked. For instance, the Interdepartmental Component Co-ordination Group, responsible for co-ordinating building dimensions and performance requirements for the entire public sector, was staffed by only 17[85] and the British Standards Institute, with whom they worked, was a voluntary body quite inadequate to the task.

The ambitions of the state expert required a degree of technological sophistication absent from the post-war building market. Thus, the pressed steel systems of the latter years of the war could not be implemented due to their considerable expense. Where dimensions and performance requirements were agreed during the 1960s, the latter were often set too high for manufacturers to meet within cost limits.[86] As the IBIS project demonstrated, the more sophisticated the product, the longer the lead-in time and the less chance of securing a sufficiently large market to justify production. Expert opinion was too optimistic of industry which could but fail to fulfill its hopes.

As they did not control industry, research and development architects could only initiate development where manufacturers stood to profit. Ultimately, the experts failed because producers had little to gain in the short and medium term from dimensional co-ordination and in the long term, it would seem, much to fear. In 1952 the Ministry of Education pointed out that "An attempt, therefore, to co-ordinate several different elements is liable to involve considerable changes in factory plant",[87] immediately increasing production costs to any producer prepared to act on expert policy and placing it at a disadvantage to less scrupulous competitors. The incentive for manufacturers to change their ways was further reduced when, in times of peak demand, a

market was ensured for all products however dimensionally disparate.

The reluctance of industry to follow the Modern
Movement's lead was evident as early as the Burt and
Standards committees cool reception to prefabrication.
The former was chaired by Sir George Mowlem Burt
(Mowlems) and included John Laing and G.W. Mitchell
(Wimpey). Dominated by building interests such as
these, the committee could hardly be expected to
support philosophies which CISPH thought might en-
danger the financial basis of the property market or
threaten to introduce firms to building such as Briggs
Motor Bodies. While each of these contractors marketed
their own building systems at one time or another, their
designs owed more to the harsh economics of building
than mass production theory, as the next chapter
describes. Furthermore, if, as earlier chapters argue,
large contractors promoted system building to assist them
in the monopolisation of state housing, the interchange
of components could but frustrate this aim. Far from
establishing a common dimensional basis, commercial
firms jealously guarded the technical details of their
systems. With reluctance and in strict confidence they
provided the information required by the National
Building Agency to assess their products on behalf of
local authorities. Indeed, a fear expressed by some
builders in the mid-1960s was that modular co-
ordination allied to the wider growth of consortia, would
provide a basis from which government could nationalise
the building industry.[88] Demands by Rene Short, MP in
1965[89] and the building unions in 1967, that the state
should set up its own component producing factories can
only have fuelled industry's fear. Concern verging on
paranoia was excited among the system building industry,
already renown for secretiveness, by the National
Building Agency's development of H1 housetypes in
1966. This led to the accusation that the Agency was
exploiting technical information provided by commercial
sponsors in the development of its systems.[90] In 1967 the
building industry Federation insisted on a reduction in
the information its system building members were
required to give the Agency.[91]

The experts, promoting science and social purpose,
were out of step with the economic rationale of the
building market they sought to influence but over which
they had little real control. While able to determine

government research policy and promote system building in its broadest sense, they could not direct prefabrication to best realise their aims. As the deputy director of the Building Research Station was forced to admit in 1972, shortly after the final rejection of the IBIS partition, "component building in the sense of catalogues of generally available components which can be readily assembled in a wide variety of ways seems a remote possibility".[92]

Chapter 7
MATERIALS AND TECHNIQUES

Throughout the thirty years of intense state house building, commercial sponsors found a number of alternatives to traditional construction for the family dwelling. Whereas state architects were guided by theoretical concepts, commercial producers were rooted firmly in practicality: the systems they developed responded both to the nuances of social policy and to economic conditions. As a result, for short periods, sponsors produced alternatives to traditional construction comparable in cost. However, it is apparent that the success of new technology relied less on its inherent efficiency than on the conditions created by the Welfare State. In the absence of these conditions, the economics of house construction in Britain has consistently favoured bricks and mortar rather than capital intensive methods of system building.

Pre-cast concrete

Perhaps the best known form of system building was based on the use of pre-cast concrete panels. Undergoing steady development since the early years of the century, pre-cast concrete reached a peak of popularity with the infamous large-panel systems of the early 1960s high-rise building boom.

A new industry

Attempts to use pre-cast concrete components in house construction were made frequently during the first half of this century. Indeed, throughout the inter-war period, a pre-cast concrete industry developed manufacturing a range of building components.

The elimination of costly shuttering and the reduction of site labour by casting concrete floor units off-site, was exploited both before and during the First World War. In the Cheap Cottages Exhibition of 1905, Cubitts demonstrated a polygonal single-storey cottage made up of a small number of reinforced concrete slabs claiming that the method assisted rapid erection.[1] The subsequent development of a pre-casting industry was signified by the formation of the British Cast Concrete Federation in 1928. In addition to the pre-cast housing systems used in the Addison Housing Programme, between the wars attempts were made to pre-cast large walling blocks. According to Marion Bowley, labour savings were insufficient to compete with brick construction and development concentrated on flooring units and non-structural components such as paving slabs and fence posts.[2]

Although little used in Britain after the Addison Programme, pre-cast concrete components were exploited in Frankfurt's municipal housing schemes of the late 1920s and in the French Mopin system used at Quarry Hill, Leeds, in 1938. British indifference to pre-cast concrete was demonstrated in 1937 when the Ministry of Health invited building firms to propose new methods of constructing working-class flats. Of the many techniques submitted, none featured large concrete elements.[3] However, the Second World War gave pre-cast concrete development new impetus in the use of large structural elements for building concrete barges and floating harbours. This experience encouraged industry to consider a scheme for constructing multi-storey buildings with large concrete panels weighing from three to five tons. Conceived by Professor Baker and V.G. Hatherly, the *National Builder* reported in August 1945 that contractors familiar with engineering methods were investigating the scheme.[4]

Bigger panels

The post-war development of pre-cast concrete housing systems was dominated by a single theme, enlarging the unit, and incorporating an increasing number of functions. From small cladding panel or structural component, developed the room-sized unit incorporating structure, cladding and finishes. This became the basic element of large-panel concrete systems which, during the 1960s, showed a clear cost saving over traditional construction for multi-storey housing.

The first post-Second World War use of pre-cast concrete in systems such as Cornish Unit and Airey, consisted of small cladding units supported off an independent structure. The basis of the Airey system had been developed as early as 1925 and like the Cornish Unit, was manufactured by a pre-cast concrete firm rather than a major building contractor, such as those who later exploited large-panel construction. The design of these houses was to some extent governed by the intention that they should be erected by small builders, often in rural areas, without the equipment to handle large structural components.[5]

The use of concrete in small units proved uneconomic.

17 Wates System, (Wates, 1946)
The first British system to use room sized self supporting panels, Wates developed its system from wartime engineering experience

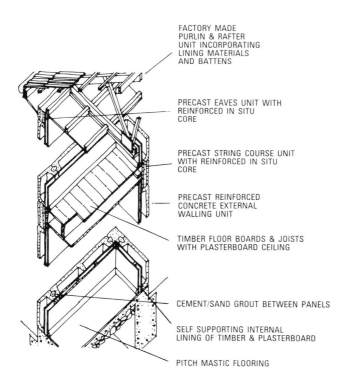

FACTORY MADE PURLIN & RAFTER UNIT INCORPORATING LINING MATERIALS AND BATTENS

PRECAST EAVES UNIT WITH REINFORCED IN SITU CORE

PRECAST STRING COURSE UNIT WITH REINFORCED IN SITU CORE

PRECAST REINFORCED CONCRETE EXTERNAL WALLING UNIT

TIMBER FLOOR BOARDS & JOISTS WITH PLASTERBOARD CEILING

CEMENT/SAND GROUT BETWEEN PANELS

SELF SUPPORTING INTERNAL LINING OF TIMBER & PLASTERBOARD

PITCH MASTIC FLOORING

The Airey house received a capital grant of £175, second only to the Aluminium and BISF houses,[6] and its use declined rapidly after the "emergency" period. In 1948 the Ministry of Works found that, of the non-traditional houses it had tested, the large concrete panel system (most certainly Wates) proved the cheapest.[7] Wates, a large building firm involved in the wartime Mulberry pre-cast concrete harbour project, was the first British building firm to use room-size external wall panels which combined both structural and cladding functions. Wates continued to produce their house in large numbers after the withdrawal of government subsidies to non-traditional houses. The next step in the British development of pre-cast concrete was made in 1948 when Reed and Mallick built their first house. Unlike the Wates system, which required a self supporting internal lining, the hollow Reema panel was cast with an inner surface ready for plastering. A further element of wall construction, the internal lining, had been incorporated into an increasingly complex panel. Whereas the Wates house required 1,500 labour hours, Reema required only 1,280.[8] By 1962, as well as over 300 village halls, Reema had constructed 20,000 houses using its hollow panels.[9]

Higher flats

By the mid-1950s a tradition of using large pre-cast concrete panels for housing had developed. However, the wider exploitation and further development of this method was stimulated by three factors; a change of government policy in favour of high-rise building, the introduction of the towercrane, and improved jointing systems.

In November 1955, the government changed the subsidy system to increase the output of multi-storey flats with the aim of achieving higher densities in redevelopment projects.[10] The "progressive storey height subsidy", as it was known, positively favoured high-rise construction: tender approvals for dwellings over five floors rose from 8,044 in 1955 to a peak of over 44,000 in 1966.[11] The Exchequer paid dearly for the desire to build high: in 1964 P.A. Stone calculated the construction cost of a small dwelling in London to be £2,737 for two storeys and £3,936 for fifteen.[12] Much of this additional cost was the requirement for a steel or concrete structural frame in buildings over five stories. This expensive feature of high-rise was eliminated in pre-cast concrete construction which combined structural and cladding functions in the same panel. For high-rise housing, it soon became apparent that large-panel system building was cheaper than traditional construction.

The lifting device essential to the newly created high-rise market was the rail mounted tower crane. Developed in Europe between the wars, the first models were introduced to Britain in 1951 and vigorously promoted by the Ministry of Works. Although no more than a means of lifting heavy components to great heights, the tower crane exercised a powerful influence on building operations. Calling for detailed preplanning and the systematisation of erection processes, the widespread use of the tower crane played its part in improving the organisation of building operations.[13] In developing the expertise to use tower cranes, building firms encompassed many of the skills needed to operate system building. By 1952, several continental makes were available in England and home produced models were being rapidly developed.[14]

As well as the lifting method, the rapid assembly of high-rise flats from concrete panels relied on a complex joint first developed by continental engineers. Where

18 Reema House (Reed & Mallick, 1953)
Reema developed the first concrete panels to combine internal and external wall surfaces. Introduced in 1948, it began a tradition of large panel construction which endured for twenty years in Britain

19 Bison Wallframe components (Concrete Ltd, 1962)
Reducing the local authority dwelling to an assemblage of standard sized pre-cast concrete floor and wall panels, with a standard bathroom/kitchen unit, Concrete Ltd built more multi-storey flats than any competitor

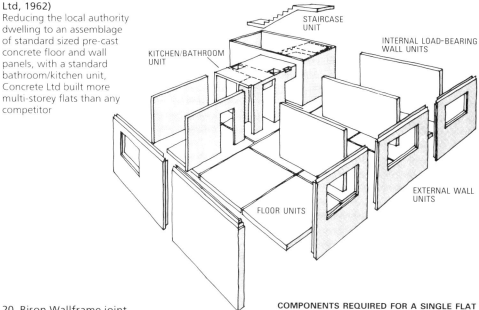

STAIRCASE UNIT

KITCHEN/BATHROOM UNIT

INTERNAL LOAD-BEARING WALL UNITS

EXTERNAL WALL UNITS

FLOOR UNITS

COMPONENTS REQUIRED FOR A SINGLE FLAT

20 Bison Wallframe joint
The dry joint, which connected up to eight panels with the minimum of site work, was essential to the economic use of pre-cast concrete

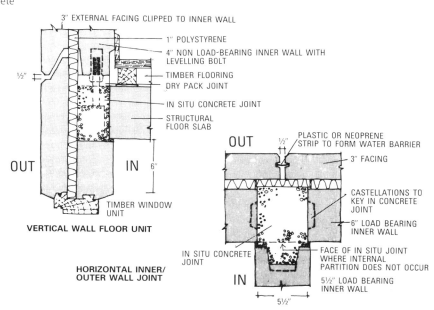

3″ EXTERNAL FACING CLIPPED TO INNER WALL

1″ POLYSTYRENE

4″ NON LOAD-BEARING INNER WALL WITH LEVELLING BOLT

TIMBER FLOORING
DRY PACK JOINT

IN SITU CONCRETE JOINT

STRUCTURAL FLOOR SLAB

½″

OUT   IN   6″

TIMBER WINDOW UNIT

VERTICAL WALL FLOOR UNIT

HORIZONTAL INNER/ OUTER WALL JOINT

OUT   ½″   PLASTIC OR NEOPRENE STRIP TO FORM WATER BARRIER

3″ FACING

CASTELLATIONS TO KEY IN CONCRETE JOINT

6″ LOAD BEARING INNER WALL

IN SITU CONCRETE JOINT

FACE OF IN SITU JOINT WHERE INTERNAL PARTITION DOES NOT OCCUR

5½″ LOAD BEARING INNER WALL

IN

5½″

internal and external walls met, eight panels abutted and the junction had both to transmit loads from one panel to another and be weatherproof. In large-panel construction it was crucial that structural components could be rapidly stacked, one above the other, the connections being made with a minimum amount of site work. Accurate casting of the panels in steel or timber moulds obviated the need for laborious setting out on site and minor adjustments to the alignment of the units were made with bolts cast into the top of the panel below. The Larsen Nielsen joint, upon which many others were based, reduced *in situ* work to join the wall and floor elements to a minimum. The panels abutted each other directly and the residual voids were either dry packed or filled with grout. Weather-proofing was achieved by a grooved channel holding a flexible tongue in the vertical plane and, in the horizontal plane, by a down-stand lip in the face of the outer leaf of the panel. The dry joint was crucial to the production of large-panel systems whose profitability required minimal site work: their hallmark is the bold orthogonal grid imposed on every visible face.

In 1962 the Building Research Station published a theoretical study comparing the costs of conventional construction and large-panel techniques. The study was of necessity hypothetical for at this time fully pre-cast large-panel systems had yet to be used on a significant scale in Britain. The panel system showed a 3.5 per cent saving over conventional construction, representing "a gross return of about 30 per cent per annum on the additional capital investment of £100,000"[15] for the purchase of the factory plant and a transport fleet. Apart from the elimination of the frame, a major factor in this saving was the reduction of plasterers' work due to the smooth internal surface provided by the pre-cast concrete panel. Should plastering be dispensed with altogether, as was common on the Continent, further savings could be expected. Provided the investor was assured of a production run of 800 dwellings, the Building Research Station speculated that "At present it appears that large-panel construction can be undertaken with prospects of saving in cost representing an acceptable return on investment and with little danger of appreciable loss." By 1964, according to government statistics, system built flats above four floors, in which large-panel construction dominated, were over two per cent cheaper than conventional construction. Indeed, in two consecutive

years, 1967 and 1968, tenders for high-rise system
building actually fell.

Bison and Camus

One of the first British large-panel systems was Bison,
manufactured by the biggest of the pre-casting specialists,
Concrete Ltd. Although the systems it manufactured
were erected by subcontracted building firms, Concrete
Ltd may be considered one of the most successful non-
building industry sponsors.

The firm was founded in 1919 and began by manufacturing pre-cast floor beams. Rather than producing
housing immediately after the Second World War
Concrete Ltd. concentrated on developing pre-stressed
floor panels. The innovatory flair and image consciousness
of the firm was evidenced in 1949 when it adopted two
bison at London Zoo, promoting the animal as a
trademark. With the introduction of tower cranes, in
1952 the company designed the Bison Wide Slab, a large
pre-stressed flooring unit up to 7ft. 6ins. wide. This was
incorporated into a complete system of construction with
the introduction of pre-cast concrete beams and columns
and used for a nine-storey block of flats for Barking
Council in 1957. In 1961, in a further development for
Barking, the frame was replaced by load-bearing wall
panels and the following year saw the introduction of the
Bison Wall Frame system with Birmingham Corporation
as the first takers. In essence the system was a collection
of pre-cast concrete panels which integrated internal and
external finishes, wiring and plumbing to form the entire
fabric of the dwelling. Stairs and bathrooms were also
cast as complete units. When it launched Wall Frame,
Concrete Ltd. had a total output of five million and had
established five casting factories throughout the country.[16]
Therefore, the first British large-panel system was
introduced by a major firm with a regional system of
manufacturing plants. Between 1964 and 1979 Concrete
Ltd. erected 31,668 dwellings in Wall Frame and within
three years of being introduced had captured 20 per cent
of the high-rise market (see Appendix 5).[17]

British manufacturers borrowed much, both directly
and indirectly, from continental practice which had
advanced further by the early 1960s. France, Scandinavia
and the Low Countries had been applying pre-cast

concrete to flat construction continuously since the Second World War. In 1949 the French engineer, R. "Camus, patented his system and by 1962 had completed 40,000 flats with factories in France, Russia, Algeria, Germany, South America and Italy. Typically, Camus jointly owned factories with indigenous contractors and industrialists.[18] Rather than develop their own systems, three British firms, Unit Construction, Mitchell and Fram Higgs & Hill all became joint owners of British factories producing panels under the Camus patent. Four other firms also licensed continental panel systems for production in Britain. Furthermore, those systems that were developed in Britain owed much to foreign experience. Indeed, in the crucial years in which Concrete Ltd. converted its frame system to loadbearing wall panels they seconded a senior engineer to the Danish offices of P.E. Malstrom, consulting engineers to Jespersen and Larsen Nielsen. Rather than pay royalties on a patented design, Concrete Ltd. studied continental practice at first hand and applied it to their own system in return for a consultancy fee.[19]

The economics of large-panel investment

Investment in large-panel production was considerable and generally greater than any other form of system building. However, sponsors adopted a range of techniques for producing large-panel systems according to their willingness or ability to invest large sums of money. Techniques ranged from modest site-based systems to sophisticated hydraulic panel-pressing machines with hitherto unheard of capacities.

The most expensive element in the production process was the concrete casting plant. The factory built by Taylor Woodrow Anglian at Lenwade in 1963 to produce components under the Larsen Nielsen patent was estimated to have cost £250,000. The factory consisted of four 330 ft. long casting shops, each making different types of component transported about the works by two overhead cranes. The stockyards included custom-built racks for the storage of panels and new sidings connecting the works to the rail network (eventually the firm purchased a road transport fleet to avoid the vicissitudes of rail travel). Concrete was mixed and conveyed from a central batching plant by a system of conveyors. Ninety five-ton steel casting moulds were imported from Germany and Denmark at a cost of between £1,000 and £1,700 each. Capital costs also included training the 120-strong workforce in pre-casting techniques.[20] Larsen Nielsen represented a standard for pre-cast panel investment. The four rather more sophisticated plants built by Laing for the production of Jespersen components were estimated to have cost between £600,000 and £750,000 each. As well as a steam curing shed, Laing's plants featured a conveyor belt system to transport the units and a travelling hopper and vibrating machine. Only fourteen workers were required to operate the highly mechanised wall and floor casting shops.[21]

Not all firms invested in this level of technology. The cost of a "crude but effective" Reema plant with an output of 500 dwellings per annum was less than £150,000.[22] By using a greater amount of labour in the production and erection process, investment costs could be substantially reduced. The setting up of temporary casting works on site further reduced investment. Although Wates had considerable experience in pre-casting by the early 1960s and studied foreign factory produced systems, it dissented from the fashion for centralised factories and developed a "mobile manufacturing unit" resident on-site for the duration of the contract. This decision was explained by Wate's Managing Director:

> a central factory will cost between half a million and three quarters of a million pounds: it will produce 2,000 dwellings per year. . . . A mobile factory costing £125,000 will produce 750 dwellings per year. The first must be amortised over at least ten years. . . . The mobile factory can be amortized over three.[23]

Furthermore, while central factories built up considerable overheads which could be justified when operating at full capacity, they were an expensive liability when production was slack. Site factories avoided much of this expense and could cope more easily with the climate of uncertain demand which eventually characterised system building. Between 1964 and 1979, Wates built 17,782 dwellings in their pre-cast concrete system and their success was second only to Concrete Ltd. (*see* Appendix 5).

The enthusiasm of British building firms for importing expensive foreign systems was not shared by the Building

Research Station which took an early and active part in panel production technology. In 1963 the Station developed the battery casting technique for use by smaller building firms and direct works departments.[24] This ingenious and cheap technique of site casting large numbers of panels vertically using the previous batch as moulds for the next, was intended for projects as low as 100-200 dwellings. Contrary to the Station's expectations the system was little used by direct works departments and a Midland Housing Consortium scheme to develop a battery casting system foundered in 1968.[25] Nevertheless the technique was willingly taken up by a number of contractors such as Wates, the Fram Group and Gleeson Industrialised Building. A later invention of the Building Research Station was a concrete panel pressing machine which expanded the technology of hydraulically pressing curb stones to large-panel proportions. Launched 1969, the 1,000 ton press, costing £250,000 alone, could produce panels for 4,500 flats per year and could be packed into twelve 13 ton sections. Impressive though this was, there were few commercial producers able to utilise this order of output.[26]

The economics of large-panel design

Large-panel concrete systems can be identified by their principle feature, the room-size units from which they were assembled. From this basic principle flowed a host of design constraints: more than any other system, the rationalisation of construction to the assembly of large concrete panels exerted an influence on design. Any departure by architects from a very specific discipline caused economic penalties to be born either by producers or clients.

The economics of large-panel design were described in 1967 by the National Building Agency.[27] Using figures obtained from a Jespersen plant, the ideal panel was room-sized and square with the minimum of projections and indentations. If, for instance, the panel were halved in width, despite the reduced size, little cost was saved. Standard variants (panels which although not standard were more common than one-offs) added between 75–85 per cent to the cost, while one-off specials might cost up to two and a half times more than standard panels. Simply moving a power point from its standard location

178

dictated the manufacture of a special panel, involving extra work in redesigning and adjusting the moulds. The more mechanised the system, the greater the cost of departure.

The implications of using economic panel sizes and shapes were numerous. In order to use the standard panel at its most efficient span, both wide and narrow frontage dwellings were prohibited. Whereas placing flats back-to-back had little effect, handing the plan simply doubled the number of component types. A standard architectural device for articulating housing layouts was thereby inconsistent with the exigencies of large-panel production. Balconies fixed to the face of external walls were preferred to those which were recessed and the staggered section or plan introduced a range of additional jointing problems. While internal layouts needed to be faithfully repeated on each floor, so that panels could be simply supported one above each other, the superimposition of two panels with large door openings required the insertion of extra reinforcement. One dwelling type popular during the 1950s, but particularly unsuited to large-panel construction, was the maisonette which placed bedrooms over living floors and thus prevented the repetition of identical layouts. Furthermore, internal stairs required floor panels with large openings concentrating stresses to an unwelcome degree. The imperatives of pre-casting concrete panels favoured cellular buildings, regular in outline and identical on each floor with modestly sized openings in compartment walls.

Typical of the large-panel dwelling was Bison's Wallframe. The core of the system was a standard kitchen/bathroom unit, emerging in one piece from the factory embodying all piped services. The basic flat had two bedrooms with the kitchen/bathroom unit against the party wall. Structural crosswalls, which could be centred at 6 inch increments between 9ft. and 16ft., divided bedrooms and living rooms. The standard practice was to join two flats back-to-back to form a wing: two wings would then be connected by lift and stairs. While adjoining flats had to be identical, the plan of each wing could be varied within the formulae. The layout could be further elaborated by separating wings with additional flats placed back-to-back. By varying the arrangement of wings about the lift and stair core, a limited set of plan shapes could be derived, the most distinctive of which was a staggered block.[28]

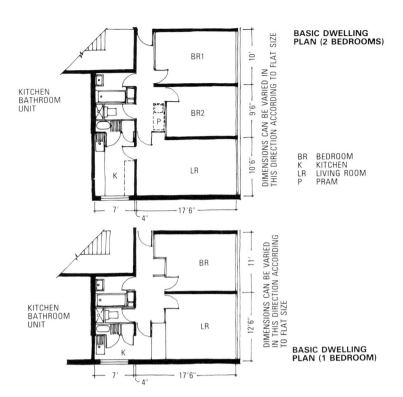

BASIC DWELLING
PLAN (2 BEDROOMS)

KITCHEN
BATHROOM
UNIT

BR1

BR2

P

LR

K

DIMENSIONS CAN BE VARIED IN
THIS DIRECTION ACCORDING TO FLAT SIZE

10'

9'6"

10'6"

BR   BEDROOM
K   KITCHEN
LR   LIVING ROOM
P   PRAM

7'   17'6"
   4"

KITCHEN
BATHROOM
UNIT

BR

LR

K

DIMENSIONS CAN BE VARIED
IN THIS DIRECTION ACCORDING
TO FLAT SIZE

11'

12'6"

BASIC DWELLING
PLAN (1 BEDROOM)

7'   17'6"
   4"

TYPICAL BLOCK
PLAN

BR   LR

LR   BR2   BR1

BR1   BR2   LR

STAGGERED BLOCK
PLAN

21 Bison Wallframe type plans
Bison Wallframe was based
on a standard layout and
produced different sized
flats using the same
components. A limited
range of block types could
be produced by different
arrangements of standard
flats around lift and stair
cores

180

The demise of high-rise

Despite the attention it has attracted, high-rise was a short-lived and comparatively limited phenomenon. Changes in government policy away from multi-storey housing in the mid-1960s caused a rapid decline in the use of pre-cast concrete systems since they were almost exclusively concentrated in this sector.

In 1966, at the peak of multi-storey construction, 75 per cent of local authority housing tenders were for less than four storeys, and thus the potential market for pre-cast concrete systems was, for this reason alone, limited.[29] Changing design policy was crucial to large-panel sponsors. Loadbearing concrete panels showed a saving over frame and cladding construction for multi-storey building, but as a simple walling technique they could not compete with brickwork. In December 1965 the government withdrew the progressive storey height subsidy over six floors to limit the construction of high flats and promote mixed development, medium-rise layouts.[30] It is important to note that this measure predated the infamous partial collapse of Ronan Point which is often cited as the factor crucial to the decline of

22 Ryde Vale, London (Bison Wallframe/LCC, 1965)
A typical Bison development consisting of two and one bedroom flats either side of the service core

multi-storey system built housing. The real significance of Ronan Point was that it focussed public attention on events whose course had already been determined.

The new policy produced a rash of six storey housing of the "deck-access" type. At these heights it was generally considered that pre-cast concrete still maintained a positive cost advantage over traditional construction. In April 1967 a yardstick system prescribed limits for local authority housing costs and re-arranged subsidies to favour low-rise high density development.[31] The effect of new policies was dramatic: between 1966 and 1974 tender approvals for housing over four storeys fell from 44,306 to 2,390.[32] Between 1970 and 1976 pre-cast concrete systems fell from 45 per cent of system built housing to 7 per cent.

Several attempts were made to use pre-cast concrete systems for two-storey housing, although this was often done to supplement the construction of high blocks in large system built mixed development schemes. The general trend reduced the amount of pre-cast concrete (often only to structural crosswalls) as a system took on lower building heights. In 1966 Concrete Ltd. modified Wallframe to accommodate the six-storey heights favoured by the 1965 subsidies. The new system featured a prestressed floor slab spanning between pre-cast party walls and a single leaf non-structural concrete spandrel panel for the front and rear cladding.[33] C.Bryant produced a low-rise pre-cast concrete crosswall system using a substantial amount of timber frame components and completed over 12,674 dwellings. However, the success of this firm must be considered in light of the corrupt relationship it entered into with its major client, Birmingham Corporation.[34] The tendency to use the more flexible systems such as Jespersen and Yorkshire Development Group for medium rise developments also slowed the decline of pre-cast concrete.

Associated as it was with a particularly conspicuous aspect of state policy – the high-rise boom – the rise and fall of pre-cast concrete constituted one of the most dramatic aspects of system building. The acute concentration on high-rise in the early 1960s undoubtedly brought about the need to hastily import systems developed elsewhere. Nevertheless, this should not obscure the fact that a tradition of pre-casting concrete panels for use in social housing had developed continuously in Britain since the war. Had continental systems not existed. British firms would have been forced to rely on their own inventive resources or the developments of the Building Research Station. This might have slowed the growth of pre-cast concrete in high-rise construction but would not have affected the outcome, which was the result of the interaction of social policy and building economics. The inability of firms to reapply pre-cast concrete to low-rise housing during the 1960s was for a number of reasons: not only had design trends changed to favour greater variety in layouts and house forms, but also traditional building had itself become more efficient than in the years of dislocation, materials and labour shortages that typified both the early post-war years and the heights of the 1960s building boom. Furthermore, a new type of system had entered the market: timber frame.

Timber frame

Despite the fact that timber is well suited to prefabrication, its use reached a peak only after the heyday of system building. The development and widespread use of timber frame established itself slowly in Britain, nevertheless, by 1976 it accounted for more than half of total system building production. Furthermore, it was the only method to be used by speculative housing developers.

Disruptions and restrictions

Timber, though suitable for prefabrication was an imported material. As a result, in early post-war years its use in building was severely limited by world trade disruptions and government attempts to control balance of payments deficits.

Timber in house construction has a long history in Britain, and was used particularly for temporary and emergency accommodation during the two world wars.[35] The introduction of plywood in the 1930s, gave considerable impetus to the use of timber in prefabricated construction. Industrially manufactured, light and strong, plywood eventually became the basis of timber frame techniques. When stiffened with softwood battens, plywood forms rigid, easily handled units of considerable strength which can be made up in modestly equipped workshops. Between 1941 and 1944 Uni-Seco Structures built five million square feet of accommodation in their plywood and timber system for government hutted programmes with thirty factories supplying timber components to 200 contractors.[36] The firm eventually constructed 29,000 bungalows under the Temporary Housing Programme in a timber and asbestos system.

The subsequent development of timber in construction was delayed at the end of the Second World War by government policy. Not only had the conflict disrupted world timber supplies but until 1953 the state drastically reduced imports through a licensing system in an attempt to improve the balance of payments. Whereas pre-war consumption of timber was 2.5 standards/dwelling, the allowance in 1947 was 1.6.[37] Although the government imported 2,444 Swedish timber houses to boost output in the emergency period, timber was severely limited in non-traditional construction. In 1945 the Burt Committee rejected British Power Boat's design for a prefabricated house which required large amounts of timber, despite the fact that it was otherwise an economic method of construction and saved skilled building labour.[38] In common with other timber prefabricators such as Riley Newsum, Uni-Seco turned to overseas markets for which timber was made available by a government eager to increase exports. The systems which this firm marketed in Britain – for schools, hospital buildings and offices – featured a gradual reduction in timber content throughout the late 1940s.[39] Government policy was undoubtedly successful for, whereas before the war Britain's consumption of timber was the highest per capita of any predominantly importing country, by 1953, with the exception of Ireland and Hungary, it had become the lowest. Rationing was reinforced by the sheer expense of post-war timber: since 1945 it had risen in price by 378 per cent compared with the average index of building material inflation of 216 per cent.[40]

Following decontrol in 1953, the Ministry of Housing and Local Government, in conjunction with Canterbury Council, carried out an experiment on the increased use of timber construction. In a development of twenty four maisonettes, loadbearing brickwork was limited to structural crosswalls with prefabricated timber frame cladding panels and plasterboard on timber-stud internal partitions. This experiment in partial prefabrication was reckoned to have saved £142 per dwelling compared with all brick construction.[41] In 1957, Unity, a firm which had previously sponsored a composite concrete and steel frame system, began marketing a two-storey house of brick cross-walls, prefabricated non-structural timber wall panels and prefabricated roof trusses.[42] Thereafter, this method of construction, referred to as "rationalised traditional" or "crosswall", became a popular form of construction both in system and traditional building.

As well as encouraging the use of prefabricated timber techniques generally, increased housing programmes of the early 1960s saw the introduction of timber frame construction. Important in the wider use of these techniques was the replacement of local building bye-laws with National Building Regulations in 1964. Although waivers could be obtained in "specific cases", the model bye-laws had effectively prohibited the use of timber for external cladding and party-wall construction. New regulations designed to encourage new techniques allowed external timber claddings and a fireproof timber party-wall was developed by the Ministry of Housing and Local Government in the 5M housing system.[43]

The platform frame

"Platform frame" dominated timber technology enabling the mechanised assembly of timber components into structural wall panels. This technique was taken up eagerly by sponsors as it required little in the way of investment compared with concrete and steel.

Originally developed in America and Canada after the war, platform frame was a considerable departure from the traditional timber house, eliminating most of its skilled labour content. Rather than using a skeletal frame constructed *in situ*, prefabricated wall panels were brought to site and, in conjunction with floor and roof units, rapidly nailed together to form a rigid box-like, weather-tight structure. Like steel frames this allowed the simultaneous working of subsequent finishing trades throughout the house. Wall panels were made up in workshops using large table jigs on which the timber studs, ply sheathing, windows and door frames, vapour barriers and insulation were assembled by unskilled labour.[44] Platform frames replaced traditional jointing techniques, such as halving, morticing and hand nailing with the universally applied buttjoint. Machine cut lengths were butted against each other in the jig and fixed with plate connectors driven home by hydraulic presses reducing drastically the amount of craftwork. The savings gained through this technique cannot be calculated precisely as reliable data on the cost of specific types of system building is not available. In 1965 the Timber Research and Development Association claimed that when used efficiently timber frame required one third to a half the labour required in traditional housing and was capable of a cost saving of 5–10 per cent.[45] Official statistics on tender costs for low-rise system built and traditional housing also suggest that timber frame was competitive with other systems and traditional construction. In 1969, by which time timber frame was a popular method for two-storey housing, system building tenders started cheapening in relation to traditional construction. During the mid-1970s, when timber frame predominated, government statistics indicate that low-rise system building tenders were less than traditional construction suggesting a possible cost advantage.

Modest investments

The eventual predominance of timber frame in system building technology was a result of its competitiveness. However, two other factors were important: that it could be made indistinguishable from traditional construction and its very modest requirement for capital investment.

While some specialists, such as Vic Hallam, both manufactured and supplied the components for large housing contracts, other sponsors restricted their involvement to distribution. The most successful timber system, Frameform, was organised on the latter lines and marketed by James Riley & Partners. If a client selected Frameform, its layout would be sent to James Riley and modified in conformity to the system's requirement. The components were then manufactured by sub-contracted woodworking firms, using standard equipment, to James Riley's specifications. A licensed building firm, whose supervisory staff were quickly trained to use the system, would erect the components which could be handled without special lifting gear. In this manner, contracts as small as two houses were feasible. Through its network of subcontractors, James Riley reckoned itself capable of supplying up to 15,000 houses each year (although successful the firm never attained this figure) without having to invest in any production plant. Capital sufficient to provide the accommodation and staff necessary to adapt local authority designs, co-ordinate suppliers and contractors was all that was needed. Furthermore, capacity could be rapidly expanded or contracted to suit the market. Compared with other forms of system building this level of investment, and hence the financial risk, was modest and within the reach of many more firms.

Tradition and timber frame

If the production characteristics of timber frame were attractive to sponsors, its design flexibility was equally attractive to clients and architects. Furthermore, that it

23 Timber frame under construction (Quickbuild Homes Ltd, 1964)
True to its name, the Quickbuild system rapidly came together on site. Lightweight panels made in modestly equipped workshops could be lifted into place without heavy craneage

was indistinguishable from traditional construction enabled its adoption by speculative developers.

Frameform's planning grid was a sixteen inch external module (coinciding with the intervals of wall studs) and a four inch internal module. However, as the manufacturer was at pains to point out, for a modest cost even these could be ignored.[46] This relative freedom in planning was accompanied by a wide choice of external finishings which included a single leaf of brickwork, render, tile hanging, asbestos cement sheets, concrete facing slabs and timber boarding. Confident of their ability to emulate traditional designs, James Riley ran a competition in which participants attempted to identify their system from photographs of traditional-looking houses. Organised at the 1968 Housing and Town Planning Exhibition, successful competitors stood to win £100.[47]

The fact that timber frame could be made indistinguishable from and competitive in price with traditional construction most certainly enabled its application to the private market. Furthermore, the minimal investment required enabled small-and medium-sized developers to incorporate it into their speculative operations. In the late 1960s Wates were using timber frame wall panels, concealed beneath a veneer of brickwork, for speculative housing.[48] The adoption of timber frame by large housing developers was rapid. A. Cullen estimates that, whereas during the 1960s and 1970s no more than 1.5 per cent of private housing was built in timber frame, by

24 Demonstration houses at Hammersmith (Frameform, James Riley & Partners, 1967) Clad in brickwork and softwood boarding, timber frame looked perfectly at home on the suburban housing estate

1979 it had reached 15 per cent with many developers making a complete switch in their techniques.[49] Unlike other methods of system building which modified the architectural character of housing, timber frame appeared an almost perfect substitute for loadbearing masonry construction.

The use of timber frame by speculative developers raises questions on the relationship between advances in traditional construction and "system building". Used by private housing developers, timber frame is best understood as limited investment in traditional methods of production. Significant in speculative development is the fact that producer and client are one, encouraging investment in methods of production. Furthermore, as Chapter Two shows, there was a close relationship between speculative development and system building sponsorship: the former often became the most successful exponents of the latter. Nevertheless, in noting this exception to the rule (that system building was only used on a significant scale in state housing), it is important to note that timber frame required minimal capital investment and produced traditional looking houses. Indeed, the form in which timber frame appears in private housing, was little more than the construction of an inner wall leaf in pre-manufactured timber panels, rather than block or brick. Were it not for the historical legacy of "system building" in social housing, a phenomenon which involved more than just the technical aspects of building, the term "system" might never have been applied to what was otherwise a comparatively modest development in housebuilding methods.

Wimpey No-Fines

Previous sections have described types of building system sponsored by various firms, this section will look at a system which was sponsored, on a large scale, by one firm only. There were many systems which used concrete poured into reusable shutters but none which proved as popular as George Wimpey's No-Fines. By June 1968 Wimpey were able to claim that three quarters of a million people were living in No-Fines houses they had built.[50]

Like most post-war systems, the basic principle of No-Fines had been in use on a small scale for many years. However, in the post-Second World War years of skilled labour shortages and sustained public housing programmes, No-Fines's virtual elimination of skilled labour and high potential production made it a remarkably successful form of building. It would appear, however, that other than to Geo. Wimpey, this potential went unnoticed in the early years during which sponsors chose to develop systems for the social housing programmes that lay ahead.

No-Fines was first developed in The Netherlands which, like Britain, was affected by shortages in skilled building labour and traditional materials immediately following the First World War. The system was imported to Britain in the early 1920s and used by a number of firms including Laing.[51] In contrast to its later success, only small numbers of No-Fines houses were built between the wars due, according to the Ministry of Health, to a shortage of the plasterers needed to complete the roughly cast walls.[52] By the end of the Second World War, both Wimpey and Holland Hannen and Cubitt had built prototypes in No-Fines,[53] but of the two, only the former pursued the system further and by 1951 the firm had reached an annual production of 10,000 houses.

No-Fines was based on a concrete mix which omitted sand (hence "no-fines") poured into reusable shutters to form external and internal walls. According to the Ministry of Housing and Local Government, No-Fines was not a particularly labour saving system, requiring on average 1,700 labour hours per house.[54] However, Bernard Gosschalk points out that the unskilled labour used afforded a considerable cost saving and suited the system to post-war skilled labour shortages.[55] Furthermore, the completion of No-Fines shells at the rate of one a day speeded the remaining building work. The omission of sand, as well as lightening and cheapening the mix, lightened the shuttering which could be manhandled into position without craneage. Shuttering was the main form of investment in the system and its application was not limited by the availability of craneage or proximity to casting plants. The lightweight shuttering and absence of plant made the system highly mobile. The omission of sand also resulted in a cellular composition which provided thermal insulation and prevented the capillary attraction of water through the wall. Due to No-Fine's lack of tensile strength, window openings were limited to modest sizes and evenly distributed throughout the walls – very much in the manner of brickwork. This, together with the rendered external finish, determined the appearance of the finished dwellings which were indistinguishable from rendered brick construction. Floors and roofs were constructed in timber.

Of perhaps most interest to prospective Local Authority purchasers was the system's design flexibility. According to the London County Council, which used No-Fines extensively in the late 1940s and early 1950s, the system was able to replicate a wide range of standard house plans.[56] By 1953, Wimpey were using eleven different house types on the Willenhall estate for Coventry City Council including a special corner unit devised by the City Architect (*see* illustration 3).[57]

High investment and good organisation

Wimpey's remarkable success resulted as much from its financial and organisational resources as it did from the technical merits of No-Fines. Over and above the fact that the system was competitive in price and virtually eliminated skilled labour, having developed expertise in constructing No-Fines, Wimpey possessed the financial resources and organisational muscle to expand production on a national scale to whatever level the social housing market demanded. Newcomers were effectively prohibited: Wimpey could absorb the demand while competitors were still learning how to use the system properly.

Simple in principle, No-Fines was an expensive system to operate. The capital investment required is not known to the author but can be guessed by looking at the similar Easiform system. Like No-Fines, Easiform was a poured concrete system, although it incorporated a cavity and used dense concrete for the inner leaf. This in turn required heavy shutters and, therefore, craneage, making the system more complex to operate and, significantly, putting it at a disadvantage to No-Fines. In 1952 an Easiform kit capable of producing thirty-four houses per annum cost £4,000. Although a single shutter set was a modest investment, large numbers were required to produce substantial quantities of housing. For instance, in 1952 the government estimated the cost of a concrete pre-casting factory with a capacity of 1,000 houses per year to be £60,000. According to government figures for Easiform, in order to produce 1,000 poured concrete houses per year, the shutter sets alone cost £116,000.[58]

For successful operation, No-Fines required organisational expertise. In 1948 the Ministry of Works noted a considerable discrepancy between the two firms who used No-Fines in their measured experiment of that year (by this time the Unit Construction Co. was also using the system in small numbers):

> Because the "no-fines" concrete houses on a particular site proved outstanding, one might be tempted to say that "no-fines" concrete construction was in itself superior to traditional construction. . . . [However] the methods and organisation used by a different firm to build "no-fines" houses on another site produced very poor results.[59]

Wimpey had both the expertise to build No-Fines efficiently and the financial resources to expand production. A director of the firm pointed out that, as the use of the system increased, so did Wimpey's selling and contracting organisation:

> a developing network of area and regional organisations made it possible to offer No-Fines to local authorities throughout the United Kingdom. All the advantages of a local contractor with the service facilities of an international organisation are thus available as required by every local authority.[60]

As the case study of Coventry indicated, in the hands of a firm with Wimpey's resources, not least of which was a large permanent workforce, No-Fines was capable of monopolising local authority housing programmes. Once established, the type of relationship which the firm developed with its municipal clients was difficult for a newcomer to dislodge. Furthermore, Wimpey's had no intention of sharing their expertise with other firms. In 1952 the government approached the company suggesting that it should license its system to smaller builders but received a curt response from the Managing Director:

192

"he was quite definite that Wimpeys will not associate with other firms: they could not be prepared to risk their goodwill . . . it has been considered carefully in the past and definitely turned down".[61]

In 1953, with the casting of a dense reinforced concrete frame into the walls, No-Fines was developed for an estate of six-storey flats at Birmingham,[62] and in 1956 a series of eleven-storey point blocks were built for Coventry.[63] While the principle of constructing the external shell remained the same, the 1960s saw the refinement of internal work, with increasing prefabrication of timber roof trusses, timber flooring, internal partition units and service installations. Indeed, the post-war development of No-Fines owed more to progress in timber technology than to any improvement in the basic principles of casting No-Fines walls.

Although outstandingly successful, the peak of No-Fines production was reached in 1967, three years before the overall decline in system building began. Furthermore, as it was essentially a low-rise system, it was less affected than many by the reduction in high-rise flat building. It is evident, therefore, that the use of No-Fines was declining in relation to other forms of construction. With the demise of pre-cast concrete the two main competitors to No-Fines were timber frame, whose post-war development had been delayed but was now catching up, and traditional construction whose productivity had improved considerably by the late 1960s. It is most likely that both these methods had overtaken No-Fines in efficiency and, as they were clad in traditional brickwork, were thought to produce visually more acceptable houses. Remarkable though its success was, No-Fines proved as vulnerable as any other method of construction to the changing economics of post-war building.

Bricks and mortar

System building presented a sustained challenge to the traditionally constructed municipal dwelling but was never able to replace it. Even though the proportion of system built dwellings exceeded 40 per cent in 1970, at all times the bulk of social housing was in fact accounted for by time honoured bricks and mortar. Not only was traditional building thought, for the most part, to enable better designed buildings, but until the late 1960s statistics indicated that it was generally cheaper. Despite the many attempts of the state, the Modern Movement and sponsors, bricks and mortar provided the most efficient homes. Furthermore, traditional construction successfully utilised many of the innovations that were exploited by system building sponsors, becoming increasingly productive and technically advanced throughout the post-war period.

Technical developments in traditional construction

It is impossible to state a precise level of productivity growth in post-war building. However, it is evident to any observation of construction methods that considerable changes took place after the war with the introduction of mechanical plant, prefabrication of standardised components and automation of materials manufacture. Each of these could not but improve building efficiency.

In assessing productivity increases in traditional building, non-technical factors must be considered. The 1948 government Committee of Enquiry Into the Cost of Housebuilding noted the deleterious effect of post-war dislocation on housebuilding efficiency. As these were overcome in succeeding years, traditional building became more productive. However, strains imposed on the building industry in the 1960s once again hampered efficiency. Nevertheless official figures for productivity suggest that traditional building improved steadily from the end of the war onwards.[64] Some sources also suggest a dramatic rise in the 1960s, with the Under Secretary of State for the Environment announcing to Parliament in 1972 that over the past decade output per worker had improved by between four per cent and eight per cent per annum.[65] However, this view was tempered by the National Building Agency in 1976 which asserted that there had been "little improvement" in housebuilding efficiency over the past ten years.[66]

Despite difficulties of measurement, it is apparent that very tangible developments in traditional house construction proceeded along a number of paths. One of these involved the introduction of mechanised plant to site operations. Many basic innovations were made before the Second World War: the portable electric drill, the powered concrete mixer and the tower crane. However, their wider application in building operations was a post-war phenomenon. Between 1948 and 1964 investment in mechanical plant by the building industry grew from £11m. to £50m. annually.[67] Nevertheless, the application of mechanical plant to building is not as easy as in other industries. While ideal for tasks such as earthmoving and heavy materials and components handling, it is less easy to use mechanical plant to construct the fabric of the conventional house. Furthermore, overall efficiency is impaired by the long periods for which plant lies idle awaiting the appropriate stages of the job to be reached.[68]

Of more significance have been advances in materials manufacture benefitting system building and traditional construction alike. The production of many basic materials, such as bricks and concrete, was highly mechanised before the Second World War. Indeed, one inter-war innovation, plasterboard, and its mass production was acknowledged by R.B. White as "perhaps the greatest single contribution to prefabrication of any period".[69] The post-war years also saw the introduction of extensive ranges of industrially produced boards such as chipboard and plywood. The impact of these advances on house building were legion, for nearly half the cost of construction was accounted for by basic materials. Indeed, as Donald Bishop pointed out in 1966, over the past decade the price of building materials had, in real terms, fallen in common with other mass produced commodities: "To this extent – amounting to perhaps 40 per cent of the cost of building – the industry is industrialised already".[70]

Also of significance was the introduction of limited prefabrication. Rather than attempting to prefabricate the entire structure or limit themselves to a predetermined kit of parts, conventional builders inserted factory-made components into a structure built by conventional means. As early as the mid-nineteenth century, Thomas Cubitt was serving building sites with centralised workshops pre-manufacturing and finishing plasterwork, marbles, steel components and joinery.[71] The pre-manufacture of windows, doors and joinery fittings was common practice among interwar speculative housing developers and, indeed, has been noted in previous histories of prefabrication. Led by Crittalls, the interwar period also saw the marketing of standard ranges of windows and doors in both timber and steel. A more recent innovation has been the widespread use of prefabricated roofing trusses during the 1960s. These have since dominated the housing market, both public and private, with the effect that a significant part of house construction – the basic roof structure – is now manufactured under industrially advanced conditions: in 1978 three million trusses were made on 250 machines. Other components such as metal lintels are also manufactured by flowline production.[72]

Management techniques constituted a further area of advance. The state was particularly active in this field. For instance, by 1948, the Ministry of Works and most local authorities were insisting on the use of Time and Progress Schedules by government contractors.[73] In view of the fact that the bulk of building work was carried out at this time directly for the state, this measure brought such procedures to the attention of a large number of firms. Most building firms, both large and medium, improved their management techniques during the post-war period. According to John MacLean & Sons the fear of competition with non-traditional producers was an important incentive towards this.[74] During the 1950s and 1960s Work Study and Network Analysis were imported from America and applied by larger firms to building operations both conventional and industrialised.

Cheap building labour

Advances in traditional building were only one of the difficulties facing investors in capital-intensive, labour-saving techniques. It was noted on a number of occasions during the 1960s that the cheapness of British building labour inhibited attempts to industrialise the housebuilding industry, consistently giving an advantage to traditional construction.

In 1962 Donald Bishop observed the need for building work to become more highly paid in relation to other types of labour for the "potential" economies of system building to be realised.[75] Three years later, in 1965, A. Tozer, managing director of Cubitts Construction Systems Ltd., anticipated that it would still be at least two years before building wage rates rose sufficiently for a real cost advantage in system building.[76] This did not take place and system building operated in a market antipathetic to capital intensive labour saving methods of production. Despite considerable demands on building resources during the mid-1960s, building in Britain continued to stay relatively cheap. Referring, in 1966 to the latest figures produced by the Organisation for European Co-operation and Development the *National Builder* proudly noted that:

> The British building industry had the best record of any in Europe for holding its prices down during the ten years, 1953 to 1963, and that during this period our housebuilding costs rose even less than that of other building works.[77]

Other sources support this boast.[78] The fact that this relative cheapening of housing costs took place before the major industrialised building drives of the mid-1960s suggests that productivity increases in house construction were not necessarily the result of system building as some advocates claimed.

The illusion of system building efficiency

In many cases system building contracts proved cheaper than contracts in traditional construction. This was assumed, by the supporters of radical innovation, to be proof that capital-intensive technology was the most reliable route to improved building efficiency. However, a number of detailed studies of building methods suggested otherwise, proposing that technical innovations had less relevance to efficiency than careful management and economic design. It would also appear that new methods of construction attracted the more efficient contractors who may have been capable of achieving the same results with traditional construction. Therefore, the apparent relative cheapening of system building in later years, according to official statistics, was not evidence of the superiority of system building technology and may well have been an illusion: the same houses might have been cheaper with or without system building.

To use a building system, sponsors had to enhance the organisation of construction operations and enforce a degree of rationality on design. The dependance of system building on good management was noted by the Ministry of Works in its measured experiment of 1948. The Ministry's verdict was that, on average, non-traditional methods of construction had indeed shown significant savings in labour content and that three had shown savings in cost. However, in achieving this, successful sponsors had developed a degree of managerial expertise uncharacteristic of the traditional builder:

> to achieve useful results with new methods of construction it is necessary to have the appropriate organisation for the design of the house, for the production of the components and for erection on site. It is probable that all three functions will need to be very closely integrated if success is to be assured, and that management of the "production engineer" type will yield the best returns.[79]

This aspect of system building was re-emphasised by the Building Research Station during the 1960s. According to Donald Bishop, the benefit of system building was its effect on the design and organisation of the building process rather than the superiority of its purely technical aspects: "the discipline imposed by large panels on the design makes operational control and high productivity more feasible than is the case with conventional construction".[80] Hence, Bishop proposed that the "average" labour productivity of building systems was likely to be higher than the "average" labour productivity of brick construction although the difference between the best exponent of each was not great. In 1968 Bishop suggested that the average labour content of a traditional house might vary from between 2,400 hours "when building is just allowed to happen" to 700 hours in the hands of a specialist. The latter figure competed easily with the best results obtainable in system building. So far as raising the productivity of the industry as a whole, Bishop's analysis suggested that either system building removed the difficulty that the average contractor had in making traditional construction as efficient as it might be or attracted the type of sponsor amenable to improved management techniques.[81]

In 1970 the National Building Agency supported the latter thesis. So far as the Agency was concerned, the technical merits of different types of two-storey house construction were less important to efficiency than the organisational ability of the sponsoring contractor:

> the productivity which is achieved by using industrialised methods is less dependent on the construction techniques adopted than on the management of design

and construction. Industrialised building is operated by contractors who are generally larger and more efficient than the average contractor. The size of industrialised housing projects is also somewhat larger than the national average. In this situation, system builders have achieved markedly faster building times and higher site productivity.[82]

Accordingly, official statistics which suggest significant cost savings through system building for two-storey housing after 1969 may well be describing an altogether different phenomenon: that of bigger, more efficient firms taking on larger contracts. The fact that they used building systems may not be the reason for their lower tender prices – these firms may well have achieved the same efficiency with conventional construction.

The degree to which building could be made more efficient without introducing capital intensive methods but by mimicking the close relationship between design, production and organisation found in system building was demonstrated by the National Building Agency in the late 1970s. The Pitcoudie I development project of 112 houses, completed in 1977, was funded by the Glenrothes Development Corporation with the Agency acting as productivity consultants. The layout, although consciously intended to avoid the extremities of design rationalisation often associated with system building, consisted of straight terraces of simply designed houses in five types varying from one to three stories. Pitcoudie combined the following productivity raising design strategy with the latest limited prefabrication techniques.

– Although the housetypes differed in layout and elevational treatment "they were designed in such a way that, as far as practicable, the same building sequence could be followed in each house" thereby allowing a more regular flow of work from one house to another.

– The building sequence consisted of fewer and larger operations than was normal, reducing the number of return visits by individual trades and reducing their interdependance: the wiring harness was delivered complete and installed in one operation.

– A high degree of standardisation was used in construction details: there was only one bathroom layout.

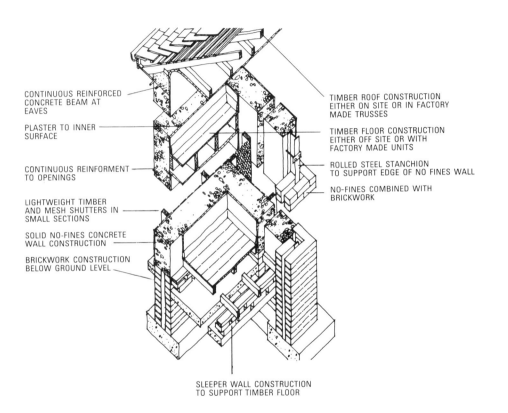

**25 Pitcoudie Phase I
(Glenrothes Development
Corporation, 1980)**
Using a range of labour
saving techniques
developed for traditional
construction, Pitcoudie was
as efficient as the most
effective forms of system
building

CONTINUOUS REINFORCED
CONCRETE BEAM AT
EAVES

PLASTER TO INNER
SURFACE

CONTINUOUS REINFORMENT
TO OPENINGS

LIGHTWEIGHT TIMBER
AND MESH SHUTTERS IN
SMALL SECTIONS

SOLID NO-FINES CONCRETE
WALL CONSTRUCTION

BRICKWORK CONSTRUCTION
BELOW GROUND LEVEL

TIMBER ROOF CONSTRUCTION
EITHER ON SITE OR IN FACTORY
MADE TRUSSES

TIMBER FLOOR CONSTRUCTION
EITHER OFF SITE OR WITH
FACTORY MADE UNITS

ROLLED STEEL STANCHION
TO SUPPORT EDGE OF NO FINES WALL

NO-FINES COMBINED WITH
BRICKWORK

SLEEPER WALL CONSTRUCTION
TO SUPPORT TIMBER FLOOR

200

– Only familiar and readily available materials and components were used reducing the "learning curve" in their installation and application.

– The house plans were dimensionally co-ordinated using only two shell sizes to aid the use of standard components: there was only one size of joist and two roof truss spans.

According to the National Building Agency this scheme was an unqualified success. Whereas between 1974 and 1977 the average labour content of a Scottish dwelling was measured at 1,584 hours for traditional construction and 1,139 for system building, the Pitcoudie I houses measured in the same survey took an average of 1,016 hours. A second phase of 283 houses completed in 1980 achieved comparable productivity using similar techniques.[83] In the light of this experiment it is no surprise that, with the benefit of hindsight, observers questioned the tendency of many sponsors to continue marketing their systems.[84] Once again it had become clearly evident that efficiency was to be sought more through the development of design and management operations in traditional construction than any of the radically new technologies available.

Chapter 8
KEEPING THE ARCHITECT TO REASON

If they were to use it efficiently, or at all, architects had no choice but to observe the limitations system building placed on design. As Clifford Culpin, Consultant Architect to Concrete Ltd, said: "To mess about with a system is as illogical as building with bricks of odd sizes".[1] As well as affecting the design of the basic dwelling unit, system building required repetition: "Investment in the capacity to repeat carries with it an obligation to accept a minimum level of repetition without any change in the design".[2] To resist this imperative, it was thought, was to oppose the very aim of mass production itself.

The ways in which architects responded to the effects of system building on design were various. Expressing Modern Movement values in 1945, Joseph Emberton advocated that the design of prefabricated houses should evolve along the lines of aeroplanes, cars or trains, where "maximum efficiency was expressed in form" so that prefabrication would "produce results equally satisfying besides providing more efficient homes".[3] A very different view was taken by Emberton's contemporary, G.A. Gellicoe, following his visit to America to see new methods at first hand. Gellicoe proposed that architects should resist what he regarded as the dehumanising effect of unbridled mechanisation:

> it is surely the fundamental task of our profession, and of ours alone, to preserve the humanities . . . we must have good design and good planning; but the main thing is the maintenance of human qualities over machine quality.[4]

These statements were those of opposing sides in a debate on the design of welfare building programmes: on the one hand, good design and efficiency were considered synonymous and required the simplification of the dwelling unit and its repetition, on the other hand it was thought that good design involved approaching each building project afresh to find the most appropriate solution to the many demands, whether functional or symbolic. But, both Emberton and Gellicoe would have agreed that it was the architect alone who was responsible for bringing about the successful resolution between architecture and mass production. The conscience of the architectural profession grappled with this more than any other responsibility in post-war years.

Architecture and social housing

The readiness with which most architects accepted the limitations placed on their creativity by system building can only be understood as the result of established attitudes to the design of social housing. Indeed, the disciplines of new technology were entirely consistent with the design orthodoxy already established for social housing by the end of Second World War. Furthermore, Modern Movement design theory, inspired by ideals of mass production, insisted that the source of architectural expression should be the process by which a building was produced. Together these attitudes created a climate in which the effect of system building on design was almost unquestioned for several decades.

The design of early state housing in Britain

A state policy toward design developed with early social housing programmes. This extended beyond standards of accommodation and construction to include a definition of what was "good". The inter-war years saw the establishment of a state design orthodoxy for mass housing which extolled order and simplicity and rejected decoration and formal device.

The topic was discussed in detail by the Tudor Walters Committee in 1917. The Committee was concerned to secure the maximum economy in construction and maintenance consistent with close attention to internal planning and orientation. The ideal cottage was thought to be "simple, straightforward" and rectangular in plan. In considering the monotony that might arise from large areas of similarly designed housing, the Committee suggested that attempts to introduce variety for its own sake "can only result in effects which in their way would be as objectionable as the monotony to which reference has already been made".[5]

A stringent model for social housing was promoted by the Liverpool School and displayed in the 1917 Dormanstown housing scheme by Adshead, Ramsey and Abercrombie. In its design the School expressed a belief that industrial society was characterised by standardisation in its products and uniformity in styles of life. This perceived collectivisation of society dictated a very distinct approach to mass housing design wherein a "standard cottage", using the Dorlonco steel frame, was universally applied without variation in a strikingly simple neo-Georgian style.[6] The success of mass housing design in Adshead's view relied not upon "its peculiarity or idiosyncrasy, nor in a word upon its individuality" but upon excellence of design in the standard dwelling unit.[7] The Ministry of Health itself promoted the neo-Georgian style used at Dormanstown from 1919, partly in an attempt to wean local authorities away from a tendency to use decoration and needless variety in the design of state housing schemes.[8] The wholesale adoption by the London County Council and other urban authorities of the neo-Georgian style for inter-war redevelopment schemes arose from its potency as a suitably austere image for municipal housing. By 1927 the government *Housing Manual on the Design, Construction and Repair of Dwellings* insisted that in good design artistic expression and idiosyncrasy should give way to reason and order:

> irregularity, which is merely want of order, is always a negative and destructive quality. Regular order is a quality within the reach of most; it should only be abandoned by those who have a clear vision of the more subtle and pleasing relationship and order which they are to provide in its place.[9]

The Modern Movement

The relationship between design and construction was a central theme in the theoretical development of the Modern Movement. Industrial models of production replaced formal composition as the accepted tool of architectural expression. As a result, external form was required to do no more than make evident the efficiency of the design: beauty, it was assumed, would automatically result.

Some of the earliest projects of the Modern Movement were in the social housing programmes of the Weimar Republic. These provided the architect with the unique opportunity, described by Walter Curt Behrendt: "Now for the first time, it became his task to develop, in accordance with actual and clearly defined needs, and with all the aid of technical science, a new type of small dwelling".[10] At its extreme, the scientific consideration of mass housing produced the *Zeilenbau* ("strip building method") used in Ernst May's *Westhausen Siedlung* at Frankfurt (1930). The *Zeilenbau* was derived from "constant attempts to lower both the cost of layout and the proportion of land coverage". With the sole aim of efficiency in mind, housing blocks were arranged in parallel rows orientated to obtain the maximum sunlight regardless of surrounding road patterns. The outcome of this approach was the standard dwelling within a standard site plan: its implicit assumption was that the needs of social housing were best met by the scientifically derived, universally applicable method in place of traditional concerns with context and form.

It would, however, be untrue to suggest that Modernism was a style devoid of composition. In 1932, H.R. Hitchcock and Philip Johnson refuted the claims of "functionalists" that their work was without style and identified a language of form which they termed The International Style.[11] Nevertheless, the source of this language, claimed *Neues Bauen* architects, was a "strict attention to utility, economy and other purely practical considerations" in which the process of construction played a central role.[12] As Bruno Taut wrote in 1929: "if everything is founded on sound efficiency, this efficiency itself, or rather its utility will form its own aesthetic law".[13] So far as the Modern Movement was concerned, the most efficient way of producing houses was through standardisation and mass production and these themes, therefore, dictated architectural form.

The architecture of early system building

Within the context of Modernism, progressive architects considered the design of early post-war non-traditional housing a grave disappointment and the result of sponsors failing to make the process of factory production a central motif in the appearance of their buildings. Indeed, it would seem that sponsors were most interested in merging their systems inconspicuously with traditional local authority housing.

According to D. Dex Harrison, while inter-war architects in Germany and France had taken new materials and "examining their design potential" produced revolutionary forms such as the open-plan dwelling supported on "pilotis":

> the pioneer prefabricators were trying laboriously to adapt these materials to the traditional plan and box like concept of the small house . . . .Here we have the origin of the deep seated mistrust of prefabrication as something which is "substitute" and lacks its own inherent [architectural] validity.[14]

In Harrison's view, architects such as Beaudouin and Lods (France), Neutra and Buckminster Fuller (USA) and Gropius (Germany) had indeed already begun to develop an aesthetic for prefabrication, primarily by expressing the jointed structure between the different

26 Assembling the Arcon House (Arcon Group, late 1940s)
Unconventional materials and techniques could not be disguised in the external appearance of many of the temporary bungalow designs

elements, the new materials and forms of construction themselves and by abandoning traditional archetypes such as the pitched roof and multipane window.

Like post-war social housing generally, non-traditional designs departed from the inter-war Neo-Georgian stereotype. However, few made obvious reference to more "efficient" methods of building. While revolutionary techniques of production used in the temporary housing programme could not be disguised, they were certainly not emphasised in their external appearance. Austerity was the order of the day, producing a functional aesthetic with understated traditional elements such as casement windows and pitched roofs.

A departure from traditional cottage imagery was to be found in the Keyhouse Unibuilt prototype, designed by Grey Wornum and Richard Sheppard in the early 1940s. With flat roof, clean rectilinear form and the minimalist porch structure, Modern Movement design is clearly evident. However, this stylistically outstanding model foundered at its prototype stage. Frederick Gibberd, another Modernist architect, was appointed by

27 Keyhouse Unibuilt, Coventry (Keyhouse Ltd, 1944)
Modernist principles of design are clearly evident in this prototype system designed by Grey Wornum and Richard Sheppard.

the British Iron and Steel Federation who, it might be assumed from this choice, intended its house to be stylistically of the moment. Gibberd's calm essay in contemporary design incorporated generous windows and a gently sloping roof. However, the uniqueness of construction was evident only in the cladding of upper floor and roof in a material new to domestic construction: profiled sheet steel.

Modernist influences were also absent from the popular pre-cast concrete systems such as Airey and Cornish Unit, neither of which were credited to well known architects. Between them, by 1955, approximately 50,000 dwellings were produced in a style which attempted to belie new production techniques through traditional archetypes. The Airey house, originally designed after the First World War, was a bland example of cottage styling with small windows and steeply pitched roof. Unless seen at close quarters, in which case the horizontal pre-cast concrete slabs were recognisable as a new walling material, it differs little from the typically austere post-war cottage. The more distinctive Cornish Unit is immediately recognisable by its mansard roof which owes more to inter-war eclecticism than post-war

28 BISF House (1945)
Frederick Gibberd's essay in restrained modernism struck a balance between new technology and traditional housing design

Modernism. It would appear that non-traditional sponsors chose to adhere to the tradition of state housing. As they no doubt intended, their products sat inconspicuously in the municipal housing landscape that had developed since the First World War.

The architecture of mass production

From the late 1950s, the architectural establishment's adherence to Modern Movement design theory strengthened rationalist trends previously evident in British social housing. Ultimately this led to designs in which system building was seen less as a restriction than the genesis itself of architectural expression.

The New Brutalism: a style for system building

29 Airey Houses at Chingford, Essex (Wm. Airey, 1946)
The flat-roofed version was little used and the majority of Airey houses conformed to the austere, cottage appearance of post-war local authority housing

The system building boom of the early 1960s was accompanied by a marked change in architectural fashion. For much of their housing, local authorities had by this time abandoned the two-storey cottage and were building blocks of flats. The aesthetic expression of multi-storey housing developed very much from techniques of construction and was guided by a particularly potent architectural movement – The New Brutalism.

This restatement of Modern Movement design theory pervaded British architecture from the mid-1950s to the mid-1970s and was the source of inspiration for architects concerned with system built housing.

Brutalism displaced early post-war Modernism, referred to as The New Humanism and described by Reyner Banham as "brickwork, segmental arches, pitched roofs, small windows (or small panes at any rate) – picturesque detailing without picturesque planning".[15] In place of this, Brutalism offered a style inspired by Mies Van de Rohe and Le Corbusier which concentrated on venerating new materials and techniques which emerged after the war. Picturesque composition was replaced by reference to the processes by which buildings were produced and an attempt was made to restore grandeur to urban planning through the use of repetition and large scale composition. hese themes provided a ready framework of architectural expression for system building.

The use of concrete, a material particularly favoured by Brutalists, had become widespread in all forms of building since the war. Indeed, it could be suggested that Brutalism's appeal to architects was its ability to give architectural coherence to the techniques and materials of multi-storey construction. As in Alison and Peter

30 Cornish Unit houses in Cheltenham, Glos (Central Cornish Concrete Co., 1946)
One of the more distinctive, non-traditional designs, the eclectic Cornish Unit adopted a mansard roof

Smithson's most influential projects, such as the Golden Lane Housing competition entry (1952) and the Sheffield University Extension scheme (1953), the buildings to which Brutalists first addressed their theories were the large urban projects of the Welfare State: the very building type exercising the minds of local authority housing architects.

Pragmatism

The type of architecture produced in the social housing projects of the Welfare State does not conform to current architectural tastes. The fact that these were accepted at the time arose from the way in which Modern Movement values reinforced existing attitudes to social housing. The resulting architectural philosophies seem alien to contemporary sensibilities: efficiency was the order of the day and the prevailing orthodoxy that architectural style should be no more than the expression of this. As the 1960s building boom gathered pace, these attitudes were compounded by a degree of pragmatism which had little regard for the architectural implications of industrialising the building industry.

For instance, in 1965 Basil Honikman fatalistically conceded that system building "must be reviewed with the same attitude that one regards any other mass-produced article designed for mass consumption. To demand more is like asking the low-priced motorcar to perform like a Rolls Royce".[16]There were also architects who happily exchanged the traditional pleasures of design for the excitement of system building. Miall Rhyss Davis, consultant to Concrete ltd., typified the mid-1960s rationalist architect more concerned with the process of production itself than extrinsic qualities in the finished dwelling:

> Let us stop and look at the piece of metal, or concrete, or plastic, or glass. It is pretty well the same whatever chunk of building grows from it. . . . So where the excitement, the fireworks? The quantity, the speed, efficient, neat, fast organisations, calculated and planned exactly. A new machine, a mechanised administration – this is the excitement . . . it lives on continuity, big investment, and requires vast pipe lines of communication.[17]

211

As building programmes increased, the calls mounted on housing architects to fall into line and compromise their architectural instinct to approach each project afresh and question previous solutions. There was never any suggestion that quality of design should be sacrificed but, rather, that experiment and variety militated against efficient production. At the 1962 Housing From the Factory conference, Cleeve Barr lamented the multitude of British social housing types which had developed over the past century. Listing eleven of these, he suggested the consequence was that

> At best this variety has led to some fine examples of good architecture which are known throughout Europe. At worst it has resulted in a waste of professional and technical skills which has caused additional expense to local housing authorities and prevented both traditional and non-traditional builders from taking full economic advantage of repetitive building operations.[18]

Throughout the 1960s an ongoing project within the Ministry of Housing and Local Government Research and Development Group was the reduction of "needless variety" in housing design. In Circular 76/65 (1965) local authorities were instructed to provide continuous programmes and larger sites to system builders and advised that, "the number of plan types in a scheme is kept down, and satisfactory types kept in use".[19]

The LCC and Morris Walk

One of the first authorities to make a clear union between new technology and Brutalism was the London County Council (LCC). The Morris Walk estate was the first of its large-panel schemes and is perhaps the purest example of Modern Movement design in this country.

The early 1950s saw an increasing concentration by the Council on mixed development and system building. Furthermore, in 1950 responsibility for the design of housing was transferred from the Valuer's Department to the Housing Architect, bringing in a large number of new staff. Among these were former Hertfordshire architects including Cleeve Barr (later Assistant Housing Architect) and others described by Kenneth Frampton as "sympathizers and colleagues"[20] of the Smithsons. According to Reynor Banham's account of Brutalism, the LCC

Architects' Department was the veritable battlefield on which Brutalism gained ultimate supremacy over The New Humanism.[21] With the battle won, the Council built a number of designs in the new style such as the Alton West slab blocks (1959). Based on a scaled down version of Corbusier's *Unité d'Habitation* (1947–52), LCC architects used *in situ* and pre-cast concrete as the principal material of construction and architectural expression. As Kenneth Campbell, Housing Architect to the LCC, pointed out a few years later:

> Concrete is a serious material, it is the building material of this twentieth century . . . there are some places in Roehampton where ordinary Portland cement has weathered as beautifully as Portland stone.[22]

31 Slab blocks, Roehampton (LCC, 1957)
The highly modelled elevations of Roehampton established the architectural respectability of bare concrete and exposed aggregate in public housing

Thus, even before it adopted large-panel building systems, the LCC was already committed to a design theory which derived its aesthetic from modern methods of production.

The Morris Walk redevelopment scheme (1963) was the first of the LCC's estates to use large-panel

32 Day production units, Morris Walk, Woolwich (Larsen Nielsen, Taylor Woodrow/LCC, 1963)
The number of panels manufactured in one day formed the basic unit of design in the LCC's first large concrete panel estate at Woolwich

SITE PLAN

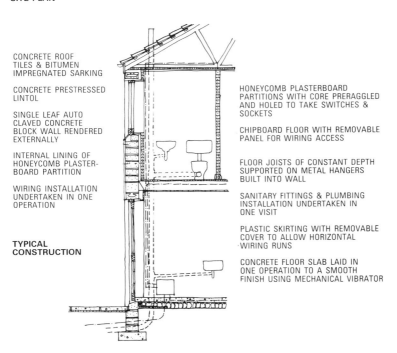

CONCRETE ROOF
TILES & BITUMEN
IMPREGNATED SARKING

CONCRETE PRESTRESSED
LINTOL

SINGLE LEAF AUTO
CLAVED CONCRETE
BLOCK WALL RENDERED
EXTERNALLY

INTERNAL LINING OF
HONEYCOMB PLASTER-
BOARD PARTITION

WIRING INSTALLATION
UNDERTAKEN IN ONE
OPERATION

**TYPICAL
CONSTRUCTION**

HONEYCOMB PLASTERBOARD
PARTITIONS WITH CORE PRERAGGLED
AND HOLED TO TAKE SWITCHES &
SOCKETS

CHIPBOARD FLOOR WITH REMOVABLE
PANEL FOR WIRING ACCESS

FLOOR JOISTS OF CONSTANT DEPTH
SUPPORTED ON METAL HANGERS
BUILT INTO WALL

SANITARY FITTINGS & PLUMBING
INSTALLATION UNDERTAKEN IN
ONE VISIT

PLASTIC SKIRTING WITH REMOVABLE
COVER TO ALLOW HORIZONTAL
WIRING RUNS

CONCRETE FLOOR SLAB LAID IN
ONE OPERATION TO A SMOOTH
FINISH USING MECHANICAL VIBRATOR

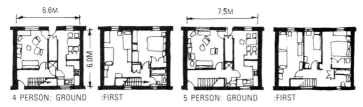

6.6M   7.5M   6.0M

4 PERSON: GROUND   :FIRST   5 PERSON: GROUND   :FIRST

TYPICAL DWELLING PLANS

construction and broke new ground in developing an architectural style based on the production methods of system building. Morris Walk consisted of 562 dwellings in the Larsen Nielsen system. In describing the scheme, while it was still on the drawing board, to the Housing From the Factory conference in 1962, the Assistant Housing Architect, J. Whittle, claimed that many of the system built schemes they had visited abroad had been "architecturally disappointing" and their layouts monotonous. In Whittle's view this resulted from architects too often adapting designs originally conceived for traditional construction. However, in his first large-panel estate, Whittle returned to first principles:

> It is our experience that many promoters of these systems delight in their claim that they can build any block designed for traditional building. But this is putting the cart before the horse; building by a special method should give rise to a recognisable architectural expression, which should develop from a rational use of the method by the architect.[23]

33 Elevations, Morris Walk
Proud of their achievement in reducing the number of panel types to a minimum, LCC architects intended Morris Walk to be the architectural expression of mass production applied to housing

Rather than purpose or setting, Morris Walk's architectural motif was derived from the number of panels the factory produced in one working day. The "day production

unit", as it was termed, comprised two living rooms, two kitchens, two bathrooms and WCs, two stores and four bedrooms. By varying the position of the party wall, a variety of dwelling sizes, ranging from three bedrooms to bedsits, could be provided. The general application of the day production unit resulted in equal-sized living rooms regardless of the overall size of the flat. This was also true of bedrooms. There were two types of kitchen and a standard bathroom/WC module for the whole project. Ten-storey blocks were formed by joining day production units back-to-back either side of a staircase and lift tower while day production units joined end-to-end, with outrigged staircases, formed three-storey linear blocks. The articulation of accommodation blocks and service cores provided advantages both intellectual and avowedly practical, enabling "the complex lift, staircase and service core . . . to be considered separately from the dwelling units" supposedly leading to greater simplification in design and erection but, more importantly, visually defining the basic unit of factory production.

Standard panels, considered essential to efficient system building, characterised the appearance of Morris Walk. Whittle boasted that only four basic sizes of cladding panel were used which, with a limited number of window sizes, gave rise to a total of seventeen standard types. The elevations marked a significant departure from preceding LCC designs, not least in the absence of modelling and lack of visual expression to individual dwellings. A particular innovation (to become more common in the future for economic reasons) was the omission of balconies. These were the dominant motif of the Alton West blocks where they articulated the broad facades and gave expression to individual maisonettes. Significantly, in its earlier system building experiments at Picton Street, Camberwell (1957) and Aegis Grove, Battersea (1962 – now demolished), the Council retained the external balcony. However, for its first design in large-panel construction, the balcony was an unwarranted extravagance which would certainly have increased the number of different panel types and introduced additional jointing problems.

Little was said of the Morris Walk site plan by Whittle, other than that "the design problem was to dispose standard units about a site which was most irregular in contour and produce an ordered scheme". Examination of the Morris Walk layout reveals two very noticeable qualities; the uniform architectural expression given to high and low blocks and their identical orientation, both of which resulted from the universal expression of day production units. In previous LCC schemes, different techniques of construction were used for blocks of different height allowing very different elevational treatments. At Alton West this varied from timber clad crosswall construction for the row houses to pre-cast concrete cladding for the point blocks. As each block at Morris Walk was made up of the same set of concrete panels, there was no opportunity within the LCC's rationalist design orthodoxy for varying orientation or architectural treatment. Indeed, despite the rich topography of the site, which includes steep slopes and the division into unequal portions by a railway line, this mixed development scheme is remarkable in having every block, both high and low, aligned uniformly. This was not the case with previous LCC estates, the layouts of which were always influenced by topography. This varied from picturesque site planning at Roehampton to the varied orientation of row houses, maisonettes and flats on the Loughborough Estate, Brixton (1953). Whether or not the LCC's intention, the degree of

34 Site layout, Morris Walk (Larsen Nielsen/LCC, 1963)
Perhaps the most thoroughly Modernist housing estate in Britain, the LCC's first large panel estate adopted the pre-war German "Zilenbau" layout with all blocks uniformly aligned

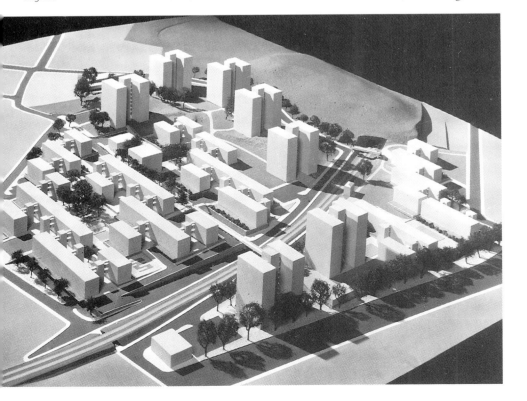

rationality which lay at the heart of Morris Walk brought it closer to the systematization of the Zilenbau than any scheme yet in this country.

While the basis of Morris Walk's design was later questioned, not least by the LCC itself, Whittle and his colleagues were, for the moment, happy with their first essay in large-panel construction: "This design demonstrates that the dull and repetitive schemes so often associated with industrialised housing are not necessarily the fault of the system". To the charge that the design was monotonous, Whittle's superior, Kenneth Campbell, might have replied with the words he used at the Housing From the Factory conference:

> There has been far too much – there is always far too much – talk about variety and monotony. These are practically meaningless terms . . . design begins in the bones of a building. It is in the total of the building that beauty lies . . . one can easily obtain variety, which is, too often, restlessness, even vulgarity, but what one has to achieve is an inner richness in one's buildings which comes from quite different things entirely . . . what counts . . . is how far the architect has grasped totally and absolutely the technique by which his building is produced(1962).[24]

Non-conformity and new values

Morris Walk emphasised the technical characteristics of system building on the assumption that efficient methods of production would produce a new aesthetic for social housing. However, there were many architects who were unhappy with this approach. Throughout the post-war period there existed a tradition in which designers expressed dissatisfaction with the degree to which system building compromised design. In most cases these architects grudgingly accepted the constraints of new technology, while, in others, attempts were made to apply system building to formally complex designs which contradicted the very ethos of efficient panel production. At first, only a few architects refused to use methods which denied them opportunities to produce designs incorporating the full range of architectural values. Nevertheless, the challenge to system building grew stronger throughout the late 1960s and early 1970s as architects increasingly kicked against the traces of new technology and questioned their earlier readiness to subordinate housing design to factory methods of production.

Non-conformity

It is evident that the aesthetic shortcomings of system building played a major part in the resistance of local authorities to new technology. Objectors received no prominence in the architectural press: the Luddite implication of their concern was in direct opposition to the adoption of a progressive professional ideology. However, these subdued voices represented a substantial body of opinion aggrieved at the effect of system building on the way in which they practised their skill as designers.

One of the first to raise his voice in protest was R.W. Brown who, in May 1944, lamented of his wartime work for the government that "prefabrication would make us stale. He had experience of that in the Office of Works, where he had to go to cupboard no.1 for section B, and so on, and copy something. He completely lost interest in his work and felt hopeless".[25] The effect of prefabrication on the diligence of architects was noted by the Department of Health For Scotland which, in 1951, found that "Architects take more care with buildings designed by themselves".[26] In his correspondence with the Ministry of Health in 1951, the Regional Production Officer for the South West, C.H.H. Smith, frequently referred to official architects, both in local authorities and his own office who were:

> not enamoured of systems which limit the scope for attractive lay-outs . . . [and] who feel no responsibility for securing rapid housing progress and will always prefer to plod slowly, so long as they can express their individuality in housing schemes of limited extent.[27]

Of the various means by which retrogressive elements of the profession frustrated system building, Smith mentioned the misinformation of lay-committees in which the faults of new methods were dwelt upon at the expense of their merits and the use of systems on sloping sites in an attempt to increase costs and bring them into disrepute.

Quite convinced that system building was an unaccept-
able alternative to traditional methods, the County
Architect and Planner for Buckinghamshire, F.B. Pooley,
was able to confess in 1968 with "some pride in being the
architect to the only county in the country not to be
muddled in a consortium".[28] Although Buckinghamshire
was a rural authority it had, according to Pooley, a
programme of building running in 1968 at three to four
million pounds a year in an expensive building area short
of skilled labour. In these respects it enjoyed the same
incentives to adopt prefabrication as the rest of the
country. Furthermore, Pooley was familiar with the
benefits offered by system building as he was formerly
employed by Coventry and had written an article on the
city's No-Fines estate at Tile Hill in 1953.[29] Pooley's
objection to system building and consortia was quite
plain: so far as he was concerned they were unsound
economic and administrative developments which had an
"unfortunate influence on design". This is not to say that
Buckinghamshire had refused to consider prefabricated
schools, it had in the early 1950s but found them "by
their very nature" incapable of providing the same
flexibility in planning as traditional construction and
without substantial economic advantages. In Pooley's
opinion, the designs produced by system building were
inherently poor:

> The trouble with the post and panel theme is that at its
> best it is a flimsy looking element with little civic
> quality about it: at its worst it is just plain and
> monotonous . . . concrete panels are not all that much
> better and, by and large, those that we can afford are
> uncivilised slabs of material, incapable of maturing in
> a satisfactory way.[30]

In preference to system building, Pooley used "simple
straightforward construction, with an emphasis on limited
standardisation" and brickwork wherever possible as in
the eleven-storey block of loadbearing brick flats he built
at Aylesbury in 1961. Nevertheless, Pooley was not
averse to using pre-cast concrete where he felt it
appropriate. For instance, a proprietary frame by Concrete
Ltd. was used at the Royal Grammar School, High
Wycombe (1964). Upholding a less restricted version of
Modern Movement values than the LCC, Pooley was
convinced that architecture which combined good design

with economy could only be achieved "if every building is designed for its site and built in a construction that is economical and sound and where the individual architect can use his skills to the full".

State sponsored systems and design flexibility

State sponsored systems designed on the basis of modular co-ordination were intended to overcome some of the design limitations traditionally associated with system building. While, on the face of it, these systems embodied a greater degree of design flexibility, they raised as many problems as they solved and merely served to underline the architectural problems associated with system building.

A keen observer of these developments and their contribution to the debate on system building was the *Architects' Journal*. Of 5M CLASP's developmental application to elderly person flatlets at Stevenage, the *Journal* pointed to "the success of the design in creating a small scale and intimate environment for old people".[31] However, as the *Journal* also pointed out, the success of 5M in eradicating the limitations of industrialised building was limited: "As so often happens with system building, however, a limited range of ceiling heights combined with the inevitable flat roof has resulted in the pavilion arrangement being blurred by the uniform eaves". Furthermore, the journal suggested that the expensive steel frame might have accounted for the poor quality of finish to the external and internal claddings. In its overall verdict, *Architects' Journal*, somewhat apologetically, admitted of this worthy attempt that "Looked at in the cold light of reason this first essay in 5M CLASP seems to raise as many problems as it solves". Indeed, in 1968, the Ministry of Public Buildings and Works admitted of its 5M barracks at Catterick that unfavourable comments "on the appearance of the finished quarters has come from some Army sources".[32]

Of 12M Jespersen's use at Livingstone New Town, *Architects' Journal* commented favourably on the range of dwelling types and richness of the staggered section in comparison to the average system built estate. Indeed, the *Journal* suggested that any constructional complexities generated by the complex forms were outweighed by the planning problems dealt with by the system and the

range of dwelling types it had provided. The *Architects'
Journal's* overall verdict was that "If the level of design
apparent at Livingstone could be achieved in a large
proportion of our public housing instead of in a pitifully
small proportion, the national standards would begin to
approach a desireable level".[33] However, the tendency of
architects to exploit 12M's design virtuosity generated a
host of expensive detailing problems and in 1967 Laing
announced that they were unable to operate the system
profitably. This news was received with dismay by one
contributor to *Architects' Journal*, J. Jordan, who like
many of his professional colleagues "saw the project as
the most hopeful of the efforts in the British industrialised
building field".[34]

New values at the GLC

The mid-1960s saw a significant change in the approach
to system building of the Greater London Council (GLC,
formerly the London County Council). This change
undoubtedly reflected larger and increasing concerns at
its effect on the urban environment. Indeed, no sooner
had the foundations to Morris Walk been laid than
Kenneth Campbell expressed misgivings on the degree to
which technology had inspired the design:

> it was an example of architects falling over backwards
> to try to look at it through the eyes of the production
> engineer, and we rather gave up the wider viewpoint
> of the architect. In our "MkII" development this is
> what we shall be doing.[35]

The "MkII" development increasingly focussed on by the
GLC during the mid-1960s was Thamesmead. One of
the first products of the Council's extended role in
planning the Greater London conurbation, Thamesmead
was the largest development it designed. Originally
known as the Woolwich Erith scheme, the intention,
announced in March 1966, was to reclaim 1,300 acres of
marshlands from the Thames flood plain to house a
population of 60,000. Two-thirds of the homes were to
be built by the GLC and a half of these by system
building. Planned to take place over fifteen years, the
first stage of the project was a system built 4,000 dwelling
contract placed later in 1966.[36]

222

Further indication that design values had changed was given by Hubert Bennett in May 1966 when he stated that strict adherence to system building manufacturing discipline was no longer the Council's policy. At Thamesmeade, Bennett intended to use irregular building forms with an emphasis on medium rise housing in line with the new subsidy system even though "Designing in this way exposes the weakness of most industrialised building systems, whether for tall or low building, which is their inflexibility in the manner in which one dwelling can be related to another".[37] Rather than continuing to derive the design of housing from production methods, Bennett warned system builders that:

> the large contracts with which the GLC is likely to be associated will, for social as well as architectural considerations, need to be carried out by building techniques which, although making full use of modern means of production will also facilitate the creation of a first rate environment.

At Thamesmeade the GLC literally inverted the design philosophy of Morris Walk. Rather than selecting the system and then designing the scheme to its production characteristics, Thamesmeade was designed first and the system chosen later. According to A. Pike, "The design team decided that the correct approach would be to design a good project without reference to a specific industrialised building scheme and then apply the use of a system".[38] By Spring 1966, design work had progressed sufficiently for the GLC's quantity surveyors to develop a cost plan based on traditional construction. Following this, in conjunction with the National Building Agency, the scheme was put out to tender. The contract was eventually awarded to Cubitts who proposed using the Balency system in October 1966.[39] Notable in this project was a special form of contract whereby the Council actually owned the on-site panel casting factory operated by Cubitts. This arrangement resulted from the GLC's policy of gaining a better understanding of the economics of large-panel construction and reflects its desire to achieve greater control over system building programmes.[40]

Balency was a typical large-panel system in all but two respects; it had an unusually sophisticated method for integrating piped services into the concrete panels

223

(which, like most systems, fixed the kitchen/bathroom arrangement) and, more importantly, had *in situ* rather than pre-cast floor slabs. This latter feature may have been instrumental in the choice of system as it increased design flexibility.

Phase I consisted of 1,500 dwellings in three block types; highly modelled five-storey linear maisonettes, thirteen-storey towers and three storey terraces. The first result of the GLC's new design orientated policy was that a large part of the scheme was not built in the system. The half-mile long, intricately shaped, two to five-storey linear block comprising 342 dwellings was staggered both in plan and section to a degree totally unsuited to large-panel construction. Rather than rationalise its form to bring it within the capabilities of the system, the block was built in traditional cross-wall construction. Where non-structural pre-cast concrete panels were used for external cladding, they were styled to match the system built part of the contract and, where the design allowed, Balency units were incorporated *ad hoc*.[41] The result was a formally complex, traditionally built housing block providing an architecturally dominant spine to the scheme.

35 Linear Housing, Thamesmeade (Balency, GLC 1969)
Adopting the principle of design first and choose the system later, parts of the Thamesmeade estate could not be built in Balency due to the irregular plan and stepped section. Nevertheless, pre-cast concrete panels were used to provide a unified "system built" aesthetic

By contrast with the linear block, the three-storey terraces conformed more to the traditional pattern of large-panel construction. However, in their alternating indentations and projections in plan and section they too flouted the conventions of system building in return for concessions to formal complexity. The same is true of the thirteen-storey point blocks which were given a far greater richness of form than at Morris Walk. This included incised corner balconies and wrap around corner kitchen windows. Neither of these – requiring cantilevered panels and awkward joints more readily solved in monolithic frame construction – owe their inspiration to the production of pre-cast concrete panels. The outcome of the GLC's rejection of its former rationalism was a highly mannered design of greater

36 Point Blocks,
Thamesmeade (Balency,
GLC 1969)
Incised balconies and corner windows: when designing Thamesmeade, the GLC rejected their earlier belief in rational prefabricated design exemplified at Morris Walk

formal richness than had hitherto been achieved in system building. Within this, it could be said that the traditionally built blocks borrowed their imagery from system building and the system built blocks their imagery from *in situ* construction. While this approach may be seen as lacking the purity of Morris Walk and a headlong retreat from the principles of Modernism, it was sufficient to gain Thamesmeade the highest international award for urban design. The Sir Patrick Abercrombie Award was given to the GLC in 1969 with the following comment from the adjudicators: "An indication of harmonious integration of human values, aesthetic expression and modern techniques is to be found in this project".[42]

The architecture of bureaucracy

The late 1960s was a turning point for popular and professional attitudes towards architecture. Rather than a panacea to the housing problem, system building was soon regarded as the nadir of post-war building and the inevitable result of Modernist design theories.

Modernism: a shattered illusion

The rejection of system building was part of a larger movement in cultural values, the precise nature of which has yet to be fully explained. Nevertheless it can be said that, following hard on the collapse of the post-war boom and the onset of economic crisis, this shift resulted from a less optimistic view of the role technology played in social and economic progress. No longer seen as social idealists, the Modernist architects who had controlled social building policies over the past twenty years were characterised as incompetent bureaucrats.

As they viewed the environment created since the war with dismay, architects and their critics increasingly questioned their former wholehearted concentration on technology and material growth. Typical of this was Ove Arup's 1968 warning that "it is only a matter of time before our society . . . [is] completely taken over by technology".[43] Only thirty years earlier Arup had been a member of CISPH vigorously promoting mass production in building methods.

The general perception that central and local government architects and system building sponsors were seen as unscrupulous charlatans "deeply implicated in all kinds of plans for the destruction of old England" was noted by Martin Pawley in 1971.[44] The association of Modernism and system building with bungling politicians and unfeeling bureaucrats was also expressed with particular clarity in Malcolm McEwan's *Crisis in Architecture* (1974).

While popular opinion saw architects as villains of the piece, the profession saw itself unwittingly enmeshed in a system beyond control that had subverted the principles for which they had struggled for two generations. At the RIBA's 1967 Annual Conference, Maxwell Fry mourned his shattered illusion, formed in the 1930s, of a fusion between architecture and industry which would enable "a renaissance of urbanism". Architects, he lamented, "are as much in the grip of the reproductive system as we are the agents of a bureaucracy, whether governmental or commercial and the buildings we design must reflect the character of both".[45] Indeed, according to Reynor Banham – another Modernist dismayed by 1971 at the course of events – the most recent apotheosis of the welfare bureaucrat's architecture was Thamesmeade. Despite their attempt to re-establish formal architectural values, Banham described the GLC's latest scheme as "Bennett's Leviathan". Significantly, as much as building technology itself, Banham's horror was the result of the sheer scale on which Thamesmeade, and other large redevelopment schemes were being carried out:

> a virtually self manufacturing city, erecting itself panel by room-sized panel out of a factory in its own entrails . . . My first reaction to the new environment being created there was a kind of numb disbelief . . . What I can't believe is that we have really created a situation in which one man can ordain the environment of so many.[46]

The tide turns

The years up to 1970 saw very little dispute by architects over the changes taking place in building technology. Up to this point a consensus existed that new technology was necessary to achieve social goals. Whether against their better judgment or not, architects out of sympathy with system building simply got on with the job. Furthermore, little space would have been afforded them by a professional press which supported the orthodoxy of industrialised building. However, this changed in the early 1970s as architects became increasingly vocal in their opposition to new methods and the press increasingly willing to allow discussion to take place in their journals. Dissent centred on two events in particular, Metric House Shells and the MACE school system.

1969 saw the publication of *Metric House Shells*, and the requirement of Circular 69/69 that it should be applied to all subsequent local authority housing. Metric House Shells should be remembered not for bringing the building industry one step nearer industrialisation – by this time a lost cause – but for the protest unleashed from an architectural profession aggrieved at yet more erosion of its design freedom by Ministerial edict and the enmeshing of architecture in another layer of official control. The RIBA declined to support the new policy out of a professed sense of social responsibility, and protested vigorously. Whereas in previous years this sense of responsibility might have led the profession to support such an initiative, in the new climate of opinion it seems to have had the opposite effect. Edward Hollamby, Lambeth Borough Architect, protested that "The whole of the country's architecture was being removed from the field of creative design".[47] Taking up the attack in *Municipal Journal* later in the month, Jane Drew launched an extended polemic against the National Building Agency describing, in the fashion of the time, a future environment of Orwellian dimensions:

> there will be no curves, no minor refinements, no visual adjustments for heights, no connections at corners . . . It is really all part of mechanisation taking command, of the Orwellian-cum-Gideon world of the future where feeling and imagination are blunted, convenience takes command and idealism is lost . . . it is noticeable that those who urge metric shells are not creators. Not being practising architects, they wish to control others.[48]

Defending the Agency, in the same issue, Cleeve Barr could do little more than reiterate his ideal of greater building efficiency and point to the fact that most council housing was already rectangular and that the National Building Agency was only rationalising the design of a product that was, in all but its finer dimensions, standardised already: "The trouble to date is that every architect, for every site, tends to use a different set of dimensions for simple rectangular houses of the same type".[49] The interchange between Drew and Barr carried over to the next issue of *Municipal Journal* but, whereas Barr and his supporters had once held the higher ground, they were now defending building policies which were becoming increasingly unpopular.

While the controversy over Metric House Shells led only to words, that over the Metropolitan Authorities Consortium for Education (MACE) school system led to positive action on the part of disaffected GLC architects. MACE was set up in 1966 and, like other consortia, immediately began to develop its own system of construction. Using a frame based on a 1m. planning grid, MACE was intended to be unique in its degree of planning flexibility.[50] Significantly, so far as future events were concerned, the GLC's membership of MACE coincided with the employment of Louis Hellman, an architect who had moved from private to public practice in 1965 "in the hope of entering a more liberal environment".[51] His hopes dashed, Hellman ran up against a hierarchy "trained in the forties and early fifties . . . cast in the orthodox functionalist and technological mould". In January 1973, Hellman published an article, "The Myth of the Machine Aesthetic", attacking the Modern Movement. In Hellman's view, system building was the quintessential outcome of a fusion between Modernist design theory and local government bureaucracy:

> This upper strata finds it hard for its part to cope with imaginative proposals or creativity. They have generally risen to high posts not through design ability or architectural merit but through political and administrative conformity – they generally go for the safe solution. For this new management class of non-architect IB is ideal. It allows them not only to control the career structure of those below them but also their architectural output. IB with its related codes, graphs, graphics, grids, manuals, financial jugglings, programming and all the other paraphernalia of "rationalism" fits in nicely with the self-perpetuating mystique of

"management" – it is a style for bureaucracy, tidy boxes to be labelled and administered.[52]

In August 1973, Dick Collins, Mayor of Camden, refused to accept the new Edith Neville Junior and Infants Mixed School at Kings Cross built in MACE. Among Camden's complaints was that there was too little stock room, corridor and teaching space.[53] Seizing the moment, Hellman joined the fray and published an attack on MACE in the *RIBA Journal* pursuing the theme of his earlier article. In Hellman's view, from the first MACE prototypes it was evident that "far from being anonymous enclosures for teaching, they were assertively 'architect-ural' with a most unpleasant brutalist prefab aesthetic".[54] The introduction of MACE was followed by a "growing wave of discontent" on the part of architects obliged to use the system. A result of this, claimed Hellman, was that "architects are so demoralised that they do not give sufficient care and attention to their work with it". Among the system's technical faults Hellman listed poor sound and thermal insulation, wall and roof leaks due to the impractical jointing system and a lack of choice in finishes. However, as damaging as these was the system's high cost which led to reductions in floor area. As Hellman pointed out, high costs allied with an inflexible planning grid had serious repercussions:

> Reduce the area of a MACE school? How can you reduce area on a 1m. planning module without chopping off valuable teaching space? How can you decrease the height of external walls when only a 2.4m. high component is available?

Following a further unsatisfactory report on the system by the Schools Division Participation Movement and in view of cuts in its capital spending programme, the ILEA announced, in April 1974, that it was withdrawing from MACE. In all, by this time, the GLC had built nine schools in the system, had seven under construction and three more due to start.[55] In its response to this decision, the MACE Development Group ascribed the revolt of GLC architects to "an inability to work within the discipline of a standard idiom . . . and a romantic desire for self-expression".[56]

230

Architecture by association

An obvious question for the architectural historian is whether there was such a thing as a style distinctively that of system building as opposed to other methods of construction. In answering this question, it is clear that our understanding of the architectural characteristics of system building was, and continues to be, very heavily influenced by changing social and cultural values.

System building varied from being identical in appearance to traditional methods to being distinctive in its own right. It is simply not the case that system building automatically generated a particular type of architecture. This is well shown by comparing a brick clad timber frame house with the archetypal traditional dwelling, or by comparing a large-panel tower block with one built in a monolithic concrete frame clad in purpose designed pre-cast concrete units. The distinctions between each are not necessarily apparent to even the most well researched eye.

Evidence suggests that having chosen to use system building, architects were more restricted in design than traditional construction. The degree to which these restrictions operated and their precise nature varied with the different methods of system building used. It was certainly a characteristic of some of the early post-war cottage systems, such as Cornish Unit and BISF that only one standard model was available. However, this was as much a product of the way in which these dwellings were marketed – nothing in their methods of production precluded the development of, for instance, special corner units as was common in traditionally constructed estates. Variety was not the overriding priority of sponsors or clients in the years of post-war austerity and the "emergency" period. Throughout the 1950s, popular, poured concrete systems, such as No-Fines and Easiform, proved capable of as wide a variation in plan types as local authorities required. In later years, at its extreme, large-panel construction imposed considerable economic penalties on the client if physical characteristics of production were ignored in the design of the basic unit, or if the required degree of repetition was not obtained. However, at the other extreme, timber frame was capable of application to projects as small as two houses and, if a sufficiently high priority of the designer, did not have to adhere to the preferred dimensional module.

What is more significant is that larger values lay behind the design of system built estates than the physical characteristics of the method of construction in use. The debate on architectural style overshadowed any simple division between system and traditional building. The manufacturing model of design was as much used in traditional construction as it was in system building with the same justification – that standardisation produced economy. Indeed, it is evident that the supposed disciplines of new technology were emphasised by architects attempting to validate Modern Movement theories of design. Nikolaus Pevsner's perception of the constraints of new technology had a philosophical as much as a material basis: "they keep the architect to reason. They eliminate neo-irrationalism".[57] The desire of the upper echelons of the public architectural service to find a unified idiom for social housing design may have prompted Kenneth Campbell to welcome the effects of system building as he saw them:

> To work within such disciplines may be just what the profession, at the moment, needs more than anything else. It would probably be good for society at large also, individuality run riot is one of the banes of our age".[58]

It could be argued that the supposed design require-ments of system building fulfilled the fantasy of Modernist architects for building methods which demanded a rationality absent in traditional construction. This was an important motif in the attempt to give architectural expression to their vision of a collectivised society. At Morris Walk, therefore, the characteristics of concrete panel production were capable of being exaggerated to an extreme by architects committed to a particular set of architectural goals. However, equally, they might be ignored or minimised as in the case of Thamesmeade.

System building was no more than a form of organisation which focussed new methods of construction on particular building types. While technology had its physical characteristics and more or less of a requirement for standardisation, it is evident that the architecture of system building exists in terms the association we have given it with one type of project – the local authority estate. To the average eye, what served eventually to set system building apart from traditional construction was its use in many of the largest individual housing projects likely ever to be seen in these isles and, frequently, for the least popular dwelling type we have known, the multi-storey flat. Characteristic of these projects, whether system or traditionally built, was the replacement of traditional housing archetypes, such as pitched roof, intimacy of scale, and street frontage with an alien set of motifs. In this respect, an "architecture" of system building, as generally perceived, is the product of its association with the largest and least popular of post-war housing developments. It was this quality of Thamesmeade's system built architecture which horrified Reynor Banham in 1971. While the individual No-Fines dwelling is indistinguishable from a rendered brick house and capable of equal variety in design, there was not, and probably never will be, anything built in traditional construction which matches the sublimity of Coventry's tracts of No-Fines housing. These literally stretch as far as the eye can see in all directions. Similarly, the large-panel tower block continues to define the skylines of our inner cities. However, these are examples of an architecture which resulted from the way in which system building was used to achieve particular social policies

37 Prototype aluminium bungalow (AIROH, 1945) Politicians and citizens of the newly formed Welfare State gather before a prototype aluminium bungalow developed by aircraft manufacturers. If science and technology had won the war, harnessed to housing, it would strengthen the social system in peace

within a very specific set of architectural values. In this sense only can system building be said to have produced its own aesthetic.

As important as whether it had an inherent visual language, was the way in which system building was affected by changing notions of acceptability. In the space of four years the same GLC architects advocated wholly different design theories for system building and produced schemes as diverse as Morris Walk and Thamesmeade in essentially the same method of construction. A detailed analysis of these schemes reveals distinctions which had less to do with differences between pre-cast concrete systems, than the relationship perceived between technology and social progress. Morris Walk was the outcome of a belief that social goals could be achieved through uncompromising application of production values, whereas Thamesmeade was determined by a belief that the hard edge of technology should be softened to create a humane environment.

Nevertheless, while massive social housing programmes remained the goal of social policy and mass production the conventional wisdom of architecture, local authorities generated their designs within the constraints of system building. Voices opposing system building were barely heard for as long as Modern Movement values held sway. But after the economic crisis of 1968, Louis Hellman was given unrestricted access to the architectural press in mounting his polemic against MACE. Housing programmes were by this time in decline and rather than looking for ways of increasing production, architects had started to enquire why society was scarred by the houses and schools it had recently built. The increasing pressure which Welfare State policies came under afforded the architectural establishment an opportunity to examine its previously unquestioning attitude to technology. In the process, opinion focussed on system building as the most obvious aspect of the single minded pursuit of technical advance in post-war housing design and production policy. Indeed, one of the most remarkable features of system building was the speed with which it was transformed in the perception of society from the most progressive aspect of architectural theory to the epitome of unenlightened bureaucracy.

CONCLUSION

System building overseas

System building was by no means confined to the British Isles and at one stage or another, the majority of industrialised economies have adopted new methods of construction. An examination of Europe suggests that factors behind the system building were similar to those in Britain, while in America it is evident that different social and economic conditions produced another approach to house construction.

Large panel pre-cast concrete systems were used on the Continent well before their use in Britain. Indeed, due either to higher labour costs or stronger state policies favouring new housebuilding methods, it appears that sponsors met with greater success abroad. This success was also related to the greater use of high-rise housing.

In 1948 the French government sponsored a competition encouraging designers and contractors to develop labour saving systems for housing. This was followed in 1953 by a further competition in which system building was applied to 50,000 low-cost dwellings; from then on a portion of the housing market was reserved for system building by the state.[1]

That system building could not compete economically with traditional construction in The Netherlands caused it to be highly dependent on government policy. The output of system built dwellings after the war rose steadily until a special subsidy paid for them was withdrawn in 1952. Production then fell until a policy of reserving continuous contracts for specific systems was adopted, after which system building rose. In 1962 10,000 out of 80,000 houses were built by just four systems. When this arrangement was abandoned, system building flagged once more.[2]

A similarly steady demand combined with restrictions

on the numbers of systems was provided by the Danish government. Larsen & Nielsen and Jespersen had production figures consistently above 1,000 units per annum in their native countries, with the former maintaining this for over twenty years.[3]

The most dramatic example of system building flourishing under state control was in Eastern Europe. In 1966 the Moscow building department comprised 11,000 professional staff, 74,000 manual workers and 100 factories producing components for 100,000 dwellings on 400 sites.[4]

Since the war, system building has been a major feature of the housing market in America: in 1964, 600 manufacturers produced 250,000 houses, 22 per cent of total production. In America, there is no state sector as such and private housebuilding is encouraged by federal subsidies. System building there seems to have been generated by the scarcity and expense of building labour wedded to abundant timber resources. The "mail-order house", in which pre-cut timber components were supplied to the purchaser, was a significant feature of the Mid-West housing market between 1900–14, with firms such as Sears & Roebuck major suppliers. Except during the Great Depression, when labour was cheap and capital dear,[5] the off-site manufacture of timber housing has continued to flourish. Building labour in America differs in three ways to Western Europe: it is comparatively expensive (judged in 1968 to be three times more so than Britain), it is more expensive than factory labour, and skill differentials are higher (judged in 1966 to be 2:1 in America and 6:5 in Britain).[6] The expense of skilled American site labour and cheap indigenous timber have generated a consistent development in the off-site manufacture of timber house components: in these the overall labour content can be reduced, unskilled substituted for skilled and factory substituted for site labour. By using timber, these benefits were gained through a relatively cheap technology which did not require the capital investment, assured markets and large contracts of the European systems. It is significant that the types of timber frame techniques used in America have also been adopted in Britain's speculative house building where the opportunity exists for producers to invest in methods of production.

The use of system building in nations which implemented extensive social housing programmes, such as France and Holland, was more akin to Britain. American

236

housebuilding, however, developed very differently as a result of economic circumstances and social policies. Nevertheless, while these produced technical developments such as timber frame, the resemblance between the two continents was superficial. It is significant that there was an absence of capital intensive methods, such as pre-cast concrete. Furthermore, there was also little attempt to revolutionise building. This was noted by one North American timber frame producer, R.J. Poirer, who suggested that the European tendency to refer to the concept of industrialising building would "mystify the average North American builder".[7] This is not surprising, however, for American social policy developed on very different lines to this side of the Atlantic.

Demand and supply

A major factor in the development of system building was the perceived imbalance between demands for social housing and the ability of the industry to supply. The superimposition of enormous housing programmes at times of strained building resources undoubtedly created an imperative to find alternative methods of construction. While system building may have brought more resources to bear on housing production, it cannot be said to have realised ambitions for greater productivity.

As a result of an upswing in the post-war world economy the period covered by this book was characterised by full employment and periods of acute labour shortage. Between 1945 and 1970 unemployment in Britain stayed below 2.5 per cent.[8] The effect of this coupled with welfare building programmes was to cause building labour shortages, particularly among skilled operatives.

In Britain, for reasons which have yet to be fully accounted for, building wage rates remained low by comparison with manufacturing industry, and job security and conditions of work poor. It is likely that the low social status and casual basis of much building work and physically harsh conditions limited its appeal to a specific sector of the male working population. Therefore, the workforce was unlikely to expand even had employers been prepared to offer higher wages. The absence of female labour in building work, only beginning to change now, exacerbated difficulties in enlarging the labour force. The weakness of building unions, plagued by labour-only subcontracting and a disparate federation structure, allowed the unattractive features of building work to persevere: it was not until 1972 that national industrial action took place with the improvement of pay as one of its aims.

Under normal conditions, the comparative cheapness of British building labour was in itself little incentive to the introduction of new technology. However, under abnormal conditions of demand it also meant that building was unable to recruit labour quickly in competition with other industries. As the building industry could not meet increased building demands with traditional methods intensive in the use of skilled site labour, the tendency was for extra resources to be sought in the form of new technology. System building reduced the need for skilled site operatives by introducing unskilled non-building labour to the construction process by the off-site manufacture of components. Furthermore, in order to manufacture the equipment and plant on which system building relied, new resources were also brought to bear in the form of engineering production. In these two ways system building supplemented traditional resources and contributed to the achievement of unprecedently large housing programmes. However, contrary to the many claims made, in the absence of consistently lower prices for much of the time it must be concluded that system building was generally less productive than traditional methods in overall terms: labour may have been saved on site but it was added at other stages of production. This conclusion is supported by the government's own figures on building costs (*see* Appendix 7), and the tendency of purchasers to return to traditional methods of building when peaks subsided.

System building and the Welfare State

Limiting an account of new technology to purely economic factors produces a distorted picture which overlooks the historical circumstances from which system building emerged and the character it took on. In particular, the supply and demand model does not account for the nature of social housing, the pursuit of individual interests by participants in the state housing system, and the ideological value of mass production in policies aimed at reinforcing the social system.

238

A historical framework for system building in Britain can only be provided by examining the nature of the Welfare State. The influence which state policy brings to bear on modern society has been described by Ralph Miliband:

> More than ever before men now live in the shadow of the state. What they want to achieve, individually or in groups, now mainly depends on the state's sanction and support. . . . It is for the state's attention, or for its control, that men compete; and it is against the state that beat the waves of social conflict . . . it is possible not to be interested in what the state does; but it is not possible to be unaffected by it.[9]

It is difficult to conceive a contemporary society without a state, for this is the political culture which binds together, whether by consent or by force, different economic classes at any one time. As "the mirror which society holds itself up to", the form taken by the state is liable to change over time as classes wax and wane in power. Despite the influence of its armies, navies and police forces, history suggests that the state is only able to maintain the status quo by enlisting the consent of major classes in society: this is the purpose of social policy.

To achieve cohesion in post-war Britain, policies were pursued which became known as those of the Welfare State. For a period of time, social policy embodied the ideal that, under a modified force of capitalism, all sectors of the population should by right share more equally in the fruits of society's labour and that poverty, poor housing and ill health should be eliminated by directing public finance into housing, hospitals and schools. In its attempt to ensure the levels of material wealth necessary to achieve these aims, the Welfare State intervened in the workings of the economic system.

The ideology of a Welfare State was given material form by the myriad of statutes legislating social policy. Physical substance was given to this legislative mantle by municipal housing estates, hospitals, schools and local and central government offices of concrete, steel, glass, bricks and mortar in which most learnt and were restored to health, and in which many lived and worked. Indeed, it could be said that, at its most tangible, the Welfare State was about building.

Looking in more detail at the actions of the Welfare State it is evident that it fundamentally affected the economy as a whole, becoming in post-war years its single largest investor. Indeed, it has been suggested that the unusually rapid growth rate experienced by post-war Europe resulted largely from the consistently high demand created by welfare expenditure. According to B. Ward, it is likely that welfare policy "was a more important stabiliser of demand and stimulator of growth than monetary fiscal policy".[10] In 1960 government investment, including that of local authorities, amounted to forty per cent of gross national production (GNP). This condition was not peculiar to Britain: at least eleven capitalist economies (including the United States) had government expenditures in excess of 25 per cent of GNP, with some, such as Austria and France exceeding even Britain.[11]

Just as it emerged the major investor in the economy, the Welfare State also became the major customer of the building industry, buying in 1968 nearly half of all new work.[12] In turn, approximately half this investment was in the form of social housing. State housing was a very different market to that which had historically produced the approach to building known as general contracting. By comparison, state housing was more highly organised and commissioned on a large scale by centrally funded local authorities on the basis of nationally declared programmes. During the 1960s these programmes were guaranteed for a number of years as an element of government policy. Social housing was a highly standard-ised product, the spatial and amenity levels of which were established centrally. The degree of variation to these was limited by ministerial loan sanction and the tendency of local authorities to provide the minimum in order to increase the number of houses provided at the least burden to the ratepayer. Social housing design was further standardised with the adoption of the *Homes For Today and Tomorrow* space standards as minima in 1965.

Of fundamental importance to the development of system building was the fact that the design of social housing was not controlled by the consumer but by the makers of social housing policy. This immediately removed a potential source of resistance to new tech-niques. For the resident, housing is more than just a commodity for dispassionate consumption, despite the tendency of architects and politicians to see it this way. It is crucially significant that no attempt was made to use the more radical forms of system building in the private housing sector. Indeed, had local authority tenants possessed more control over the houses in which they lived, building technology in state housing would have developed on very different lines. For instance, it is inconceivable that some housing forms associated with system building, such as high-rise, would have occurred in the first place. In contrast to private building, social housing during this period was a more certain market typified by the large scale purchase of standardised products and amenable to centralised policy making.

The characteristics of state housing were evident in the preference many local authorities displayed for system building from the mid-1950s onwards. Initially, they resisted new methods in general needs programmes, typified as they were by conventional housing forms in comparatively low densities. In smaller quantities, this type of housing has always been well served by local builders using traditional methods. However, it was necessity that forced housing committees to take advantage of the systems offered by national contracting firms: quickly producing large quantities of acceptable, if uninspired dwellings. As housing forms became more complex in high density redevelopment schemes, local authorities relied on the technical expertise of individual sponsors, and in some cases considered their organisation and production methods superior to those of local firms. Nevertheless, while the state apparatus produced the conditions under which system building could operate, the relationship between central and local government allowed a degree of freedom in the implementation of national policies at local level. This allowed housing committees to exercise individual policies in relation to design, contract size and selection of systems, which, despite central government advice, led to the frustration of many sponsors. While more organised than traditional building, state housing in post-war Britain ultimately proved insufficiently organised and centrally controlled to make the most efficient use of capital intensive methods of house production.

System building was undoubtedly the response of large building firms to the conditions created by welfare policy. Robbed of pre-war speculative markets by state controls, building firms used new technology to make the most effective use of skilled labour resources. System building was also attractive to speculative firms, as it created the conditions under which they could invest in new technology and control the design of their products at a national scale. After the war many of these speculative firms also moved into civil engineering where new technology played an important part. Other accounts, such as P. Dunleavy's *The Politics of Mass Housing In Britain*, have tended to see system building during the 1960s as a diversification into housing by civil engineering firms.[13] However, this view neglects the *continuous* involvement of major post-war contractors in system building from the 1940s onwards. Many of these firms moved into civil engineering and system building *simultaneously* as a result of the curtailment of private housebuilding by state policy and the potential offered by new technology.

The use of system building required the sponsor to invest in methods of production for use in markets over which they had no control. However, despite this risk, the potential market in state housing was huge for the sponsor who invested in the right system and raised the possibility of the audacious firm achieving a partial monopoly of the market. This was the case with Wimpey No-Fines and was, possibly, the ambition of many other firms.

The final ingredient to the system building bonanza of the early 1960s was confidence that a market of sufficient size and of the right character existed. This was provided by the anticipation that economic growth would continue as it had for the past generation, by the establishment of large scale state housing as an enduring component of welfare policy and by the commitment of the state to the technical transformation of the building industry.

The view that central government played a significant part in the development of local authority housing policy during the post-war period is not shared by all. J.B. Cullingworth describes the government's role in policy formulation as "remarkably weak".[14] But the state did forge an intimate relationship with the industry upon which its social policy goals rested. This was symbolised by the Ministry of Works' exhibition, "The Builder and the State", held at Olympia in 1947. As Geoffrey Rippon pointed out later: "The social and economic progress of this country depends on an ever-increasing output from the building industry".[15] For this reason governments were unable to ignore the way in which buildings were constructed, creating the imperative for intervention in

242

the efficiency of the building industry. State policy was essential to the use of new technology in local authority housing in the immediate post-war years which depended on the subsidies offered. During the 1960s policy was not as effective as the government itself might have wished, but even so, the Court of Inquiry into the Collapse of Flats at Ronan Point observed that under such policies, system building "naturally blossoms".[16]

Stability in society and revolution in technology

The concentration in contemporary and subsequent accounts of system building on increased housing supply has left unexplored the part it played in Keynesian economic management policies. These policies were considered essential by the Welfare State in order to create the full employment and material prosperity which would retain the consent of all classes for the existing social structure. Furthermore, it is evident that the claims made for new technology in housing served an ideological purpose in reassuring the population that their needs could be met by the present system. In the minds of welfare politicians, the promise of a revolution in building was a potent slogan in their efforts to ensure social cohesion.

System building was intended to meet the "vast and ever increasing need for housing"[17] without endangering the stability of the economy by allowing demand to exceed the limits of supply. Were this to happen, it was expected to inflate building prices or hold back economic expansion as a whole. Fear of this was evident during the post-war stabilisation period when the War Cabinet was intent on doubling the prewar rate of house production without creating inflation in the building industry. To this end it retained the framework of wartime controls to restrain private demands at the same time as ensuring the production of temporary and permanent state housing through the use of redundant munitions factories. During the early 1950s system building was promoted as part of a policy designed to protect employment in manufacturing from demands for labour created by welfare housing policy. The larger aim in this instance was to maximise exports in order to combat the balance of payment deficit. The impact of housing policy on manufacturing industry again concerned the state during the 1960s when it feared that shortages in building labour would hold back plans for overall economic expansion. The levying of Selective Employment Tax on "service" industry and its incongruous application to building, like the policy of the early 1950s, was considered necessary to enlarge the manufacturing workforce and protect its potential labour supply from demands imposed by construction. To increase the manufacturing workforce was considered essential to produce the goods which would both pay for increased housing programmes and raise living standards. Although not appreciated at the time, the fundamental flaw in this policy was that, in the absence of significant gains in overall productivity, system building's requirement for plant and equipment used the very manufacturing labour it was supposed to protect. System building did not raise the overall productivity of construction significantly and in this sense, while it may have produced more houses, did not fulfill government economic policy in its broadest sense.

The survival of the Welfare State rested on reconciling the attempt to produce abundantly for the home market, in order to meet the demands of all classes for increased living standards, at the same time as producing enough goods for export to maintain a balance of payments equilibrium and resist the very inflationary pressures which welfare policy created. The dilemma created by attempting to meet these opposing forces engendered the hope that technology would bridge the gap between enormous demands for material goods and the economic system's capacity to produce. This hope was nowhere more evident than in the expectation held of new building methods and in particular system building. System building was the most direct application of what was understood to be mass-production to the practical reality of building houses. Housing was thought to be the remaining mass consumed commodity which had so far eluded modern methods of industrial production and organisation. What mass-production did for the automobile industry, the Ford Motor Corporation and the American economy, it was thought capable of doing for housing production. This belief in technology was particularly evident at times when the social structure was felt to be under greatest pressure; following the two World Wars, during the Great Depression and in the 1960s when Britain's declining world position became increasingly evident.

Not everyone was convinced of the proposition that buildings could be mass-produced. As early as 1919 *The*

Builder pointed out that "The economy to be attained by repetition in building is limited, and cannot be compared to that which is effected in turning out machines or domestic implements".[18] Indeed, as late at 1965 C. Pratten and R.M. Dean suggested that as a concept "mass-production" was still comparatively poorly understood despite its long existence and claimed benefits: "Economists have long written about economies of large-scale production, and every economics textbook has a section on the subject. Very few, however, give any particular quantitative notion of how important these economies are in any particular industry".[19] For the most part, system building did not cheapen housing and only increased supply by bringing more resources to bear in its production. Nevertheless, architects and politicians displayed a tendency to proselytise the application of mass production through system building, forecasting "miraculous" gains in housing output for little additional labour and dramatic reductions in cost. The fact that such evidence as there was questioned these views was ignored in the belief that the building industry stood on the verge of a revolution in the throes of which the fetters of tradition would be cast aside and practical difficulties overcome. Such beliefs were inevitably fed into government policy by ministers ideologically disposed to listening unquestioningly to briefings by Modernist technical advisors. Had they been inclined, they could easily have sought advice and listened to opposing arguments which would have dispelled the myth that buildings were anything but capable of mass-production in the normal sense, and that system building was anything but capable of "miraculous" gains in housing output.

However, this would have shaken the belief that the Welfare State could at once provide housing in abundance, manufacture sufficient consumable goods to distract its working class from fundamental inequities in the distribution of wealth, and preserve the value of its currency in a world economy. Without a belief in technical breakthrough, politicians and housing experts would have lost the substance of speeches in which they persuaded the electorate that their policies held the solution to class inequality without fundamentally changing the social structure. If anything, it was fear of revolution in society, everpresent throughout the years covered by this book, which created the imperative for system building to be promoted as the long sought after revolution in building.

REFERENCES

ABBREVIATIONS

AAS	Annual Abstract of Statistics
A&BN	Architects and Building News
AD	Architectural Design
AMA	Association of Municipal Authorities
AMC	Association of Municipal Corporations
AR	Architectural Review
AJ	Architects' Journal
BD	Building Design
BISF	British Iron and Steel Federation
BPC	British Productivity Council
BRS	Building Research Stations
BSI	British Standards Institute
C&CA	Cement and Concrete Association
CISPH	Council for the Industrial and Scientific Provision of Housing
CLASP	Consortium of Local Authorities Special Project
CMR	Centre for Modern Records, University of Warwick
CSO	Central Statistical Office
CR	Conference Report
DOE	Department of the Environment
DSIR	Department of Scientific and Industrial Research
EDC	Economic Development Committee
EPA	European Productivity Agency
GLC	Greater London Council
GRO	Gloucestershire Records Office
HCM	Housing Committee Minutes
HCP	Housing Committee Papers
H&CS	Housing and Construction Statistics
HSGB	Housing Statistics Great Britain
ICCG	Interdepartmental Component Co-ordination Group
IBSAC	Industrialised Buildings Systems and Components
ILO	International Labour Office
ISO	International Standards Organisation
JRSA	Journal of the Royal Society of Arts
LCC	London County Council
MHC BOCO	Midland Housing Consortium, Board of Chief Officers
MHLG	Ministry of Housing and Local Government
MJ	Municipal Journal

246

MOE	Ministry of Education
MOH	Ministry of Health
MOL	Ministry of Labour
MOW	Ministry of Works
MPBW	Ministry of Public Buildings and Works
MR	Municipal Review
NB	National Builder
NBA	National Building Agency
NBS	National Building Studies
NEDC	National Economic Development Council
NEDO	National Economic Development Office
NFBTE	National Federation of Building Trades Employers
NFBTO	National Federation of Building Trades Operatives
NUCUA	National Union of Conservative and Unionist Associations
OA	Official Architecture
PEP	Political and Economic Planning
PP	Parliamentary Papers
PRO	Public Records Office
PWBS	Post War Building Studies
RIAI	Royal Institute of Architects of Ireland
RIBA	Royal Institute of British Architects
RIBAJ	Royal Institute of British Architects' Journal
SCOLA BOCAM	Second Consortium of Local Authorities, Board of Chief Architects Minutes
TS	Team Spirit
UN	United Nations
WCHCM	War Cabinet Housing Committee Minutes

NOTE: To avoid repetition, only the first of consecutive quotes taken from the same source are referred to. Evidence and quotes repeatedly taken from a single source are also referred to collectively with a note at the beginning of the discussion.

INTRODUCTION

1. Reported in AJ 102 (1945), p.253.
2. E.D. Simon, *Rebuilding Britain: A Twenty Year Plan* (London, Gollancz, 1945), p.69.
3. BRS, NBS No.36 (1965).
4. MHLG, Circular 76/65 (1965).
5. PP 1918, Cmnd 1919, p.50.
6. PP, 1964–5, Cmnd 2764, p.57.
7. D. Bishop, in RIBAJ, LXXIII (1966), p.513.
8. BD, 8 Feb. 1985, p.1.

CHAPTER ONE

1. F. Engels, *The Housing Question*, C.P. Dutt (ed.), London, Martin Lawrence, 1935, Lawrence and Wishart, 1942), p.5.
2. M.C. Swenarton, *Homes Fit For Heroes* (London, Heinemann Educational, 1981), pp.1–10.
3. P. Thane, *The Foundations of the Welfare State* (London, Longman, 1982).

4. S. Merrett, *State Housing in Britain* (London, Routledge & Kegan Paul, 1979), p.31.
5. T. Carlisle, *Signs of the Times* (1829).
6. E.J. Hobsbawm, *Industry and Empire* (London, Weidenfeld & Nicolson, 1981), p.176.
7. J. Cornes, *Modern Housing in Town and Country* (London, B.T. Batsford, 1905), p.xiv.
8. W. Thompson, *The Housing Handbook Up-to-date* (London, National Housing Reform Council 1903), p.154.
9. F.W. Taylor, *The Principles of Scientific Management* (New York and London, Harper & Bros, 1911), p.15.
10. H. Ford, *My Life and Work* (London, Heinemann, 1922), p.80.
11. J. Merkle, *Management and Ideology* (Berkeley and London, University of California Press, 1980), p.244.
12. S.D.Adshead, in *Town Planning Review*, VI (1916), p.246.
13. Hansard (Commons), 5th ser. 114, Apr.7 1919, col.1791.
14. Swenarton, op.cit., p.34.
15. Merrett, op.cit., p.47.
16. PP 1918, Cmnd 9191, p.48.
17. MOH, *Standardisation and New Methods of Construction Committee: Report on the First Years Work of the Committee* (1920), p.4.
18. F.M. Lea, *Science and Building: A History of the Building Research Station* (1971), pp.35–69.
19. MOW, PWBS No.1, 1944.
20. MOH, *Committee on New Methods of House Construction Interim Report* (1924), p.4.
21. PP 1924–5, Cmnd 2392, p.16.
22. R. Miliband, *Parliamentary Socialism* (London, Merlin Press, 1973), p.148.
23. Merret, op.cit., p.320.
24. A. Maddison in C.M. Cipolla ed., *The Fontana Economic History of Europe: The Twentieth Century*, vol.2 (London, Collins, 1981), p.452.
25. J. Stevenson, *British Society 1914–45* (Harmondsworth, Penguin Books, 1984), pp.103–43.
26. G. Wersky, *The Visible College* (London, Allen Lane, 1978).
27. J.D. Bernal, *The Social Function of Science* (1939).
28. W. Gropius (1910), translation in T. and C. Benton, *Form and Function* (n.d.), p.189.
29. M. Macleod, *The Art Journal* 43 (1983), pp.132–47.
30. R.A. Brady, *The Rationalisation Movement in German Industry* (1933).
31. B. Miller Lane, *Architecture and Politics in Germany: 1914–1945* (1968), pp.87–129.
32. G. Ciucci, *Oppositions* 24 (1981), pp.87–129.
33. F.R.S. Yorke, *The Modern House* (Cheam, Architectural Press, 1934), p.168.
34. F.R.S. Yorke, *The Key to Modern Achitecture* (London and Glasgow, Blackie and Son, 1939), p.124.
35. *AD* 97 (1943), p.390.
36. CMR, transcipt of interview with H. Weston, 23 Nov. 1978.
37. CISPH, *Housing Production: 1st Report* (1943), pp.5, 11.
38. PRO HLG 37/66, CISPH, (Oct. 1943).
39. M. Fry, *Fine Building* (London, Faber & Faber, 1944), p.63.

248

CHAPTER TWO

1. PRO CAB 87/1 (RP[41]1).
2. PRO CAB 87/56 (IEP[42]65).
3. D. Fraser, op.cit., p.212.
4. PP 1943–4, Cmnd 6527, p.3.
5. PRO CAB 87/56 (IEP[42]65).
6. PRO CAB 87/3 (RP[43]24].
7. N. Rosenburg, *Economic Planning in the British Building Industry 1945–49* (1960), pp.21–38.
8. PP 1943–3, Cmnd 6428, p.2.
9. W. Churchill, in the *Listener* XXXI (1944), p.343.
10. *Hansard* (Commons), 5th ser. 402, 1 Aug. 1944, col.1255.
11. PRO CAB 66/55 (WP[44]536).
12. PRO CAB 87/6 (R[44]59th).
13. MOH, *Temporary Accommodation* (1944), p.4.
14. PRO CAB 87/9 (R[44]153).
15. PP 1944–5, Cmnd 6609, p.2.
16. Unless noted otherwise the following discussion of policy is taken from PRO CAB 87/36 (H[45] 2nd, 7th & 21st) and 87/37 (H[45]55).
17. MOH, Circular 182/45, (1945).
18. PP 1947–8, Cmnd 7279, pp.27–8.
19. MOH *The Cost of Housebuilding: First Report* (1948), p.50.
20. MOW, PWBS No.25 (1948), pp.63–73.
21. BRS, NBS No.36 (1965), pp.32–45.
22. A. Ramsay Moon, *Structural Engineer* 25 (1947).
23. R.J. Mainstone, in T.I. Williams, *A History of Technology* (Oxford, OUP, 1978), p.932.
24. PRO CAB 87/54 (IEP[41]14).
25. J. Hurstfield, *The Control of Raw Materials* (London, HMSO, 1953), p.347.
26. PRO CAB 117/43 BISF (7 Feb. 1943).
27. PRO HLG 94/6 (BC3).
28. MOW, PWBS No.25 (1948), pp.63–73.
29. PRO HLG 94/6 (BC29).
30. A.M. Gear & Ass., *The Arcon Group 1943–67 Report* (1967), p.39.
31. Arcon, *Arcon Mk.V. Prefabricated House* (1946).
32. E.G. Goldworthy, *Light Alloys in Post-War Britain* (n.d.), p.5.
33. B. Finnimore, *Construction History* 1 (1985), pp.60–72.
34. PRO CAB 124/476 Ministry of Reconstruction (5 Nov. 1947).
35. MOW, PWBS No.23 (1946), pp.46–8.
36. B. Finnimore, "The Industrialisation of Building" (PhD. thesis, University College, London, 1985), pp.92–6.
37. RIAI, *Prefabrication* (1945), p.3.
38. PRO CAB 117/95 War Cabinet Committee on Reconstruction Problems (28 Apr. 1941).
39. A. Cooke, *Letters From America 1946–51* (Harmondsworth, Penguin Books, 1981) pp.7, 8.
40. *AD* 11 (1941), p.186.
41. *The Builder* 163 (1942), p.365.
42. MOW, *Methods of Building in the USA* (1946).
43. Anglo-American Council on Productivity, *Building* (1950).

44. L.F. Urwick, *The Life and Work of F.W. Taylor* (1957).
45. A.C. Bossom, *JRSA* 93 (1944), p.23.
46. *Structural Engineer* 25 (1947), p.214–5.
47. *AD* 12 (1942), p.88.
48. *AJ* 97 (1943), p.391.
49. R. Sheppard, *Prefabrication in Building* (Architectural Press, London, 1946), p.9.
50. J. Madge, *Tomorrow's Houses* (Pilot Press, London, 1946), p.206.
51. W. Churchill, in the *Listener* XXXI (1944), p.343.
52. *Hansard* Commons, 5th ser. 398, 15 Mar. 1944, col.354.
53. *Hansard* Commons, 5th ser. 402, 1 Aug. 1944, col.1258.
54. MOH, *Housing Progress* (1948).
55. N. Vig, *Science and Technology in British Politics* (Oxford, Pergamon Press, 1968), p.13.
56. *Hansard* Commons, 5th ser. 416, 30 Nov. 1945, col.1857.
57. Association of Building Technicians, *Homes For the People* (1946), Foreword.

CHAPTER THREE

1. PRO CAB 128/17 (21[50]).
2. Rosenburg, op.cit., p.47.
3. *Hansard* Commons, 5th ser. 475, 22 May 1950, col.1718.
4. MHLG, *Houses* (1952), Foreword.
5. PRO HLG 68/110 MOH (3 Nov. 1946).
6. PRO HLG 101/371 MOH (17 Nov. 1951).
7. M. Bowley, *The British Building Industry* (Cambridge, CUP, 1966), p.203.
8. Unless noted otherwise the following case study of Coventry is taken from Coventry City Architect's Department, *Development and Redevelopment in Coventry* (1956); Coventry City HCM 11 Sep. 1941; 18 Nov. 1943; 21 Mar. 1946; 26 Aug. 1947; 28 Apr. 1949; 15 Feb. 1950; 8 Feb., 29 May, 13, 21 Sep. 1951; 19 Jun., 11 Sep., 11 Dec. 1952; 12 Nov. 1953; 8 Apr. 1954.
9. *MJ* 59 (1951), p.122.
10. Coventry City, *6,000 No-Fines Dwellings* (1958).
11. R. Isacharoff, "The Building Industry in the Interwar Years" (School of Environmental Studies, University College London, u.d.).
12. H. Richardson and D.W. Aldcroft, *Building in the British Economy Between the Wars* (1968), p.35.
13. National Federation of Registered House Builders, *Physical Reconstruction in Britain* (1944).
14. H. Beaver, *NB* 30 (1950), p.93.
15. Isacharoff, op.cit.
16. R. Coad, *Laing* (1979) and A. Jenkins, *On Site: 1921–71* (London, Heinemann, 1971).
17. C.M. Kohan, *Works and Buildings* (London, HMSO, 1952).
18. Bowley, op.cit., pp.213, 214.
19. Unless noted otherwise the case study of Laing's is taken from Coad, op.cit.; *TS* Dec. 1946, Dec. 1947, Jun. 1950, May, Jul., Nov. 1951, Dec. 1952, Jan., Nov. 1953, May, Nov., Dec. 1954, Jul., Sep., Nov. 1955, Jul. 1956, Dec. 1957, Jan. 1958, Nov. 1959, Dec. 1960.

20. MOH, *The Cost of Housebuilding 1st Report* (1948), p.57.
21. PRO HLG 102/204, Committee of Officials (12 Oct. 1948).
22. PRO CAB 130/59, Working Party (25 Apr. 1950).
23. *Hansard* (Commons) 5th ser. 475, 22 May 1950, col.1718.
24. PRO CAB 130/59, Working Party (25 Apr. 1950).
25. MOH Circular 6/48 (1948).
26. PRO CAB 128/23 (CM[20]51).
27. *Hansard* (Commons) 5th ser. 497, 4 Mar. 1952, col.190.
28. PRO CAB 128/25 (CC[70]3).
29. *Interbuild* I (Dec. 1953), p.19.
30. Unless noted otherwise the following discussion of Ministry Policy is taken from PRO HLG 101/371 MOH (17 Nov. 1951, 2, 16, 22 & 24 Jan, 5 Feb. 1952).
31. MHLG Circular 28/52 (1952).

CHAPTER FOUR

1. M. Shanks, *The Innovators* (London, Pelican Books, 1967), p.17.
2. MHLG *Homes For Today and Tomorrow* (1961).
3. PP 1961–2, Cmnd 1725, p.14.
4. AAS 101 (1964), tab.193.
5. PP 1963–4, Cmnd 2235, p.6.
6. PP 1964–5, Cmnd 2764.
7. *MJ* 62 (1954), pp.899–902.
8. *MJ* 65 (1957), p.588.
9. A. Freind, *Failed Strategies, Falling Investment* (Watts House, 1981), p.17.
10. The Civic Trust, *Industrialised Building* (London 1963), p.12.
11. HCS1 (1972), TAB.XXVII.
12. *Hansard* (Commons), 5th ser. 744, 10 Apr. 1967, co.134.
13. Unless noted otherwise the case study of the LCC is taken from LCC Housing and Public Health Committee Minutes 8 Nov. 1944; 3 Apr. 1946; LCC HCP 9 Jul. 1953; 3 Dec. 1956; 28 Jun., 14 Nov. 1961; 1 and 6 Mar., 28 Jun., 8 Sep., 1962; 15 Feb. 1965; 6 Jan. 1966.
14. *MJ* 61 (1953), p.2169.
15. R. McCutcheon, "Modern Construction Policy in Low Income Housing" (PhD. thesis, University of Sussex, 1979), p.222.
16. C.H. Walker, *Prefabrication* I (1953), p.32.
17. *NB* 26 (1947), p.284.
18. *IBSAC* I (1963), p.27.
19. *MJ* 76 (1968), p.205.
20. *IBSAC* 3 (May 1966), p.11.
21. L. Carter and J.C. Holliday, *Post War Council Housing in Coventry* (1970), p.8.
22. CRO AP/CF/1/126, City Architect (n.d. c.1959).
23. Coventry City HCP, City Architect (7 Jul. 1966).
24. CRO AP/CF/1/126, City Architect (9 Dec. 1965).
25. J.A. Maudsley, *MJ* 76 (1969), p.1289.
26. D. Bergman, in NEDO EDC For Building, *The Building Industry and the Public Client* (CR 1968), p.7.
27. *HCS* 2 (1972), tab.XII.
28. Concrete Ltd., *Bison Survey Three* (1964), p.16.

29. R. Opie in C. Feinstein, *The Managed Economy* (Oxford, OUP, 1983), p.149.
30. NEDC, *The Growth of the UK Economy to 1966* (1963), p.29.
31. G. Rippon, *RIBAJ* LXX (1963), p.373.
32. PP 1963–4, Cmnd 2228, p.3.
33. NEDC, *The Construction Industry* (1964), p.22.
34. G. Brown, *In My Way* (Harmondsworth, Penguin Books, 1971), p.87.
35. PP 1964–5, Cmnd 2764, p.57.
36. MOL, *Manpower Studies No.3* (1965), p.7.
37. P.A. Stone, in MPBW, *The Maintenance of Buildings* (CR 1965).
38. PP 1963–4, Cmnd 2279, p.13.
39. Reported in NFBTO, *Report of the Annual Conference June 1964* (CR 1964), p.26.
40. MOW, *A Survey of Problems Before the Construction Industry* (1962), p.21.
41. Reported in *Interbuild* 9 (1962), p.46.
42. PP 1963–4, Cmnd 2050, p.4.
43. *Hansard* (Commons), 5th ser. 676, 2 May 1963, col.1328.
44. MHLG, Circular 21/65 (1965).
45. PP 1963–4, Cmnd 2228, p.4.
46. T.V. Prosser, *IBSAC* 3 (May 1966), p.16.
47. *Hansard* (Commons), 5th ser. 758, 5 Feb. 1968, cols 71 and 98.
48. *OA* 31 (1968), pp.1434–47.
49. Friend, op.cit., p.19.
50. *The Economist*, 215 (1965), p.1039.
51. MHLG, Circular 21/65 (1965).
52. MHLG, Circular 76/65 (1965).
53. *NB* 47 (1966), p.576.
54. *Hansard* (Commons), 5th ser. 782, 23 Apr. 1969, col.237
55. Friend, op.cit., p.16.
56. McCutcheon, op.cit., p.215.
57. *Hansard* (Commons), 5th ser. 698, 14 Jul. 1964, cols 191–2.
58. R. Crossman, *Diaries of a Cabinet Minister*, vol.1 (London, Hamish Hamilton/Jonathan Cape, 1975), pp.90, 131.
59. *NB* 40 (1960), p.545.
60. *NB* 36 (1957), p.242, 387.
61. *AR* 120 (1956), p.25.
62. Reported in *NB* 44 (1963), p.717.
63. *Interbuild* 9 (Oct. 1962), p.9.
64. *NB* 44 (1963), p.1012.
65. P. Dunleavy, *The Politics of Mass Housing* (Oxford, Clarendon Press, 1981), pp.110–14.
66. Unless noted otherwise the following discussion of Laing's is taken from *TS* May, Jul. 1951; Jul. 1956; Jan. 1960; Sep. 1962; Apr. 1963; Jan. 1966; Jul. 1967.
67. B.L. Gosschalk, "Industrialised Building: Concrete Systems in Great Britain" (MA thesis, University of Manchester, 1970), p.17.
68. *NB* 45 (1964), p.590.
69. *IBSAC* 2 (Sep. 1965), p.46.
70. *IBSAC* 2 (Jan. 1967), p.5.
71. *IBSAC* 3 (Apr. 1966), p.5.
72. *HCS* 18 (1970), tab.24.
73. *IBSAC* 3 (Apr. 1966), p.5.
74. M. Laing, *Philosophical Transactions of the Royal Society of*

London, A.272 (London, Royal Society, 1972), p.498.

75. *Hansard* (Commons) 5th ser. 676, 2 May 1963, col.1333.
76. MPBW, *Production of Building Components in Shipyards* (1963).
77. A.M. Gear & Ass., *The Arcon Group 1943–67 Report* (1967).
78. *IBSAC* 4 (Oct. 1967), pp.7–9.
79. *Interbuild* 3 (1956), p.513.
80. A. King, in T. Williams, *A History of Technology*, Vol.VI (Oxford, Clarendon Press, 1978), p.117.
81. Q.M. Hogg, *Science and Politics* (London, Faber & Faber, 1963), p.11.
82. N. Vig, *Science and Technology in British Politics* (1968), p.37.
83. *Hansard* (Commons) 5th ser. 676, 2 May 1963, cols 327–8.
84. H. Wilson, *The Relevance of British Socialism* (London, Weidenfeld and Nicolson, 1964), pp.28, 41.
85. P. Foot, *The Politics of Harold Wilson* (Harmondsworth, Penguin Books, 1968), p.146.
86. H. Wilson, *The New Britain: Labour's Plan* (1964), pp.57.
87. *Hansard* (Commons) 5th ser. 673, 5 Mar. 1963, col.195.
88. K.J. Campbell, in CCA, *Housing From the Factory* (CR 1962), p.138.
89. A.W. Cleeve Barr, in CCA, *Housing from the Factory* (CR 1962), p.7.
90. *AAS* 105 (1968), tab.194.
91. *Interbuild* 11 (1964), p.11.
92. Cleeve Barr, op.cit., pp.3–5.
93. A.W. Cleeve Barr, "Architecture and Industrialised Building" (manuscript for a lecture, 1963).
94. Cleeve Barr, *Housing From the Factory*, op.cit., pp.3–5.
95. Reported in Civic Trust, *Industrialised Building* (CR 1963) p.19.
96. PRO HLG 101/172, MOH 1 May 1952.
97. MHLG Circular 59/63 (1963).
98. MHLG Circular 76/65 (1965).
99. R. Wilson, *AD* 37 (1967), p.158.
100. J. Carter, *RIBAJ* LXXIV (1967), p.477.
101. *MJ* 73 (1965), p.659.
102. *Hansard* (Commons) 5th ser. 715, 5 Jul. 1965, cols 1102–3.
103. MHLG Circular 21/65 1965.
104. PP 1965–6, Cmnd 2638, p.14.
105. *MJ* 75 (1967), p.1194.
106. *MJ* 72 (1964), p.2219.
107. Association of Municipal Corporations, *Annual Conference 1966* (CR 1966) pp. 31, 37, 39, 26–44, 94–105.
108. A.W. Cleeve Bar, *MR* 36 (1966), p.738.
109. MHLG Circular 76/65 (1965).
110. HCS 18 (1970), tab.24.
111. *Interbuild* 13 (Nov. 1966), p.9.
112. *MJ* 75 (1966), p.1605.
113. Reported in *IBSAC* 2 (Dec. 1965), p.20.
114. *TS* Apr. 1963, Jan. 1966, Jul. 1967.
115. *AJ* 147 (1968), p.86.
116. *IBSAC* 4 (Jan. 1966), p.5.
117. L.W. Madden, *IBSAC* 4 (1967), pp.21, 115.
118. *Building* 212, (7 Apr. 1967) p.174, (14 Apr. 1967) p.173, (28 Apr. 1967) p.133; 213 (27 Oct. 1967), p.127, (24 Nov. 1967), p.216.

119. *Building* 213 (17 Mar. 1967) p.176.
120. *TS* (Jul. 1965), p.8.
121. Gosschalk, op.cit., p.55.
122. *NB* 47 (1966), p.123.
123. NEDC, *Productivity Prices and Incomes* (1967), p.2.
124. *NB* 50 (1969), p.20.
125. *Building* 231 (10 Sep. 1976), p.74.
126. *Hansard* (Commons) 5th ser. 795, 16 Feb. 1970, col.50.
127. *Hansard* (Commons) 5th ser. 934, 13 Jun. 1977, col.65.
128. S. Lyle, *BD* (10 Jun. 1977), p.10.

CHAPTER FIVE

1. MOH, *Committee on New Methods of House Construction Interim Report* (1924), p.4.
2. PP 1924–5 Cmnd 2392.
3. CMR MSS 78/BO/4/5/19, R. Coppock (1944).
4. NFBTO, *Annual Conference 1945* (CR 1945), pp.71–4, 122.
5. PRO CAB 134/320, Minister of Labour and National Services (26 Mar. 1946).
6. R. Fitzmaurice, *RIBAJ* LIV (1947), p.310.
7. NFBTO, *Annual Conference 1950* (CR 1950), pp.157–8.
8. MOW, *Payment By Results in Building and Civil Engineering During the War* (1947), pp.1, 16.
9. L.W. Wood, *A Union to Build* (1979), p.71.
10. T. Marsh, *Master Builder's Journal* 12 (Jun. 1967), p.23.
11. NFBTO, *Annual Conference 1962* (CR 1962), pp.44, 119.
12. NFBTO, *Annual Conference 1966* (CR 1966), p.97.
13. CMR MSS 78/BO/1/1/112–197, NFBTO Executive Committee Minutes, (3 Jul. 1962).
14. CMR MSS 78/ASW/3/2/131, Amalgamated Society of Woodworkers, (10 Apr. 1963, 7 Apr. 1964).
15. CMR MSS 78/BO/1/2/23–45, NFBTO General Council Minutes, (21 Mar. 1963).
16. The following discussion is taken from NFBTO, *New Techniques in the Building Trades* (CR 1959).
17. BRS, *Building Operatives' Work* (1966), p.51.
18. NFBTO, *Annual Conference 1963* (CR 1963), p.52.
19. NFBTO, *Minutes of a Conference on New Techniques* (CR 1964), pp.3–4.
20. Amalgamated Union of Building Trades Workers, *National Delegates Conference 1963* (CR 1963), pp.98–9.
21. NFBTO, *Minutes of a Conference on New Techniques* (CR 1964), pp.19–21.
22. NFBTO, *Annual Conference 1966*, (CR 1966), p.114.
23. Reported in *RIBAJ* LI (1944), p.169.
24. PRO HLG 37/66, RIBA (Aug. 1943).
25. *AD* 13 (1943), p.242.
26. PRO WORKS 45/24, R. Stradling (11 Nov. 1940).
27. P. Malpass, *RIBAJ* LXXXII (1975), pp.9–10.
28. Reported in *RIBAJ* XLIII (1936), p.9.
29. Leader, *AD* 14 (1944), p.49.
30. M. Pawley, *New Society* 17 (1971), p.719.
31. Anon., *The Economist* CLXVIII (1953), p.241.

32. R. Banham, *New Statesman and Nation* 61 (1961), p.26.
33. RIBA, *The Architect and His Office* (1962), p.173.
34. Reported in *RIBAJ* LXX (1963), p.359.
35. RIBA, *The Industrialisation of Building* (1965), p.9.

CHAPTER SIX

1. Reported in *RIBAJ* LXII (1954), p.4.
2. H. Emmerson, *The Ministry of Works* (1956), p.13.
3. PRO CAB 87/37, Prime Minister (15 Aug. 1945).
4. PRO WORKS 45/24, Chief Scientific Advisor (11 Nov. 1940).
5. J.D. Bernal, *RIBAJ* LIII (1946), pp.236–8.
6. MOW, *Production in Building and Civil Engineering* (1945).
7. *Hansard* (Commons) 5th ser. 396, 2 Feb. 1944, col.1258.
8. MOW, *Demonstration Houses* (1944).
9. PRO CAB 87/6 (R.[44]59th).
10. PRO CAB 87/36 (H.[45]20th).
11. E. Neel, *AD* (1944), p.130.
12. PRO CAB 87/37 (H.[45]2).
13. PRO HLG 101/54, Bernal Committee, (Dec. 1945).
14. PRO CAB 87/36 (H.[45]18th).
15. Coventry City HCM (30 Mar. 1945).
16. A.W. Cleeve Barr, *Local Authority Housing* (1958), p.119.
17. PRO 94/7, DSIR, (u.d. C.1943).
18. MOW, NBS Special Report No.4 (1948), p.13.
19. J.C. Weston, *RIBAJ* LXVII (1960), p.124.
20. MOW, PWBS No.2, (1944), p.2.
21. MOE, Circular 191, (1948).
22. PRO ED 150/43, MOE, (13 Apr. 1950).
23. A. Saint, *Towards a Social Architecture*, (London and New Haven, Yale University Press, 1987).
24. MOE, *The Story of Postwar School Building* (1957), App.II.
25. MOE, Building Bulletin No.6 (1953).
26. MOE, *Report of the First Technical Working Party on School Construction* (1948).
27. MOE, *The Story of Postwar School Building*, p.25.
28. PRO HLG 68/129, Cabinet Building Committee (31 May 1952).
29. R. Walters, *RIBAJ* (1961), p.274.
30. W.D. Pile, *AJ* 129 (1959), pp.578–9.
31. G. Hodgkinson, *Sent to Coventry* (London, Maxwell, 1970), p.172.
32. D.E.E. Gibson, *RIBAJ* LVI (1947), p.405.
33. PRO EDU 154/193, MOE (u.d.).
34. *Hansard* (Commons) 5th ser. 673, 5 Mar. 1963, cols 187–8.
35. PP 1963–4, Cmnd 2233, p.22.
36. Reported in *MJ* 67 (1959), p.69.
37. Cleeve Barr, *Built Environment* 2 (1973), p.12.
38. Cleeve Barr, *Local Authority Housing* (1958), p.21.
39. E. Sharp, *The Ministry of Housing and Local Government* (1969), pp.82–100, 208–19.
40. D.E.E. Gibson, *The Builder* 200 (1961), p.1242.
41. C.H. Aslin, *RIBAJ* LVIII (1950), p.12.
42. D.E.E. Gibson, *The Builder* 200 (1961), p.1244; *Prefabrication and New Building Technique* 5 (1957), p.80.

43. MOH, *Second report of the Committee on the Standardisation and Simplification of the Requirements of Local Authorities* (1935), p.2.
44. H. Swain, *AJ* 131 (1960), p.131.
45. *AJ* 94 (1941), p.59.
46. A. Saint, *Towards a Social Architecture* (London and New Haven, Yale University Press, 1987), pp.58–112.
47. *AR* 136 (1964), p.384.
48. Coventry HCM (7 Dec. 1961, 12 Jul. 1962, 2 Dec. 1963).
49. D.R. Polding in RIBA/NBA, *Industrialised Housing and the Architect* (CR 1967), p.9.
50. MHLG & DOE, *Housing Groups and Consortia* 3, 4, 5, 6, 7 (1968, 1969, 1970, 1971, 1972).
51. *Hansard* (Commons) 5th ser. 810, 25 Jan. 1971, cols 27–8.
52. B. Kelley, *The Prefabrication of Houses* (1951), p.24.
53. MOW, *The Use of Standards in Building: First Report of the Standards Committee* (1944), p.1.
54. PRO HLG 94/1, Building Research Station, Feb. 1943.
55. D. Dex Harrison in J. Madge, *Tomorrow's Houses* (1946) p.132.
56. PRO HLG 101/54, Bernal Committee, Dec. 1945.
57. D. Dex Harrison, *An Introduction to Standards* (1947), p.83.
58. MOE, *Report of the First Technical Working Party on School Construction* (1948), p.iii.
59. ILO, *Social Aspects of Prefabrication in the Construction Industry* (1968), p.91.
60. *Hansard* (Commons) 5th ser. 659, 15 May 1962, col.119.
61. *Hansard* (Commons) 5th ser. 686, 17 Dec 1963, col.1015.
62. MPBW, *Industrialised Building: 5M Housing for the Army at Catterick Camp* (1968).
63. MHLG, *AD* 36 (1966), pp.380–92.
64. R. Walters & I. Iredale, *RIBAJ* (1964), p.273.
65. *AJ* 147 (1968), p.86.
66. *Interbuild* 13 (Apr. 1966), p.31.
67. *Interbuild* 13 (May 1966), p.20.
68. *IBSAC* 3 (Aug. 1966), p.48.
69. P. Tindale, *RIBAJ* LXXVI (1969, pp.112–114.
70. *Hansard* (Commons) 5th ser. 732, 21 Jul. 1966, col.131.
71. G.H. Wigglesworth, *RIBAJ* LXXIII (1966), p.265–72.
72. GRO K568/1/3, SCOLA BOCAM, 4 Jul. 1967, 25 Jan. 1968, 24 Oct. 1968, 5 Dec. 1968, 27 Mar. 1969.
73. GRO K568/1/3, SCOLA Chief Architects Quarterly Meeting Minutes, 30 Oct. 1969.
74. P. Tindale, *RIBAJ* LXXVI (1969), p.114.
75. NBA, *Official Architect* 31 (1968), pp.1449–50.
76. NBA, *Metric House Shells* (1969).
77. *IBSAC* 5 (May 1968), p.5.
78. MHLG, Circular 69/69 (1969).
79. Concrete Ltd., *The Function of I.B.* (Bison Bulletin No.1., u.d. probably 1964), p.5.
80. *AJ* 140 (1964), pp.661, 666, 786, 1039, 1290.
81. Unless noted otherwise the following discussion is taken from *The Builder, Consortia* (1964).
82. L. Hellman, *RIBAJ* LXXX (1973), p.397.
83. *JRSA* 114 (1966), p.570.
84. PRO HLG 102/204, Report of a Committee of Officials (12 Oct. 1948).

85. *Building* 211 (Dec. 1966), p. 103.
86. V. Cox, *RIBAJ* LXXX (1973), p.xvi.
87. MOE, *Wokingham School*, p.5.
88. I.M. Lesley, *Bison Survey 3* (n.d. c.1964), p.9.
89. *Hansard* (Commons) 5th ser. 715, 5 Jul. 1965, cols 1102–3.
90. *Building* 211 (1966), p.75.
90. *Building* 212 (1967), p.113.
92. K.W. Pepper in BRS, *Golden Jubilee Congress* (1972), p.359.

CHAPTER SEVEN

1. J. Cornes, *Modern Housing in Town and Country* (1905), p.184.
2. M. Bowley, *Innovations in Building Materials* (London, Duckworth, 1960), pp.205–55.
3. MOH, *Construction of Flats for the Working Classes: Final Report of the Departmental Committee* (1937), p.6.
4. NB 25 (1945), p.15.
5. MOW, PWBS No. 25 (1948), p.64.
6. MOH, *The Cost of Housebuilding: First Report* (1948), p.50.
7. MOW, NBS Special Report No.4 (1948), p.7.
8. PRO HLG 101/371, MOH (u.d. c.1952).
9. W.E. Reed in CCA, *Housing From the Factory* (CR 1962), pp.80–6.
10. *Hansard* (Commons) 5th ser. 546, 17 Nov. 1955, col. 796.
11. P. Dunleavy, *The Politics of Mass Housing in Britain 1945–75* (Oxford, Clarendon Press, 1981).
12. P.A. Stone, *Urban Development in Britain* (London, CUP, 1970), p.150.
13. BPC, *A Review of Productivity in the Building Industry* (1954), p.26.
14. *Prefabrication*, 3 (1956), p.207.
15. W.J. Reiners and D. Bishop, *Builder* 204 (1962), p.880.
16. Concrete Ltd., *Bison Survey 62* (n.d. c.1962), *Bison Survey 3* (u.d. c.1965).
17. *The Economist* 215 (1965), p.1040.
18. R. Camus in CCA, *Housing From the Factory* (CR 1962), p.12.
19. J. Langrishe, *Wealth From Knowledge* (1972), p.194.
20. *IBSAC* 1 (Jan. 1964), pp.35–6.
21. *IBSAC* 2 (Sep. 1965), p.46.
22. B.L. Gosschalk, "Industrialised Building" (unpublished MA thesis, University of Manchester, 1970), p.95.
23. N. Wakefield, *IBSAC* 6 (Apr. 1969), p.74.
24. BRS, *Golden Jubilee Congress* (1962), p.166.
25. MHC BOCO, "10th Report to Elected Representatives", July 1968.
26. *IBSAC* 6 (Jul. 1969), p.43.
27. I. Fraser in RIBA/NBA, *Industrialised Housing and the Architect* (CR 1967), pp.8–12.
28. K.M. Wood in CCA, *Housing From the Factory* (CR 1962).
29. D. Embling and J. Marlow, *IBSAC* 1 (Jan. 1964), p.10.
30. *Hansard* (Commons) 5th ser. 722, 15 Dec. 1965, cols 1285–90.
31. MHLG, Circular 36/67 (1967).
32. HSGB 19 (1970), tab.10; HCS 14 (1975), tab.XXIII.
33. *Builder* 209 (1966), p.133.

34. Dunleavy, op.cit., pp.293–4.
35. *AD* 96 (1942), p.107.
36. Uni-Seco Structures Ltd., *Postwar Housing* (1944).
37. Timber Development Association, *Timber Supplies and the Housing Programme* (1947).
38. PRO HLG 94/8, Interdepartmental Committee on House Construction Minutes (27 Sept. 1945).
39. Uni-Seco Structures Ltd, *Design in Seco* (u.d., c.1948).
40. P.O Reece, *RIBAJ* LXI (1953), p.64.
41. J.L. Berbiers, *MJ* 65 (1957), p.2653.
42. *MJ* 65 (1957), p.2659.
43. R.C. Purdew in RIBA/NBA, *Industrialised Housing and the Architect* (CR 1967).
44. *IBSAC* 2 (May 1965), p.30; (Dec. 1965), p.16.
45. *IBSAC* 1 (Jan. 1964), p.55.
46. R.E. Diamante, *A&BN* 219 (1966), pp.445–7.
47. *MJ* 76 (1968), p.2618.
48. *IBSAC* & (Jan. 1967), p.54.
49. A. Cullen, in *Proceedings of the Third Bartlett Summer School: 1981* (CR 1982), pp.4–12.
50. *IBSAC* 5 (Jun. 1968), p.51.
51. MOW, PWBS No.25, pp.63–73.
52. MOH, *Second Interim Report of the Committee on New Methods of House Construction* (1925), p.4.
53. K. Hajnal-Kony in J. Madge, *Tomorrow's Houses* (1946), p.197.
54. PRO HLG 101/371, MHLG (u.d. c.1952).
55. Gosschalk, thesis, p.121.
56. C.H. Walker, *Prefabrication* 1 (1953), p.34.
57. Coventry City HCM (26 Oct. 1953).
58. PRO HLG 101/371, MHLG (4 Feb, 1952).
59. MOW, NBS Special Report No.4 (1948), p.3.
60. Reported in *IBSAC* 5 (Jun. 1968), p.51.
61. PRO HLG 101/172, MHLG (1 May 1952).
62. *MJ* 61 (1953), pp. 889–900.
63. *AR* 120 (1956), p.25.
64. RIBA *The Industrialisation of Building* (1965), p.34.
65. *Hansard* (Commons), 5th ser. 830, 1 Feb. 1972, col.92.
66. NBA, *Productivity in Housing and Construction* (1976), p.7.
67. *IBSAC* 1 (May 1964), p.12.
68. P.A. Stone, *Building Economy* (Oxford, Pergamon Press, 1976), p.105.
69. R.B. White, *Prefabrication* (London, HMSO, 1965), p.46.
70. D. Bishop, *Chartered Surveyor* 99 (1966), p.196.
71. H. Hobhouse, *Thomas Cubitt Master Builder* (London, Macmillan, 1971), p.283.
72. R. Hill, in *Proceedings of the First Bartlett Summer School 1979* (CR 1980), pp. 126–9.
73. PRO HLG 102/204, MOH (12 Oct. 1948).
74. G. MacClean, *Interbuild* 1 (1954), p.36.
75. D. Bishop in CCA, *Housing From the Factory* (CR 1962), pp.68–71.
76. Reported in *IBSAC* 2 (May 1965), p.7.
77. *NB* 42 (1966), p.767.
78. D.V. Donnison, *The Government of Housing* (Harmondsworth, Penguin Books, 1967), p.146.

79. MOW, NBS Special Report No.4 (1948), p.7.
80. D. Bishop, *The Builder* 206 (1964), p.134.
81. PP 1967–8, Cmnd 3714, p.176.
82. NBA, *Industrialised Two-Storey Housing* (1970), p.5.
83. Anthony Williams and Partners, *Building* 239 (Aug. 1980), pp.27–34.
84. D.W. Cheetham in IAHS, *Cairo Workshop on Evaluation of Industrialised Housing Systems* (CR 1976), pp.11–17.

CHAPTER EIGHT

1. C. Culpin in RIBA/NBA, *Industrialised Housing and the Architect* (CR 1967), p.5.
2. LCC HCP, Architect to Council (15 Feb. 1965).
3. PRO HLG 101/54, J. Emberton (Dec. 1945).
4. Reported in *RIBAJ* LI (194), p.163.
5. PP 1918 Cmnd 1919, p.36.
6. S. Pepper and M. Swenarton, *AR* 168 (1980), pp.87–91.
7. S.D. Adshead, *Town Planning Review* VI (1916) p.245.
8. M. Swenarton, *Homes Fit for Heroes* (London, Heinemann Educational, 1981), p.146.
9. MOH, *Housing Manual* (1927), pp.3–4.
10. W.C. Behrendt, *Modern Building* (1937), p.202.
11. H.R.H. Hitchcock and P. Johnson, *The International Style* (New York, W.W. Norton & Co, 1932).
12. J.M. Richards, *An Introduction to Modern Architecture* (Harmondsworth, Penguin Books, 1940), p.34.
13. B. Taut, *Modern Architecture* (London, The Studio, 1929), p.9.
14. MOW, *A Survey of Prefabrication* (1945), p.14.
15. R. Banham, *AR* 118 (1955), p.855.
16. B. Honikman, *Official Architecture* 28 (1965), p.1299.
17. Miall Rhys Davis, *Bison Survey IV* (n.d., c.1965), p.21.
18. A.W. Cleeve Barr in CCA *Housing From the Factory* (CR, 1962), p.2.
19. MHLG, Circular 76/65 (1965).
20. K. Frampton, *Modern Architecture* (London, Thames & Hudson, 1980), p.273.
21. R. Banham, *AR* 118 (1955), p.855.
22. K.J. Campbell, *The Builder* 203 (1962), p.1040.
23. J. Whittle, *Housing From the Factory* (CR, 1962).
24. K.J. Campbell, *The Builder* 203 (1962), p.1040.
25. Reported in *RIBAJ* LI (1944), p.169.
26. Department of Health for Scotland, *Design and Workmanship in Non-Traditional Houses* (1951), p.27.
27. PRO HLG 101/371 C.H.H. Smith (17 Nov. 1951 and 5 Feb. 1952).
28. F.B. Pooley, *RIBAJ* LXXV (1968), p.106.
29. F.B. Pooley, *MJ* 61 (1953), pp.2236–8.
30. F.B. Pooley, *RIBAJ* LXXV (1968), p.106.
31. *AJ* 136 (1962), p.147.
32. MPBW, *Industrialised Building: 5M Housing For the Army at Catterick Camp* (1968), p.4.
33. *AJ* 147 (1968), p.97.
34. *AJ* 145 (1967), p.808.
35. Reported in *The Builder* 204 (1963), p.655.

36. GLC, *GLC Architecture 1965–70* (1970), pp.16–20.
37. H. Bennett, *IBSAC* (May 1966), pp.13–14.
38. A. Pike, *AD* 39 (1969), p.602.
39. *MJ* 74 (1966), p.3913.
40. GLC HCP Architect to Council (29 Oct. 1965).
41. *MJ* 76 (1966), p.1296.
41. *MJ* 77 (1969), p.1360.
43. Reported in *IBSAC* 5 (1968), p.74.
44. M. Pawley, *New Society* 17 (1971), p.718.
45. E. Maxwell Fry, *RIBAJ* LXXIV (1967), p.333.
46. R. Banham, *New Society* (Apr. 1971), p.595.
47. Reported in *RIBAJ* LXXVI (1969), p.462.
48. J.B. Drew, *MJ* 77 (1969), p.2827.
49. A.W. Cleeve Barr, *MJ* 77 (1969), p.2829.
50. *AJ* 160 (1974), pp.101–114.
51. L. Hellman, *RIBAJ* LXXX (1973), p.397.
52. L. Hellman, *Built Environment* 2 (1973), p.32.
53. *RIBAJ* LXXX (1973), p.371.
54. L. Hellman, *RIBAJ* LXXX (1973), p.397.
55. *Building* 226 (1974), p.774.
56. *AJ* 159 (1974), p.774.
57. Reported in *AR* 127 (1960), p.383.
58. K.J. Campbell, *Bison Survey II* (u.d., c.1963), p.23.

CONCLUSION

1. R Walters in UN ECE *Proceedings of the Seminar on Changes in the Structure of the Building Industry Necessary to Improve its Efficiency and to Increase its Output* (CR 1965), p.134.
2. D.V. Donnison, *The Government of Housing* (Harmondsworth, Penguin Books, 1967), p.294.
3. *NB* 43 (1962), p.728.
4. *IBSAC* 3 (1966), p.129.
5. A.F. Bemis, *The Prefabrication of Houses* (1951), p.50.
6. MHLG, *Housebuilding in the USA* (1966), p. 12.
7. R.J. Poirer, *IBSAC* 2 (1965), p.61.
8. A.J. Youngson in C.M. Cipolla, *The Fontana Economic History of Europe: Contemporary Economies*, Vol.1 (Glasgow and London, Collins, 1980), p.160.
9. R. Miliband, *The State in Capitalist Society* (London, Weidenfeld & Nicolson, 1973), p.3.
10. B. Ward in C.M. Cippolla, *The Fontana Economic History of Europe: The Twentieth Century*, Vol.2 (Glasgow and London, Collins, 1976), p.723.
11. E. Hobsbawm, *Industry and Empire* (1981), p.247.
12. *Hansard* (Commons), 5th ser. 761, 18 Mar. 1968, cols 43–4.
13. P. Dunleavy, *The Politics of Mass Housing in Britain: 1945–75* (Oxford, Clarendon Press, 1981).
14. J.B. Cullingworth, *Housing and Local Government* (1966), p.61.
15. Reported in NFBTO, *Annual Conference 1963* (CR 1963), p.26.
16. MHLG, *The Collapse of Flats at Ronan Point* (1968), p.57.
17. PP 1964–5, Cmnd 2764.
18. *The Builder* CXIV (1918), p.5.
19. C. Pratten and R.M. Dean, *The Economics of Large Scale Production in British Industry* (1965), p.9.

APPENDIX 1

Houses Completed in England and Wales by Type of Agency 1924–81

	Permanent Local Authority	Permanent Private Enterprise	Permanent Others	Temporary Local Authority	TOTAL
1924–28*	59,739	127,539**			187,278
1929–33*	59,923	150,837**			210,760
1934–38*	69,081	264,915**			333,996
1945***	508	937	nil	8,939	10,384
1946	21,202	29,720	168	70,931	122,021
1947	86,576	39,626	1,348	34,351	161,892
1948	170,821	31,210	4,374	10,746	217,151
1949	141,766	24,688	5,326	3	171,783
1950	139,356	26,576	6,428		172,360
1951	141,587	21,406	8,190		171,903
1952	165,637	32,878	11,260		208,975
1953	202,891	60,528	15,812		279,231
1954	199,642	88,028	21,282		308,952
1955	162,525	109,934	10,867		283,326
1956	139,977	119,585	9,162		268,724
1957	137,584	122,942	8,127		268,653
1958	113,146	124,087	4,292		241,525
1959	99,456	146,476	3,449		249,381
1960	103,235	162,100	3,891		269,226
1961	92,880	170,366	5,586		268,832
1962	105,302	167,016	6,349		278,667
1963	97,015	168,242	5,398		270,655
1964	119,468	210,432	6,605		336,505
1965	133,024	206,246	7,911		347,181
1966	142,430	197,502	9,548		349,480
1967	159,347	192,940	10,611		362,898
1968	148,049	213,273	10,404		371,726
1969	139,850	173,377	10,938		324,165
1970	134,874	162,084	10,308		307,266
1971	117,215	179,998	12,563		309,776
1972	93,635	184,622	9,037		287,294
1973	79,289	174,413	10,345		264,047
1974	99,423	129,626	12,124		241,173
1975	122,857	140,381	15,456		278,694
1976	124,152	138,477	16,031		278,660
1977	121,246	128,688	26,077		276,011
1978	96,752	134,578	22,671		254,001
1979	77,192	125,306	18,224		220,722
1980	78,405	114,377	20,175		212,957
1981	58,933	103,156	17,398		179,487

Notes:
*averages; ** includes any not built by local authorities; *** April to December
Source: CSO, *AAS* (1952, 1960 & 1983)

APPENDIX 2

Houses Completed in Building Systems by Local Authorities and New Towns in England and Wales 1946–79

	A Completions total	B Completions systems	C Completions systems %tage	D In tender systems	E In tender systems %tage
1946	21202	2767	13.0		
1947	86576	20452	23.6		
1948	170821	52759	30.8		
1949	141766	34279	24.1		
1950	139356	20640	14.8		
1951	141587	20178	14.2		
1952	165637	26365	15.9		
1953	202891	41662	20.5		
1954	199642	52119	26.1		
1955	162525	34033	20.9		
1956*	139977	29000	20.0		
1957*	137584	29000	20.0		
1958*	113148	27000	18.0		
1959*	99456	17000	17.0		
1960*	103235	15000	15.0		
1961*	92880	14000	15.0		
1962*	105302	15000	15.0		
1963*	97015	14000	15.0		
1964	119468	17171	14.4	30047	21.0
1965	133024	25527	19.2	46564	29.1
1966	142430	37494	26.3	65481	38.3
1967	159347	49049	30.8	71465	42.6
1968	148049	50569	34.2	59574	39.4
1969	139850	53150	30.0	34766	30.1
1970	134874	55701	41.3	19382	19.4
1971	117215	38314	32.7	19320	20.6
1972	93635	24557	26.2	16243	21.0
1973	79289	17660	22.3	22430	24.4
1974	99423	24536	24.7	23067	19.1
1975	122857	25792	21.0	22970	17.5
1976	124152	23780	19.6	14863	12.1
1977	121246	19697	16.2	4153	5.5
1978	96752	10313	10.7	3243	4.5
1979	77192	4566	6.3	1214	3.1

Notes:
Col. A is taken from the *AAS*; Col. B up to 1955 from *Housing Returns for England and Wales* and from 1964 from *HSGB* and *H&CS*; Col. C up to 1955 is computed from cols. A&B and from 1964 is taken from *HSGB* and *H&CS*; Cols. D&E are taken from *HSGB & H&CS*. For years marked with an asterisk official statistics for completions by systems were not compiled; the figures in column B&C for these years represent estimates made by the MPBW presented to Parliament, *Hansard* (Commons)

Sources: CSP *AAS* (1952, 1960 and 1983)
MOH *Housing Returns for England and Wales* (1946–55)
Hansard (Commons), 5th ser. 735, Nov. 1 1966, Cols. 235–7
MHLG, *HSGB* (1964–70)
DOE *H&CS* (1970–80)

APPENDIX 3

Percentage of Houses Completed in Building systems by Local Authorities in England and Wales by Region 1945–54 and Percentage of Houses Started in Building Systems by Local Authorities in England and Wales by Region 1965–79

	A 1945–end 1954	B 1965–end 1969	C 1970–end 1979
Northern	13.75		
North West	14.50		
East & West Ridings	22.00		
North Midlands	24.80		
Midlands	23.50		
Eastern	13.80		
Southern	21.60		
South East	9.50		
South Western	46.70		
London	8.50		
Wales	32.20		
North		27.7	9.8
North West		40.6	21.0
Yorks & Humberside		37.1	11.7
West Midlands		46.9	24.9
East Midlands		35.4	24.4
East Anglia		9.8	12.3
South East (excluding London)		28.2	18.0
South West		17.9	6.5
Greater London		38.6	12.3
Wales		32.8	16.0

Notes:
Col. A is taken from *Housing Returns for England and Wales*; Cols. B&C from *HSGB* and *H&CS*
Sources: MOH *Housing Returns for England and Wales* (1946–55)
 MHLG, *HSGB* (1964–70)
 DOE *H&CS* (1970–79)

APPENDIX 4

Houses Completed in Building Systems in England and Wales by Individual Systems 1946–55

System	1946	1947	1948	1949	1950	1951	1952	1953	1954	1955	
PCC 4 Airey	168	612	7815	18643	21259	22161	23012	23963	25431	25991	RT
		444	7203	10828	2616	902	851	951	1468	560	YT
ALU 7 Aluminium	nl	138	9340	13461	14749	16785	nl	nl	nl	nl	RT
			9202	4121	1288	2036					YT
S/F 3 BISF	94	13045	29828	31046	31120	31320	nl	nl	nl	nl	RT
		12951	16783	1218	74	200					YT
PCC 23 British Steel Construction	16	138	360	716	1234	1730	2682	2886	3636	4317	RT
		122	222	356	518	496	952	204	750	681	YT
PCC 5 Cornish Unit	nl	80	573	2416	4833	7693	11242	16226	22024	25601	RT
			493	1843	2417	2860	3549	4984	5798	3577	YT
S/F 20 Cussins	20	185	864	1196	1259	1347	nl	nl	nl	nl	RT
		165	679	332	63	88					YT
I/S 27 Dyke Clothed Concrete Construction	—	—	—	236	396	nl	nl	nl	nl	nl	RT
					160						YT
I/S 2 Easiform	717	2650	7411	11523	15917	20602	26208	33133	41433	47820	RT
		1933	4761	4112	4394	4685	5606	6925	8300	6387	YT
S/F 25 Hill	16	125	449	649	nl	nl	nl	nl	nl	nl	RT
		109	324	200							YT
S/F 19 Howard	458	1225	1404	1404	nl	nl	nl	nl	nl	nl	RT
		767	179	—							YT
COM 26 Kingston	nl	nl	nl	nl	nl	nl	102	202	244	402	RT
								100	42	158	YT
T/F Lamella	6	50	183	nl	nl	nl	nl	nl	nl	nl	RT
		44	133								YT
S/F 16 LC System	—	—	122	760	1610	2000	2004	2296	2668	2856	RT
				638	850	390	4	292	372	188	YT
COM 18 Newland (inc. Tarran for 47)	nl	47	1250	2122	2329	2391	nl	nl	nl	nl	RT
			1203	872	207	62					YT
PCC 10 Orlit	109	778	3720	6287	7230	7377	7495	7772	8424	8524	RT
		669	2942	2567	943	147	118	277	652	100	YT
PCC 9 Reema	nl	nl	nl	392	800	1510	2428	3810	6539	8608	RT
					408	710	918	1382	2729	2069	YT
T/F 22 Scottwood	nl	nl	nl	nl	nl	600	732	924	1029	1135	RT
							132	192	105	106	YT
T/F 14 Spooner	nl	124	579	909	1352	1450	1773	2412	3067	3920	RT
			455	330	443	98	323	639	655	853	YT
S/F 29 Steane	—	—	14	91	136	nl	nl	nl	nl	nl	RT
				76	45						YT
PCC 21 Stent	nl	nl	nl	nl	2	930	1197	1253	1253	1253	RT
						928	267	56	—		YT
T/F 17 Swedish	809	2122	2408	2420	2420	2444	nl	nl	nl	nl	RT
		1313	286	12	—	24					YT

264

System	1946	1947	1948	1949	1950	1951	1952	1953	1954	1955	
S/F 15 Trusteel	2	62	764	1149	1190	1222	1720	2290	2707	3392	RT
		60	702	385	41	32	498	570	417	685	YT
I/S 24 Unit No-Fines	nl	nl	nl	nl	nl	650	1407	1981	3282	4310	RT
							757	574	1301	1028	YT
COM 8 Unity	2	107	838	1766	2619	3677	5069	8679	12808	15573	RT
		105	731	928	853	1058	1392	3610	4129	2765	YT
PCC 6 Wates	60	409	2495	4329	5628	6764	9159	12759	18063	19831	RT
		349	2086	1834	1299	1136	2395	3600	5304	1768	YT
I/S 1 Wimpey No-Fines	58	371	2923	4254	7177	10966	18284	33348	50538	61197	RT
		313	2552	1331	2923	3789	7318	15064	17190	10659	YT
PCC 11 Woolaway	10	96	419	824	1013	1444	2282	3369	4396	5336	RT
		86	323	405	189	431	838	1087	1027	940	YT
Others	224	857	2221	3666	6628	6014	60980	61801	63681	65190	RT
TOTAL	2767	23221	75980	110259	130899	151077	177442	219104	271223	305256	RT
		20452	52759	34279	20640	20178	26365	41662	52119	34033	YT

Notes:
Housing Returns for England and Wales list completions in running totals, and only list systems individually for the periods in which they were most frequently used. If not listed individually, a system's completions are included in "others". If a system is not listed to the end of the period, the last figure represents the total completions to that date and does not necessarily represent an absolute total. An attempt has been made to extract yearly totals, but in many cases these can only be computed for a limited number of years. The number preceding the name of the system refers to its ranking in total production over the period covered.
Key:

RT	running total	COM	composite steel and concrete structure
YT	yearly total	I/S	in situ concrete
nl	system not listed separately for this year	PCC	precast concrete structure
—	no completions for this year	S/F	steel frame
ALU	aluminium structure and cladding	T/F	timber frame

Source: MOH, *Housing Returns for England and Wales* (1946–56)

APPENDIX 5

Houses Completed in Building Systems in England and Wales by Individual Systems 1946–79

	1964	1965	1966	1967	1968	1969	1970	1971	1972	1973	1974	1975	1976	1977	1978	1979	TOTAL
The Amey Chivers Housing Co. Ltd, Modus PCC L	nl	nl	nl	32	—	65	46	125	10	nl	nl	nl	nl	nl	nl	nl	278
Anvil Enterprises Ltd, Anvil T/F PCC L	nl	nl	nl	nl	nl	nl	nl	nl	nl	nl	nl	167	287	347	30	8	831
Barry High Ltd, Belfry PCC LM	nl	—	48	151	182	471	258	32	2	nl	nl	nl	nl	nl	nl	nl	1144
Bernard Sunley & Sons Ltd, Sunley Albetong I/S LMH	—	—	250	346	182	91	241	54	—	nl	nl	nl	nl	nl	nl	nl	1164
Blyth Dry Dock & Shipbuilding Ltd, Blyth COM L	—	24	24	72	—	nl	nl	nl	nl	nl	nl	nl	nl	nl	nl	nl	120
British Lift Slab Ltd, (Robert M. Douglas Ltd), Lift Slab I/S MH	129	94	128	128	128	128	—	nl	nl	nl	nl	nl	nl	nl	nl	nl	735
C. Bryant & Sons Ltd, Bryant Low Rise/Wallframe PCC L	—	225	1123	1593	1689	2689	1786	1158	461	721	753	20	—	127	281	48	12674
Building Research Station, BRS (Battery Casting) PCC MH	nl	nl	nl	282	599	694	744	526	741	—	nl	nl	nl	nl	nl	nl	3586
Building Systems Ltd, (British Ropes Ltd) PCC L	7	111	180	12	nl	nl	nl	nl	nl	nl	nl	nl	nl	nl	nl	nl	310
Calders Ltd, Calder Homes T/F L	24	297	21	207	14	nl	nl	nl	nl	nl	nl	nl	nl	nl	nl	nl	549
Camus (GB) Ltd, Licensees: Unit Camus Ltd, Mitchell Camus Ltd, Fram, Higgs & Hill, Camus PCC LMH	—	2	696	614	352	1034	1143	1205	671	521	24	nl	nl	nl	nl	nl	6262
Carlton Contractors Ltd, Carlton PCC LM	nl	8	12	95	141	91	—	nl	nl	nl	nl	nl	nl	nl	nl	nl	347
Centerprise Building Systems Ltd, Cebus PCC MH	nl	—	12	194	95	—	240	80	—	nl	nl	nl	nl	nl	nl	nl	621
Concrete Ltd, Bison Wallframe PCC H	612	1595	2733	2573	3624	5009	6227	4666	1308	497	904	571	652	688	9	—	31668
Cosmos PCC L	nl	nl	nl	—	—	—	154	—	nl	nl	nl	nl	nl	nl	nl	nl	154
Costain Concrete Ltd, Siporex PCC L	2	10	519	338	—	nl	nl	nl	nl	nl	nl	nl	nl	nl	nl	nl	869
Crudens Ltd, Skarne PCC LMH	—	27	187	328	1414	814	1404	1701	913	508	70	—	nl	nl	nl	nl	7384
Crux Developments Ltd, (English China Clay Group of Industries) Crux R/T LM	nl	nl	nl	—	—	—	36	179	105	102	—	nl	nl	nl	nl	nl	422
Cubitts Construction Systems Ltd, (Holland Hannen & Cubitts Ltd), Balency PCC LMH	nl	nl	—	—	7	291	605	504	448	507	393	274	452	54	—	—	3535
Cubitts Construction Systems Ltd, (Holland Hannen & Cubitts Ltd), Lowtown-Cubitt S/F L	4	238	468	441	278	877	1455	831	802	936	1465	447	181	70	33	—	8526

	1964	1965	1966	1967	1968	1969	1970	1971	1972	1973	1974	1975	1976	1977	1978	1979	TOTAL
Dorran Construction Ltd, Dorran COM L	—	—	94	192	354	23	nl	nl	nl	nl	nl	nl	nl	nl	nl	nl	663
Drury Building Service Ltd, Drury System 3 R/T LM	nl	nl	nl	—	14	16	642	891	830	302	345	—	nl	nl	nl	nl	3040
Dudley Coles Long Ltd, Faculty R/T L	nl	nl	—	—	17	58	53	—	nl	nl	nl	nl	nl	nl	nl	nl	128
Dudley Coles Long Ltd, Trim T/F LM	—	—	106	10	101	—	nl	nl	nl	nl	nl	nl	nl	nl	nl	nl	217
Engineered Homes (GB) Ltd, Engineered Homes T/F L	nl	6	106	245	264	128	58	2	nl	nl	nl	nl	nl	nl	nl	nl	809
Fram Gerrard Ltd, Gerrard Incon	nl	nl	nl	—	—	28	226	—	nl	nl	nl	nl	nl	nl	nl	nl	254
Fram Gerrard Ltd, Gerrard Intrad I/S LMH	nl	—	—	88	—	nl	nl	nl	nl	—	—	268	148	115	—	—	619
The Fram Group Ltd, Fram/BRS PCC LMH	144	189	63	59	109	272	1226	385	11	nl	nl	nl	nl	nl	nl	nl	2458
The Fram Group Ltd, Fram Components PCC MH	—	192	288	248	51	51	—	100	—	nl	nl	nl	nl	nl	nl	nl	930
Fredericks and Pelhams Timber Buildings, Fredericks T/F L	nl	nl	nl	nl	nl	nl	—	8	51	—	nl	nl	nl	nl	nl	nl	59
W & C French Construction Ltd, Lecaplan PCC LM	—	120	4	—	470	669	275	4	nl	nl	nl	nl	nl	nl	nl	nl	1542
Gee, Walker & Slater Ltd, (Sir Robert MacAlpine & Sons Ltd), Arcal G.80 PCC L	nl	46	125	220	85	79	55	42	95	75	54	251	24	—	nl	nl	1151
George Calverly & Sons (Contractors Ltd), CM T/F LM	nl	nl	6	33	176	272	241	161	102	—	nl	nl	nl	nl	nl	nl	991
Gilbert Ash Ltd, (Bovis Ltd), Tracoba PCC MH	—	—	462	142	—	69	—	nl	nl	nl	nl	nl	nl	nl	nl	nl	673
Gleeson Industrialised Building Ltd, Gle-system PCC LMH	nl	—	38	24	180	243	164	265	246	157	227	204	474	549	432	76	3279
Greater London Council, SFI S/F LMH	nl	nl	nl	—	300	—	—	—	95	—	nl	nl	nl	nl	nl	nl	395
Gregory Housing Ltd, Gregory Housing PCC LM	—	127	590	323	118	201	35	—	nl	nl	nl	nl	nl	nl	nl	nl	1394
Guildway Ltd, Guildway T/F L	—	25	129	404	384	420	253	227	72	145	241	296	286	150	95	40	3167
Hawthorne Leslie (Buildings) Ltd, (The Hawthorne Leslie Group Ltd, HLB S/F L	—	186	618	969	248	5	nl	nl	nl	nl	nl	nl	nl	nl	nl	nl	2026
Homeville Co. Ltd, Homeville Industrialised S/F L	—	24	171	285	195	21	31	—	nl	nl	nl	nl	nl	nl	nl	nl	727
Housing Development & Construction Ltd, HDC PCC LM	40	278	141	65	—	—	—	nl	nl	nl	nl	nl	nl	—	—	nl	524
Industrial Building Services (Northern) Ltd, Peak Homes T/F LM	—	—	86	637	628	178	539	–715	—	nl	nl	nl	nl	nl	nl	nl	1353

Cont.

	1964	1965	1966	1967	1968	1969	1970	1971	1972	1973	1974	1975	1976	1977	1978	1979	TOTAL
James Riley & Partners Ltd, Frameform T/F LM	nl	—	—	39	189	405	876	298	855	1048	1629	1724	1818	2195	1112	637	12825
James Riley & Partners Ltd, Rileyform T/F LM	nl	nl	nl	nl	nl	nl	nl	nl	nl	—	—	240	886	769	548	439	2882
John Laing Construction Ltd, Easiform I/S LM	2520	2269	2763	2499	1080	1075	272	97	—	nl	nl	nl	nl	nl	nl	nl	12608
John Laing Construction Ltd, Laings Rat-trad R/T L	nl	nl	nl	nl	nl	—	—	70	—	nl	nl	nl	nl	nl	nl	nl	70
John Laing Construction Ltd, Sectra I/S MH	120	505	333	730	10	414	153	88	182	—	nl	nl	nl	nl	nl	nl	2535
John Laing Construction Ltd, Storiform I/S MH	—	51	421	983	620	905	182	145	—	nl	nl	nl	nl	nl	nl	nl	3307
John Laing Construction Ltd, 12M Jespersen PCC LMH	nl	—	133	765	1588	702	1893	1445	774	426	577	—	—	340	—	—	8643
John Lynn & Co. Ltd, (Duxford & Sunderland Shipbuilding & Engineering Group), British Housing S/F L	nl	2	10	62	nl	nl	nl	nl	nl	nl	nl	nl	nl	nl	nl	nl	74
Kenkast Buildings Ltd, Kenkast PCC L	nl	115	54	226	196	100	39	164	7	40	24	44	—	nl	nl	nl	1009
Kier Ltd, BDC R/T L	nl	—	6	—	30	—	nl	nl	nl	nl	nl	nl	nl	nl	nl	nl	36
J.E. Lesser Building Ltd, Lesser R/T LM	—	221	139	281	435	843	1109	694	284	189	—	80	122	159	—	—	4556
Sir Lindsay Parkinson & Co. Ltd, Parkwall I/S L	—	38	722	289	276	691	491	511	141	—	nl	nl	nl	nl	nl	nl	3159
The Lilleshall Company Ltd, Lilleshall PCC L	nl	nl	nl	nl	—	21	85	68	64	44	102	—	nl	nl	nl	nl	384
Lovell Housing Ltd, Lovell T/F L	nl	nl	nl	nl	nl	—	—	17	60	95	407	282	414	251	281	188	2001
J. McLean & Sons (Wolverhampton) Ltd, Mactrad T/F LM	nl	—	141	531	798	537	362	138	—	nl	nl	nl	nl	nl	nl	nl	2497
J. McLean & Sons McLean R/T L	nl	58	42	—	nl	nl	nl	nl	nl	nl	nl	nl	nl	nl	nl	nl	100
J. McLean & Sons McLean Rat-trad R/T L	nl	—	—	49	35	188	139	117	54	—	nl	nl	nl	nl	nl	nl	582
Mathews & Mumby Ltd, M2 PCC MH	—	38	158	206	178	74	198	156	228	80	nl	nl	nl	nl	nl	nl	1316
Medway Buildings Ltd, Medway T/F L	nl	—	—	154	100	52	130	—	nl	nl	nl	nl	nl	nl	nl	nl	436
Midland Housing Consortium, MHC R/T L	nl	153	106	770	855	1033	713	1292	605	271	564	1139	1857	631	468	711	11168
Ministry of Housing and Local Government, 5M S/F LM	214	33	349	670	1010	568	624	—	nl	nl	nl	nl	nl	nl	nl	nl	3468
Minox Structures Ltd, Minox R/T LM	nl	nl	—	126	73	261	314	38	213	94	57	206	314	230	150	145	2221
Modern Building Wales Ltd, Modern Building T/F LM	nl	nl	nl	nl	11	14	201	520	191	19	nl	nl	nl	nl	nl	nl	931

Cont.

	1964	1965	1966	1967	1968	1969	1970	1971	1972	1973	1974	1975	1976	1977	1978	1979	TOTAL
Mowlem Buildings Ltd, Mowlem I/S LM	382	519	460	657	1472	1179	1622	825	893	665	1485	1269	1253	1092	985	42	14800
North Eastern Major Authorities, NEMA R/T L	nl	nl	nl	nl	—	24	41	23	nl	nl	nl	nl	nl	nl	nl	nl	88
The Northwest Construction Co. Ltd, Norwest S/F H	—	142	234	8	nl	nl	nl	nl	nl	nl	nl	nl	nl	nl	nl	nl	384
Open Systen Building Ltd, OSB S/F L	nl	nl	—	8	54	288	113	19	nl	nl	nl	nl	nl	nl	nl	nl	482
Pearce & Barker Ltd, Surebuilt T/F LM	nl	nl	—	33	617	308	327	112	22	nl	nl	nl	nl	nl	nl	nl	1419
Precast Associated Constructors Ltd, PAC, PCC, MH	nl	nl	—	114	95	45	—	35	1	nl	nl	nl	nl	nl	nl	nl	290
Purpose Built Ltd, Purpose Built T/F L	nl	4	40	379	440	402	235	71	93	31	279	183	266	443	474	208	3548
Reema Construction Ltd, Contrad PPC L	nl	nl	nl	nl	nl	nl	nl	nl	47	14	64	—	nl	nl	nl	nl	125
Reema Construction Ltd, Reema PPC LMH	638	613	1071	1544	1141	1138	928	177	103	209	539	282	36	171	—	—	8678
Rigid Frame Constructions Ltd, Rigid Frame S/F LM	17	10	98	201	9	182	97	—	nl	nl	nl	nl	nl	nl	nl	nl	614
Rowlinson Constructions Ltd, Rowcon R/T LM	—	13	307	367	278	231	430	306	82	—	nl	nl	nl	nl	nl	nl	2014
Rush & Tomkins Ltd, Rat-trad R/T L	nl	nl	—	—	79	156	205	—	nl	nl	nl	nl	nl	nl	nl	nl	440
SLP Industrialised Buildings Ltd, HSSB, PCC, LMH	—	50	—	310	345	196	—	nl	nl	nl	nl	nl	nl	nl	nl	nl	874
Selleck Nicholls Williams Ltd, Cornish Unit PCC, LM	nl	55	112	22	—	30	—	nl	nl	nl	nl	nl	nl	nl	nl	nl	219
Selleck Nicholls Williams Ltd, Metracon T/F L	nl	nl	nl	nl	nl	nl	nl	nl	—	—	13	25	nl	nl	nl	nl	38
Selleck Nicholls Williams Ltd, Multilite I/S H	nl	nl	nl	nl	nl	nl	nl	nl	—	—	19	946	2414	1634	650	500	6163
Selleck Nicholls Williams Ltd Metratim T/F L	—	52	38	218	114	—	nl	nl	nl	nl	nl	nl	nl	nl	nl	nl	422
Selleck Nicholls Williams Ltd, Selleck Nicholls	nl	nl	nl	nl	nl	nl	nl	nl	nl	—	27	328	317	—	54	—	726
Selleck Nicholls Williams Ltd, Selleck Nicholls Rat Trad R/T LM	—	10	125	373	1029	1489	915	465	327	471	470	98	—	nl	nl	nl	5772

Cont.

	1964	1965	1966	1967	1968	1969	1970	1971	1972	1973	1974	1975	1976	1977	1978	1979	TOTAL
Selleck Nicholls Williams Ltd, Selleck Nicholls Timber Frame T/F L	nl	nl	nl	nl	nl	nl	nl	—	—	—	564	—	nl	nl	nl	nl	564
Selleck Nicholls Williams Ltd, XW I/S LM	—	—	37	511	1026	520	876	904	104	—	nl	nl	nl	nl	nl	nl	3978
The Shepherd Group Ltd, Shepherd's Rat Trad R/T L	—	38	363	381	246	125	123	363	16	126	12	nl	nl	nl	nl	nl	1793
The Shepherd Group Ltd, Spacemaker PCC M	184	228	132	784	550	665	101	—	nl	—	23	171	98	nl	nl	nl	2936
W.J. Simmcast & Cooks Ltd, Simmcast PCC MH	nl	nl	—	—	225	436	137	—	nl	nl	nl	nl	nl	nl	nl	nl	798
W.J. Simmcast & Cooks Ltd, Simms GDA R/T LM	17	309	787	601	60	34	—	nl	nl	nl	nl	nl	nl	nl	nl	nl	1808
Spooners Hull Ltd, Spooner T/F L	nl	—	17	305	nl	nl	nl	nl	nl	nl	nl	nl	nl	nl	nl	nl	322
Spooners Hull Ltd, Spooner/Caspon T/F L	123	606	375	196	540	588	592	571	157	144	155	460	516	284	117	51	5484
Spooners Hull Ltd, Spooner Urban T/F L	nl	—	—	332	265	24	nl	nl	nl	nl	nl	nl	nl	nl	nl	nl	621
Stanley Miller Ltd, MWM I/S MH	nl	311	119	96	—	136	383	422	—	111	463	—	—	—	109	—	2150
Stoners Appliances Ltd, Canadian Timber Frame T/F LM	nl	—	—	8	122	45	—	nl	nl	nl	nl	nl	nl	nl	nl	nl	175
Geo Stubbings Ltd, Studdings Industrial Low Rise PCC LM	nl	—	—	13	63	—	nl	nl	nl	nl	nl	nl	nl	nl	nl	nl	76
Geo Stubbings Ltd, Stubbings Rat Trad R/T L	nl	95	546	484	260	—	nl	nl	nl	nl	nl	nl	nl	nl	nl	nl	1385
Sundh (Great Britain) Ltd, Sundh I/S MH	nl	—	—	35	58	23	56	104	110	—	nl	nl	nl	nl	nl	nl	386
F. & H. Sutcliffe, Shadow Wall	nl	73	17	—	nl	nl	nl	nl	nl	nl	nl	nl	nl	nl	nl	nl	90
Swiftplan Ltd, (The Taylor Woodrow Group), Multiflex H12 T/F L	—	20	—	88	2	—	nl	nl	nl	nl	nl	nl	nl	nl	nl	nl	110
Taylor Woodrow Anglian (The Taylor Woodrow Group Ltd, Anglian PCC LM	nl	nl	53	32	231	111	35	16	32	114	237	—	nl	nl	nl	nl	867
Taylor Woodrow Anglian (The Taylor Woodrow Group Ltd), Larsen Nielson PCC MH	40	406	664	1056	875	480	632	1528	880	393	669	457	—	nl	nl	nl	8080
Wm Thornton & Sons, Prometo I/S H	nl	—	—	144	—	nl	nl	nl	nl	nl	nl	nl	nl	nl	nl	nl	144
Timber Research & Development Association, TRADA T/F LM	—	—	40	91	5	—	47	52	64	60	224	465	444	224	146	127	1989

Cont.

	1964	1965	1966	1967	1968	1969	1970	1971	1972	1973	1974	1975	1976	1977	1978	1979	TOTAL
Truscon Ltd, Truscon PCC LMH	16	—	304	—	126	108	158	—	nl	nl	nl	nl	nl	nl	nl	nl	712
Trusteel Corporation (Universal) Ltd, Trusteel Mk.II S/F LMH	52	132	133	282	529	450	238	—	nl	nl	nl	nl	nl	nl	nl	nl	1816
Trusteel Corporation (Universal) Ltd, Trusteel 3M S/F LMH	nl	5	40	530	412	537	392	423	428	245	352	364	84	147	107	—	4066
The Unit Construction Co. Ltd, Unit System 66 R/T L	nl	—	113	567	772	461	261	80	—	nl	nl	nl	nl	nl	nl	nl	2249
Vic Hallam Ltd, Vic Hallam Mks I, II & III T/F LM	158	1002	1107	248	602	512	1398	1143	4	nl	nl	nl	nl	nl	nl	nl	6174
Vic Hallam Ltd, Vic Hallam (Homepack) T/F L	nl	nl	nl	nl	nl	nl	nl	nl	nl	nl	—	19	116	154	56	27	372
Wale Sindall Developments Ltd, SB2 PCC LM	—	—	73	91	—	nl	nl	nl	nl	nl	nl	nl	nl	nl	nl	nl	164
Walter Llewellyn & Sons Ltd, Quikbild T/F L	—	20	168	213	442	385	547	272	777	878	1130	2222	2676	1817	744	293	12584
Wates Ltd, Wates High Rise PCC MH	1234	1160	1980	2181	2476	3290	2503	1156	672	460	473	177	—	nl	nl	nl	17762
Wates Ltd, Wates Low Rise T/F L*	nl	nl	nl	nl	nl	688	764	526	236	84	303	361	51	—	nl	—	3013
Weir Housing Corporation Ltd, Weir T/F L	nl	nl	nl	nl	nl	nl	nl	nl	—	—	57	383	149	—	nl	—	586
William Moss & Sons Ltd, MFC PCC LM	nl	—	—	128	129	53	305	249	—	nl	nl	nl	nl	nl	nl	nl	864
William Old & Co. Ltd, Resiform GRP LM	nl	nl	nl	—	20	54	177	161	178	43	86	660	68	14	—	—	1461
Williams & Williams Ltd, (British Steel Corporation), Rofton S/F L	nl	—	—	63	229	87	7	19	67	59	37	33	—	nl	nl	nl	601
Geo. Wimpey & Co. Ltd, Wimpey No Fines I/S LM	9085	10271	12085	14420	10031	11077	9906	7204	6477	5496	8018	9565	6066	5782	2803	612	128898
Geo. Wimpey & Co. Ltd, Wimpey 6M I/S H	nl	—	—	270	1805	706	337	234	5	nl	nl	nl	nl	nl	nl	nl	3357
Yorkshire Development Group, YDGH MKI PCC M	—	—	—	541	730	2007	456	nl	nl	nl	nl	nl	nl	nl	nl	nl	3734

Notes;
The figures for yearly completions of individual systems have been taken from *HSGB* and *H & CS*.
The table lists 121 of the 153 systems listed and are confined to those systems where the sponsoring company, the type of structural system and its housing form could be identified. The 32 "unidentified"

Cont.

271

systems are mainly those with small production figures, often introduced during the 1970s during which time catalogues of systems, giving their details, tended not to be published. The "unidentified" systems listed by the MHLG and DOE, with their total completions throughout the period covered by this table, as as follows: Beal & Son (360), Boro (82), Bury Boulton (49), Discus (74), Eurodean (581), Framecourt (82), Grayhome (148), Hales Rat Trad (140), Wellbuilt (146), F.J. Halliwell (33), 4H/7 (183), Housing System Design (508), Howard Mersham Housing (58), ISEC (258), Martin Construction (39), M.C. Meyer (235), Middleton Rat Trad (740), Mucklow (190), Multi Storey Construction (354), J. Murphy Rat Trad (280), Plus 3 Contracts (49), Ridgeway (69), Rowland (zero), Scan (225), Shanly Rat Trad (622), Spaceway (48), Timber Frame Ltd (zero), Trygon Rat Trad (981), Volumetric (zero), Lawrence Weaver Rat Trad (6), W.G. West & Sons (1329), C.M. Yuill (460). It may be assumed that most of the "unidentified" systems were of timber framed or rationalised traditional construction. The names of the sponsoring companies, type of structural system and building form have been taken from sources too numerous to mention individually. The names in brackets refer to the larger industrial groups to which sponsors belonged in cases where these have been identified.

*Figures for this system were included in Wates High Rise until 1969.

Key:
L	1–2 storeys	COM	composite steel and concrete sturcture
M	3–6 storeys	GRP	glass reinforced plastic panels
H	6 and above storeys	I/S	*in situ* concrete
nl	system not listed for this year	PCC	precast concrete
—	no completions for this year	S/F	steel frame
		T/F	timber frame

APPENDIX 6

Houses Completed in Building Systems in England and Wales by Structural Type of System 1964–79

	In situ Concrete	Pre-cast Concrete	Steel Frame	Timber Frame	Rationalised Traditional	TOTAL
1964	13280	3234	291	347	19	17171
1965	15647	6021	886	2073	898	25527
1966	17058	13043	2370	2545	2443	37494
1967	20354	16471	3759	3632	4821	49049
1968	15774	19231	3469	5958	6101	50569
1969	16138	21794	3154	5189	6874	53150
1970	13204	25566	3012	6681	7238	55701
1971	9158	18265	1334	4380	5177	38314
1972	7773	8004	1487	3181	4112	24557
1973	6161	4914	1315	2727	2543	17660
1974	9503	5503	1908	5995	1627	24536
1975	11102	2255	1120	10230	1086	25792
1976	7467	1766	332	13139	1076	23780
1977	6991	1955	223	9971	559	19691
1978	3788	922	140	5171	292	10313
1979	654	188	—	3571	97	4510

Notes:
The categories of system defined by these statistics may be described as based on the following principles: *In situ Concrete*, concrete placed into reusable shutters assembled on site; *Precast Concrete*, concrete components caste either on site or in factories and then lifted into position; *Steel Frame*, loadbearing steel frame supporting a non-structural cladding; *Timber Frame*, loadbearing timber frame or panels supporting a non-structural cladding; *Rationalised Traditional* (or crosswall), loadbearing masonry construction reduced to the minimum necessary to support timber frames and roof components and non-structural cladding panels.
Sources: MHLG, *HSGB* (1964–70)
        DOE, *HSGB* (1970–80)

APPENDIX 7

Average Costs of Local Authority Housing in England and Wales 1964–77

	Houses & Bungalows			Flats under 5 st.			Flats 5 st. & over		
	IB	Trad	All	IB	Trad	All	IB	Trad	All
Shillings/sq. ft.									
1964	55,3.5	52,0.5	52,7.5	71,5.5	69,3.5	69,6.5	94,4	96,8.5	95,11
1965	59,0.5	59,9.5	57,5	76,0	75,4	75,6	99,3.5	104,4.5	102,3.5
1966	61,6	60,3	60,9	83,4	79,10.5	80,7.5	106,0.5	109,11.5	107,10.5
1967	65,0.5	63,9	64,4	84,7.5	80,3	81,7.5	105,0.5	110,1	106,11
1968	65,6.5	65,5	65,5.5	85,3	83,3.5	83,10.5	99,10.5	114,11	105,6.5
Pounds/sq. M.									
1969	36.06	37.35	37.03	49.62	50.38	50.27	59.53	63.62	61.25
1970	38.54	40.04	39.72	51.13	54.36	53.82	68.35	62.97	64.48
1971	42.84	46.50	45.75	55.76	63.08	61.89	68.14	80.19	77.93
1972	53.28	55.44	55.00	72.87	77.50	76.64	111.19	95.37	96.02
1973	71.37	74.16	73.41	89.13	104.95	102.04	105.92	147.90	143.91
1974	83.06	88.99	87.63	112.18	123.25	121.84	132.66	213.03	179.97
1975	94.39	96.33	96.02	125.35	134.76	133.51	193.27	186.93	187.24
1976	97.89	101.71	101.13	136.03	142.54	142.16	239.60	234.58	234.82
1977	112.67	115.46	115.35	109.48	167.18	165.37	—	226.83	226.83

Sources: MHLG, *HSGB* (1964–70)
DOE *H&CS* (1970–78)

INDEX

277